Holding the Center

MIT Portrait of Howard Johnson. Artist: George Augusta, 1991

Holding the Center
Memoirs of a Life in Higher Education

Howard Wesley Johnson

The MIT Press
Cambridge, Massachusetts
London, England

This book was set in Sabon by Achorn Graphic Services, Inc.

Printed and bound in the United States of America.

Library of Congress Cataloging-in-Publication Data

Johnson, Howard Wesley, 1922–
    Holding the center : memoirs of a life in higher education /
Howard Wesley Johnson.
        p.   cm.
    Includes index.
    ISBN 0-262-10079-7 (alk. paper)
    1. Johnson, Howard Wesley, 1922–   . 2. Massachusetts Institute
of Technology—Presidents—Biography.   3. College presidents—
Massachusetts—Biography.   4. Massachusetts Institute of
Technology—History.   I. Title.
    T171.M49J62   1999
    378′.0092—dc21
    [B]   98-50199
    JK   CIP

Picture credits will be found on p. 329.

This book is for
my wife, Elizabeth,
who made the whole passage worthwhile
and is dedicated to
the men and women of the Massachusetts Institute of Technology

Contents

Foreword by John S. Reed   xi
Preface   xvii
Acknowledgments   xxi

1 Growing Up in South Chicago during the Depression   1

2 College and Going to War   15

3 The University of Chicago after the War: Student and Faculty
   Member   59

4 Becoming a Part of the Massachusetts Institute of
   Technology   79

5 The School of Industrial Management Becomes the Sloan
   School   91

6 Early Years as President of MIT   123

7 Grim Years for the Nation and the Universities   153

8 Education in the Midst of Turmoil: The Close of a
   Presidency   185

9 Chairing the MIT Corporation and Other Challenges   215

10 Boston's Museum of Fine Arts in a New Era   243

11 MIT Goes On   263

Coda: A Note for Students on Leadership   277

Sources   281
Registry of Names   283
Index   309
Picture Credits   329

"Things fall apart; the center cannot hold;
Mere anarchy is loosed upon the world,
The blood-dimmed tide is loosed, and everywhere
The ceremony of innocence is drowned;
The best lack all conviction, while the worst
Are full of passionate intensity."

William Butler Yeats, *The Second Coming*

Foreword

John S. Reed

As we approach the end of the twentieth century, we are beginning to see coming together a literature of contemporary memoirs, biography and autobiography. On the surface, much of this literature may seem unremarkable. But on other levels it sketches out a fascinating story about our era—the development of the world as we now experience it.

Much of this writing leaves us with a deep appreciation of seemingly simple things: how events confronted and dealt with have cumulating impact, how character—rather than judgment, raw talent, or energy— is critical in the shaping of outcomes and how seemingly unremarkable solid values, basic aspirations, and personal experience of events like the depression and World War II have defined many of the important actors who have shaped our twentieth-century world.

The understanding and practice of management has been in constant development throughout this century. Most importantly, it is broadly taught. For years, management, that simple practice of deciding what to do and then making it happen, was something to be learned through apprenticeship and experience. But that has changed. Today, there is a body of research-based literature that illuminates the practice of management. Would-be and practicing managers are taught as they start and progress through their careers.

In the beginning, manufacturing practices focused on the development of processes, and that gave rise to industrial engineering. Business greats like Alfred P. Sloan brought the development of process and decision-making beyond the factory floor into immensely large, complex, and growing enterprises. After World War II, and into the fifties and sixties, the notion of management was decisively expanded beyond its origins in industrial engineering. A number of key figures involved in industrial relations drew attention to the realities of the human side of management and introduced insights drawn from the social and behavioral disciplines, which in turn has led to the study of organization.

Also, in the fifties and sixties, the study and teaching of management practices were importantly shaped by two different approaches. The first rested on learning through pattern recognition, the codification of best practices, and an intense immersion in the culture of business as illustrated by case studies. The second relied on theories and observations developed by focusing core intellectual disciplines—economics, sociology, psychology, statistics, and applied mathematics—on the practice of management. Both approaches continue to have relevance to management sectors that make up a framework of business practices: marketing, production, finance, personnel administration, and so forth.

In recent decades, the realm of management has been expanded beyond the conceptual confines of the "profit maximizing firm." Management is now seen to be an essential function in institutions of all forms, both profit and nonprofit, those with defined functions and roles, such as schools, hospitals, and police departments, as well as those settings with less specific missions, such as universities, cultural institutions, and governments.

At the same time, it has been recognized that the borders within which management is practiced in all of these settings have become permeable. Management and the institutions that are managed form a part of society. As a result, decisions about what to do and how it is to be done must fit within a set of social permissions that themselves change with time. The values of society are intrusive—indeed the culture of the firm cannot be too different from that of society at large. Thus, the changes that caused social friction in the sixties, race, gender, family, and the environment, are fully reflected in today's management challenges and practices.

Furthermore, as I write, we are globalists. We recognize that the world is interconnected. Things flow: information does, as does intellectual capital. Scholarship, the arts, the environment, human concerns, all are global in nature. So are aspirations, the desire for a decent life, for education, for access to the tools that lead to economic growth. We must respond to the realities of globality in our thinking, in living, and in shaping our institutions. The living evidence of our globalism can be seen every day in the corridors of MIT.

As will be clear in the pages of this book, the multi-dimensional, unstructured, and borderless agenda of management in these settings and changing environment makes the challenges even more daunting. At the same time, learning from experience is more important.

In the past, the practice of management considered attitudes and behavior as givens, part of the environment that was accepted as management concentrated on other things. Then came competition from Japan, where workers were seen to be more constructively, creatively, and interactively linked to the production process. Global competition clearly changed that narrow view of management scope.

Today, behavior and attitudes, indeed the culture of a firm, are consciously developed. Job requirements are defined in terms of skills, knowledge, attitude, and behavior. Behavior often refers to group as well as individual activities.

Practitioners such as Jack Welch of GE seem likely to go down in business history not because of the genius of their corporate strategy, but rather because of their ability to excite constructive activity across a large and diversified portfolio of businesses. They succeed by creating a class of responsive managers who are carefully selected, trained, and then stimulated to implement a cumulating agenda of action and change that produces performance quite separately and in addition to that which comes from driving individual businesses through the traditional chain of command.

Similarly, technology-based companies drawing from the same core literature of organizations and behavioral studies have challenged traditional structures, particularly command and control hierarchies. The alternative is contracting; the question becomes: Which is more effective, vertical integration mediated by traditional structure and process, or a web of contracts with outsourcing and strategic partnerships carefully thought out and executed?

These issues and practices frame management at the end of the century. Their origins trace to activities and decisions that are very much at the heart of Howard Johnson's story.

While management is a special domain of direct interest to a relative few, it is clear that the twentieth century will be known for the impact of its science. It is almost shocking to recall that it was only in 1899 that Ernest Rutherford described the electron.

As will be seen in these pages, science and its development during this century has been a most human enterprise. While the frontiers of each scientific discipline have been pushed to almost unbelievable points, the thrust of science has also transformed and become embedded in two more traditional fields—engineering and medicine—that relate most closely to human activity. The great research universities and laboratories that lie at the center of science, engineering, and medicine have been shaped to make continued progress possible. They have also been shaped to be global enterprises tightly linked to society, its desire for improvement and change, and its changing values and moods.

What comes alive on these pages are the professionalism of science and engineering research and education, the dynamics of peer review, and the role of plain old leadership. MIT, the national agenda, and the nation's mood are at the heart of Howard Johnson's story.

One has the sense that in the prewar years MIT was a school of engineering. By the end of this book, science, the humanities, management, and the arts have come to be integral parts of the institute. Science is now at the core of engineering. Biology and the health sciences are central to the school.

The impact of the sixties: The Vietnam war, the student protests, gender and race issues mediated by the institute's president have changed and shaped today's MIT. At the end, it has been strengthened by them.

The same factors have shaped MIT's relationship with the government, again to our collective benefit.

Howard Johnson's story is that of a practitioner and builder. He practiced management throughout his life, shaping agenda and getting things done. By the time he became president of MIT, this practice was sophisticated and multifaceted, with arguably superior outcomes. After his presidency, the managerial challenges were, and are, in different settings: at the Boston Museum of Fine Arts, in board rooms, and as a "player" in the world community.

This is a story of a shaper as well as a practitioner. Howard Johnson played a central role in shaping MIT's approach to management, education, and research. He also was central to the "architecture" of that education, not only what was to be taught but how and when—undergraduates, graduate students, young executives, and senior managers. As president of the institute, he was also very much "present at the creation" as science, and particularly, the biological and health sciences, took on their particular form in MIT.

Throughout the whole story, we are left with a sense of wonder about how much was done by a quiet, friendly, unassuming, and profoundly decent person. This story has lessons for us all.

Preface

"Philosophy is perfectly right in saying that life must be understood backward. But then one forgets the other clause—that it must be lived forward."
Søren Kierkegaard, *Journals and Papers*

I began these memoirs because I felt that an accounting would be useful, describing what those of us at the center saw and did during the upheavals in the nation and the colleges in the late sixties and early seventies. Future historians with better perspective than we deserve a firsthand account of the period by eyewitnesses. Few such accounts exist from professors, students, or others who were present, and very few from presidents, provosts, or deans. With this in mind, and as time allowed, I proceeded to write a report of what happened at MIT during my years there.

I soon found that it was essential to analyze my own mind-set during these conflicted times, and in the process to recall my own life both before and after my administration. It is a complex exercise, but, once involved in the process, I found I enjoyed the study and recollection it entailed. In any case, the second theme of this book is a personal set of memoirs, of living life "forward" as well as understanding it "backward."

A third theme deserves more space than it received. It is about management and leadership in modern times, about organizing to achieve goals, about generating sound decisions. These are not trivial topics. On a wider scale, we must recognize that managing and holding the community together so that it can accomplish the high goals of adaptation and self-control in a shrinking world is a major need in our society. Its fundamental purpose is not profit but quality survival for everyone.

Many styles for achieving effective results exist, and I make no general case for my own approach. Much depends on the setting, the times, and, always, the people involved. The new requirements of leadership make older patterns incomplete and ineffective. These points are woven into the general account because they are integral to the situation. My main intention was to set goals, assemble the decision process, and then make the decision clearly, unambiguously, in a timely way. My aim was to inspire confidence in order to facilitate progress. I value highly the skills in all of the fields of analysis that make up management and lead to sound decision making; after all, I was one of the builders of a management school. But I believe the first requirements are to communicate clearly with as many people in the organization as possible and to present goals fairly in an atmosphere of high ideals. Whether an organization holds together in the midst of crisis depends on the unspoken, wide commitment of the majority to the common responsibility. Great organizations possess that mutual commitment, and excellent management makes that commitment an important goal. Teaching and learning these complex skills represent a formidable intellectual task. These memoirs relate my thoughts on these matters.

The reader will note that I record no personal peaks of academic achievement. But I have had the opportunity to be in the center of an institution that makes great achievements possible for a great many people.

Reading about the lives and events described here will bring back these times to the many who lived through them. For others, these memoirs may provide insight into situations in which it is critical to maintain the trust and confidence of many people who are under fearsome pressure. It is important in turbulent times that the centers hold.

I remember John Burchard, MIT's former Dean of Humanities and Social Science, telling me of his brief meeting with Winston Churchill. Churchill came to MIT in 1949, at the peak of his worldwide popularity, and spoke to a packed house at the Boston Garden. The speech drew resounding applause. Churchill was quickly hustled out of the Garden and into a car where Burchard awaited him to escort him back to the Ritz for a brief rest before yet another appearance. Burchard wondered what the great man's first words would be as he settled back into the seat and lit a cigar. Churchill turned to Burchard and said, "How did I do?" I suppose that is a natural question for anyone to ask, at least at the end of the day.

Most of my life has been centered at the Massachusetts Institute of Technology, that singular place of higher learning. There I have worked and taught for more than forty years. Most of what follows will describe that time and how, in the years of my presidency, my colleagues and I dealt with the events that whirled around us out of the social, political, and economic pressures on the country and on the world. In the United States, the war in Vietnam was the most obvious center of the storm. At MIT, events and issues arose out of research sponsored by the Department of Defense; the ROTC; civil rights and the equitable treatment of minorities; the boundaries of protest and of civility and common respect for the rights of others in a university. We faced the overarching problems of advancing knowledge and fostering high standards in all aspects of higher education in the midst of upheaval.

The whole community—faculty, trustees, students, staff, and alumni—struggled with these issues, often in the heat of emotion and power plays. But it was usually up to the administration, and in the end to the president, to make the critical decisions. Other institutions had many of the same problems, often with greater organizational storm and vibration than occurred at MIT. Little has been written about these events on other campuses by those with organizational responsibility. It seems to me now that it would be worthwhile to review what happened at one institution during these stormy times—to return, in a sense, to Churchill's question, "How did I do?" History never repeats itself precisely, but there will be upheavals on campuses again in the future, and what follows may be helpful to others.

Acknowledgments

Memoirs are an intrinsically personal matter, but in my case, this book could not have been written without the encouragement and help of many friends and colleagues. I am especially grateful for the indispensable help and support of Elizabeth J. Whittaker and Muriel A. Petranic of MIT. Miss Whittaker, my executive assistant for the full seventeen years during my terms as president and chairman of MIT, tabled her other activities to help in review of the text and took the responsibility for the development of the biographical notes. Mrs. Petranic, my administrative assistant during the last ten years, cheerfully pressed through the innumerable and difficult tasks of producing the book. I am grateful to both of them.

I also am deeply indebted to MIT colleagues and friends who read the early drafts of the book and made the final work better by their suggestions: John M. Wynne, Walter and Judy Rosenblith, Paul E. Gray, Glenn P. Strehle, Kathryn A. Willmore, Walter L. Milne, Robert M. Metcalfe, Samuel J. Keyser, Robert C. DiIorio, Warren A. Seamans, Charles H. Ball, and Victor K. McElheny.

I wish to thank some old friends and colleagues who, from other vantage points, read the draft and gave me invaluable advice: Warren G. Bennis, David G. Moore, Arnold R. Weber, Nils Y. Wessell, and Thomas Winship. Our sons, Stephen and Bruce, our daughter, Laura, and my sister, Evelyn Harvey, read the manuscript and gave me both encouragement and helpful criticism.

I acknowledge with gratitude the guidance and wise counsel of Frank Urbanowski, the director, and Michael Sims, the managing editor, of the MIT Press.

At a critical time I was much heartened by access to modest but necessary funding from MIT for expenses, and by a grant from the Alfred P. Sloan Foundation whose president, Ralph E. Gomory, has given me unfailing encouragement in this project from the beginning.

I wish it had been possible to name all the people who have helped me over the years—colleagues and friends who were essential to so many of the endeavors recorded here, and whose friendship I treasure. In expressing my thanks to all who have helped, I am very much aware that I alone am responsible for errors that may remain.

HWJ

With sister Evelyn and brother Kenneth, 1923

1

Growing Up in South Chicago during the Depression

I remember thinking as a boy that I had surely been born in the wrong century. I had missed, I thought, all the excitement. To have lived during the American Revolution or the nation's westward expansion would have been an opportunity to witness and participate in events that shaped the nation. Suspended between those dreams of coming of age in the eighteenth or nineteenth century and the Buck Rogers fantasies of the twenty-fifth century to come, I felt, as many children must feel, doomed to living in prosaic times.

I long ago changed my mind. Now, as we come to the ebbing of our own times and lives, I see the century just ending as having been at the same time great and tragic, splendid and disastrous, as the world inexorably continued to shrink. Sometimes I sat in a bleacher seat, and sometimes in the front rows, at some of the massive events that define these past years: the Great Depression, World War II, the Cold War, the revolutionary discoveries in science, technology, and management, and the upheavals that engulfed the whole world, including higher education, with the Vietnam War.

I was born on the south side of Chicago, the city by the lake, still in those decades a reflection of Carl Sandburg's "Hog Butcher, Tool Maker . . . Player with Railroads." My father and mother had grown up and lived there, and my grandparents had lived there for most of their lives. It was a noisy, diverse place when I entered the city on July 2, 1922, born at home as many babies were in those days. I spent the next twenty years there before I went off to war; and, in fact, the scene, the buildings, and the people hardly changed during those years. The neighborhoods of the south shore, as we called it, were still marked by nationalities and languages and religious denominations that gave them identity and character, including large communities of Poles, Lithuanians, Serbs and Croats, Swedes and Germans and Irish, Jews and Catholics and Protestants. The melting pot still worked in those days, except for the terrible schism between blacks and whites. The blacks lived north of 33d Street, and tales of the disastrous riots of 1919 were occasionally whispered.

Most of the men of the neighborhoods worked in the "mills"—the sprawling steel mills that began at 79th Street and continued, unbroken, to Gary, Indiana. They were dominated by the U.S. Steel Company, but also included such giants as Inland Steel, Wisconsin Steel, Republic Steel, and dozens of specialty subsidiaries. The mills had been busy through the twenties as they emerged from World War I and continued to boom with prosperity and confidence as well as noise and dirt to the end of the decade. Beginning in 1930 they slumped into a deepening and all-encompassing depression that marked every endeavor and every individual and continued until the onset of World War II. To the west and north sprawled the huge stockyards of Chicago; sandwiched between was an enormous variety of large and small specialty and assembly plants. On days when the winds blew from the west, we could smell the stockyards and marvel at the fortitude of the people who lived close to them.

Scattered around all of these huge enterprises and settled in the precise checkerboard of the Chicago street grid were myriad neighborhoods of great variation and vitality. We lived in a few of them over the sixteen years of my youth. We rented apartments or houses, in the typical pattern of those days, changing every three years or so, and finally ending up with a house of our own on 78th Street near the lake. I was fourteen and in high school. Families—ours and thousands like it—were the essential centers of life in the community. Of course, we always thought that our family was special, and being part of it defined the lives of all of us.

My father, Albert Johnson, worked at the mill, but—big distinction—in the "office" as a bookkeeper and accountant, a crucial difference from most of the families around us. It made his status in life, and thus ours, different from many of our neighbors and relatives who worked shifts in the mills: 7 A.M. to 3 P.M., 3 P.M. to 11 P.M., and 11 P.M. to 7 in the morning—three shifts a day, seven days a week, fifty two weeks a year. My father worked five and a half days a week, and I can see him now—a solid and steady man with a great sense of humor and an infectious laugh. He was not really himself without a buttoned collar and a tie. He was vigorous, walking to work in all weather, smoking his pipe, happy with life and proud of his wife and family. He worked at U.S. Steel and its predecessor for fifty years, and when he retired at seventy, he was proud of his new wristwatch and of shaking the hand of one of the "big shots" at the farewell dinner. I never knew him to be ill, he rarely complained, and I can't remember him ever raising his voice.

He and his twin brother were the youngest in a family that had five boys, all, finally, employees at the steel mills. His mother, widowed when "the boys" were young, was a stern-featured Norwegian, usually wearing dark clothes, her gray hair pulled tautly across her head. Born in Wisconsin to parents who had come from Norway in the 1830s, she was the stuff of the pioneer. As a young woman, she had been swept off her feet by a friend of her older brother who had come to visit the farm outside Beloit, Wisconsin. Her husband-to-be was a pioneer of a different kind: a Swede who as a boy had run away from his home in Stockholm to sign on as a crew member of a sailing ship bound for America. In New York, he joined the crew of an American clipper ship on its way around the Horn to San Francisco. He left the ship at that point to seek gold during the waning days of the last gold rush, but he left after a few years downhearted and empty-handed except for a ring made for him, according to family legend, from a single nugget. He apparently decided to settle down and, fortunately, met my grandmother-to-be, returned to South Chicago to set up a home and eventually a family. He died young at age forty-seven when my father was only nine. I see him now only in a faded photograph—a flinty Scandinavian whose face reflected hardship.

My grandmother lived with her two bachelor sons in a pleasant but formal house on the east side of Chicago until her death in 1931. A bit distant from us, in our infrequent visits she never seemed to know which of Albert's sons I was. I remember visiting her house every Christmas, snow on the ground, the streetcar ride that entailed at least one transfer, and being carried on the several-block walk by my father when we finally arrived back home. At my grandmother's house we would have a variety of traditional Norwegian baked goods and goodies, and a heavy, humorless conversation. The snow always seemed to be there at Christmas, crunching beneath our feet, and the Christmas trees, alight in the neighborhood windows, would cast a spell.

Two of my father's brothers were special to Kenneth, my older brother, and to me. Ed was our favorite. He had served in the 7th U.S. Cavalry for eight years in the late nineties and early part of this century when there were remnants of a few Indian tribes outside the reservations at Ft. Riley, Kansas. We enjoyed his tales of horse cavalry days, and he made great ceremony of his old sergeant's uniform and his hog-leg Colt. He was a champion-class trapshooter and often would bring our family a holiday turkey—his prize for a trapshooting contest.

Gullick, his younger brother, was, like Ed, a bachelor, but he was Ed's opposite in demeanor and outlook. He was a gentle, soft-spoken man who loved books and fishing and history. Since his mother and brother would not allow him to bring any more books to his own home, he would buy them for us, and we would often receive, sometimes without warning or notice, wooden crates of books: encyclopedias, histories, biographies, and Civil War and nature books. The selection had a heavy bearing on my own interests and hobbies. I still have the four-volume E. T. Seton work *Wild Animals I Have Known*. How I would bury myself in all of those books! My father's twin, Albin, was as close to an identical twin as I have ever seen. From twenty feet away he looked exactly like our father. Occasionally, as youngsters, we would sidle up to him at church and take his hand, thinking he was our own dad. For many of their acquaintances, such confusion in identifying the two was common.

My mother, Laura Hansen Johnson, was the tower of strength, compassion, and intelligence in our family, and she quietly dominated it. She was a handsome woman in her younger days, and even after we were grown we all thought her profile was identical to that of the head of Liberty on the U.S. half dollar. We all depended on her for her common

With brother Richard and Bowser, July 1935

sense, guidance, and an invisible push. We were taught discipline, but rarely in an overt way. We were "expected" to do things, and that usually carried the day.

My mother's father and mother had emigrated to America from Flensburg on the Danish-German border when they were young children, with their respective families. Both families settled in South Chicago before the great fire of 1871, and, in time, her parents, Andrew Hansen and Christina Nommensen, met and married there. My grandfather worked for the Illinois Steel Company, U.S. Steel's predecessor. He and my grandmother lived for most of their married life in the home they had built in South Chicago, raising seven children who lived to be adults. I never knew the youngest son, who died at nineteen in the 1918–1919 flu epidemic. My grandparents lived with us during their last years. My mother and father had taken them into our smaller house as though it were the most natural sequence of events. They were our honored guests and had the best room in the house. It was great fun for us, still young children, to have grandpa and grandma with us. Their deaths left a large void in the household.

We were four children: my sister Evelyn, the oldest, born in 1914, my brother Kenneth, born in 1919, myself, and younger brother Richard, born in 1928. We were sufficiently separated in age so that we had our own lives, friends, and school experiences. But we got on well and only occasionally did annoyance or anger disrupt our times. Once, when I was a boy of ten or eleven, as my sister went into the house in a huff over something I had done, I shot her in the bottom with my BB gun, right through the screen door. It was a great shot, but it cost me my BB gun and nearly put an end to my career as a marksman. We put on a united front at church or in visiting the wide circle of relatives that described the boundaries of our lives. I always felt we had an unspoken invisible agreement that none of us would ever let the family down.

The Great Depression hit the United States in 1929–1930, and it dominated the life of the nation until after the war began in Europe. In 1933, one fourth of the men and women in the country were out of work; jobs for women were almost nonexistent. Unemployment remained extreme for the entire decade. Incomes were low and uneven, and cash was scarce. Our father had a steady job, and we had a certain security, but many, if not most, in our circle in the neighborhood and among our relatives were occasionally laid off, had their work reduced to three days a week, or lost their jobs. New clothing was scarce, and food, while cheap and plentiful, had a certain plainness. We felt comparatively well off, I suppose, although my father's cash income was never large. When we had a house with a backyard of our own, beginning in 1932, a week would not go by without one or more men stopping at the back door offering to do work for a meal. My mother never turned one away. Thinking back to the people of our neighborhood, it struck me that the women grew stronger and more resolute while the men grew less sure of themselves and less buoyant. The miracle was that the American society hung together so effectively in the midst of all that grimness.

Automobiles were common, but not every family had one. Airplanes were a rare sight when I was a little boy; I can still remember people running into the streets to point at a high-flying plane. To me, the most spectacular aircraft, as I now remember, were the big dirigibles *Akron* and *Macon* and the flight of twenty-four Italian military airplanes to Chicago in 1933 led by Italo Balbo.

We did not get our first auto until 1938 when I was sixteen—a Chrysler sedan that the family continued to use for a dozen years. We had much to do for recreation: Apart from family activities were the movies, which one could enjoy for ten cents, going to the beach, or going to the forest preserves for hiking and games.

Our lives outside the family centered on two institutions: the Lutheran church and our schools. We belonged to the Windsor Park Lutheran Church, begun as an offshoot of our grandparents' church in South Chicago, where services were still in German. Even after the sermon and worship switched to English there, the hymns and the liturgy were in German, and the sonorous melodies of Bach were part of our visits to our grandparents' church. We never missed a Sunday service or Sunday school, and we knew all of our fellow churchgoers—their families, their troubles, and their achievements. We sang in the choir, went to the social events, and attended the annual picnics. It was a major focus for us.

School was the other organizing influence for our family. Despite our frequent moves, I stayed in the same school district throughout my elementary and high school years. The three oldest of us were graduated from Edward Coles Elementary School. Each day, I walked to school with my older brother until I was old enough to go alone; later, in my turn, I accompanied my little brother to school. School was a long distance away for small boys, about a mile and a half each way. Most of the time we would move diagonally across prairie lots, hurrying over the B & O train tracks, and crossing the busy 83d Street corner in all seasons, all weather. There were no buses in those days; one had to go on foot. We seldom missed school, were seldom late, and returned home at lunch time, returning to school for two hours in the afternoon. We often played on the school grounds after school, and went to activities at YMCAs and clubs, occasionally battling a rival group on the way home. Once I took a licking from a local tough named Archie Fisher, and I never forgot it. He was surrounded by his pals and I was alone except for my younger brother. I learned that day that one needed allies. After that, I usually had them.

My classmates were mixed. In our early days, most were Polish Americans, their parents having emigrated to the United States in the years since World War I. They were trying desperately to shed their Polish heritage, although many spoke Polish at home. When we finally moved north of 79th Street, the cast of ethnicity changed a bit to Irish, Swedish, and Jewish.

As a little boy I had a distinct speech problem, but it had nothing to do with an accent: I simply could not say the sound "r"; it came out as a "w." I suppose that was cute when I was a kindergarten boy and in first grade as a star in our Arbor Day play, emoting about "our fwends the twees." Elsie Krewitz, my second grade teacher, who saw that my speech defect could be a problem in later years, schooled me for a full hour after three o'clock every day for a full semester until my trilled "r's" had a ring of authenticity. I skipped along through grade school and went on to James H. Bowen High School, named for an early governor of Illinois, where I spent four years and had a relatively easy time. Studies came easily for me, and since I got along well with my fellow students, I was one of the leaders in the class. My teachers were, as always, of mixed talent and energy, but most were competent and a few were first-rate. It was public high school education in America at its best in those days, with the opportunity to learn, to play, and to grow up if one made the effort.

Bowen bordered on the mill district, and most of the 350 students in our class were white, but there were sizable numbers of blacks and Mexicans among us. Most friendship groups were segregated, but teams, clubs, and activities were usually mixed. A sense of security filled our tough school. Occasional petty thefts took place, but rarely was there violence or even the threat of it. When the football team played our arch-rival, some brief scuffles might break out, but even these were seldom serious. In my years of walking and bicycling the two miles back and forth to school, I passed through fairly tough neighborhoods, but there was never a feeling of being on guard. The standard sexual awakenings were going on, but overt expressions of them were strongly muted in comparison to today. Hand-holding with one's girl, some mild petting, and some close dancing were as far as we could go in those days when pregnancy out of wedlock in middle-class America was a death knell for one's future.

Miss Worthen, the head English teacher, taught me and many others a love for the great writers. Mr. Kurtz, Mr. Huebner, and Mr. Clark taught me precise and rigorous physics and math. Miss Miller taught me about putting out our newspaper, *The Bowen Arrow*, on a deadline. I did miss some things. R.O.T.C. would have come in handy in the next few years. Had I gone out for band, I would have learned earlier about music, which I came later to appreciate so much. Little was available in the fine arts at Bowen, and I satisfied my creative urge by drawing cartoons for the school newspaper and for the yearbooks, with an eye toward a career in that field. I often went downtown to the Art Institute of Chicago on Saturday mornings. By patiently waiting at his office door in the Tribune Tower, I became acquainted with John T. McCutcheon, the famous cartoonist of the *Chicago Tribune*. I pursued Vaughn Shoemaker of the *Chicago Daily News* for an interview to be published in the *Arrow*. They both looked at my work and gave me much encouragement.

I had several close friends, and I still think of them as good friends even though I have not seen them for nearly sixty years. My two locker mates were Jack Kimball and Jack Jenkins. Kimball was a star student who beat me for second place in the class by a hundredth of a point. We both trailed Jean Urbanowicz whose straight A average in four years of high school was unbeatable. Kimball and I both achieved straight As in science for four years and tied for first place in mathematics and science. He went to the University of Chicago, and eventually attended West Point instead of directly entering the ranks of the service. He was graduated from the academy late in World War II, and the last time I saw him was soon after the Korean War, an unhappy major wondering whether he should have entered a different field.

Jenkins went into the navy after graduation from Bowen, was taken prisoner at Clark Field in the Philippines, and later died in a Japanese prisoner of war camp. The war also meant death for my friend George Boyle, who was my opponent for the office of treasurer of the class. He never quite forgave me for winning the post. Bill DeWitt, who was in the class ahead of me but a close companion in our section of the locker room, was killed in a tank battle in North Africa. I found, at the fiftieth reunion of our class in 1989, that several others had been killed during the war. But that was not foreseen in June of 1939 when we graduated, full of spark and eager to go on to the next chapter. My two closest friends were Bob Levin, who was to be badly wounded in Normandy, and Bruce Fluegge, and we hung together both in school and after school in a variety of extracurricular activities. My time at Bowen had been productive and, by and large, a happy one. Ten percent of the class, it turned out, would go on to college, which was typical of that period.

Besides high school there was a second interest that occupied all my spare time: the Boy Scouts of America. At twelve, I had joined Troop 523, sponsored by the Windsor Park Church, and I quickly immersed myself in the lore and the excitement of scouting. I found the oath and the law of the Boy Scouts absolutely credible, and I believed in them as much as anything. I can recite them both today. My patrol, the Beavers, included my closest friends, and we met not only at the time of the troop meeting on Friday evenings, but for other meetings at least once, and occasionally twice, a week. Bobby Powers, my assistant patrol leader, was a good friend but also a fierce competitor in most of the Boy Scout activities. When we went off to camp, we were tent mates, swimming buddies, and close companions. We entered the Order of the Arrow one year apart. When I reached Eagle rank, he was close behind me, and although we drifted apart after high school, we remained good friends. Powers, the pilot of a B29, was killed during the war along with his crew. Buddy Price, the "kid" in the patrol, was severely crippled as a marine during the battle of Iwo Jima. Buddy really belonged in the Beaver patrol; he had large white buck teeth and a wonderful smile that showed them off. Powers and I got the Lifesaving Merit Badge together, swimming off the 79th Street beach in June in Lake Michigan under the tutelage of an instructor who took great delight, it seemed to us, in keeping us under water. It was the toughest of the badges for me.

Bird study was the most fascinating of them all, and it began an interest in my life that has never receded. Sixty years later, my wife Betty

As a Boy Scout, at age twelve, 1934

and I are dedicated birders, traveling the country to observe new and old species, and taking great delight in seeing these magnificently independent creatures whether in our own backyard or in far-off places. At this point, in addition to having seen many species of birds outside North America, we are approaching our 600th bird species within North America, and we hope to reach that magic number before we finish.

Scouting was one of the great formative influences on my life. For me, living on the south side of Chicago in the midst of a crowded city, scouting opened windows and doors on the natural world and brought me closer to the outdoor history and character of America in a way that nothing else could have.

The summer of 1939 was a hot one, as usual, in Chicago. I was now free of high school and just turned 17 in July, eager to get on with my life. My close high school friends, Bruce Fluegge and Bob Levin, and I had talked of bicycling to all the state parks in Wisconsin and spending the summer camping. The cold reality, however, was that we all needed to earn some money, and I settled, happily, for a few weeks of bass fishing on the Paint River in upper Michigan, including a week of running the Net River and the Paint River with Kenneth, my brother, and his pal Harley. We liked the solitude of the river, where we would seldom see another fisherman.

We had excellent fishing and the frequent thrill of running the rapids, which would appear suddenly when we rounded a bend in the river. The large rapids gave forewarning and when the menacing roar of fast-moving water would sound ahead, we had to decide quickly whether to run it or portage around it. The best known of the swift water rapids on the Paint was Horse Race Rapids, which had a roar and growl that one could hear from a mile away. The rapids ran for a full thousand yards through narrow rocky banks, and going through them was a heart-pounding experience. Occasionally we would portage around a falls, and that meant a few hours of sweating the equipment through the woods in a detour around the river. In the late afternoon, we would pull into the bank and find a place to camp for the night.

Ken and I were both at home in the woods. My several years in the Boy Scouts had given me the skills I needed to enjoy the river and the company. The fishing was good in those days, and Paint River bass were known for their combativeness, as well as their tastiness. The experience was marred by a type of worm that had invaded the bass; one had to cut a few of them from the fillet before sautéing the fish. Overall, though, our time on the river was a wonderful experience that we remembered warmly for years. Harley, a city boy through and through, told Ken many years later that the trip was one of the great experiences in his life. We came back to Chicago full of vigor and ready, we thought, for the next chapter. Few could predict that the next six years would be a life-and-death epoch for everyone.

Within days, the war in Europe began with the German invasion of Poland on September 1, 1939, and the British and French declaring war on Germany on September 3. Almost nothing would ever be the same.

On the Andorran border with France, September 1944

2

College and Going to War

Ken and I had the large attic room in our house, and we soon had a big map of the world and one of Europe on which we pinned the latest war happenings. Our list of ship sinkings was as accurate as the newspapers would allow, and we also kept track of the few land fronts that, until June 1940, remained fairly stable. The country and the city of Chicago were divided on whether America should enter the war. The words *Roosevelt* and *war monger* were often linked in the headlines of the *Chicago Tribune,* Colonel McCormick's isolationist and dominant newspaper. Most of the Midwest seemed to agree. World War I veterans and American Legionnaires were mostly in their forties, and in the Midwest antiwar feeling among them was high. I had traveled in 1937 to the Chicago Loop to be part of a large crowd that heard Roosevelt's "Quarantine the Dictators" speech on the Outer Drive bridge. It was well received nationally but not in that Chicago crowd, as I remember it. The Chicago Democratic political machine, while actively supporting Roosevelt on domestic matters, seemed to follow the McCormick line on involvement in the war. I had entered Central College in Chicago, now Roosevelt University, in the fall of 1939 and the war would remain the most important item in the news for all my college years.

In June of 1940 everything about the war changed. The German blitzkrieg that defeated France in a matter of weeks, the British retreat at Dunkirk, and the subsequent Battle of Britain made me and everyone else see that we were now on the slippery slope to war. Another dynamic was at work around us; industry was picking up and the mills of South Chicago and Gary were beginning to run at higher rates again. Unemployment was beginning to decrease for the first time in years.

I had gone to Central on a one-year scholarship, and it was largely because of that award that I entered college at all. I also had been awarded a four-year scholarship to Drake University in Iowa because of my journalism record, but the award did not include any expenses. I would have to live at home and earn all other expenses. My folks never had to tell me that; we all knew what the situation was without being told. Ken was a year ahead of me, and he was studying mechanical engineering in the Co-op Program at Armour Tech, later the Illinois Institute of Technology, which meant he alternated between work and school each semester.

I had no trouble getting jobs in downtown Chicago, and I worked forty hours a week doing low-skill tasks. I soon got a job at F. W. Dodge, the construction data company in the Merchandise Mart on the Chicago River, running their mimeograph machines. The minimum wage in those years was forty cents per hour, so twenty hours produced $8.00. But I soon arranged the job so that I could start at 4 P.M., when my classes were essentially over, and work until 8, and then worked out an arrangement for finishing the day's mimeographing in two hours by running two or three machines and still drawing the same daily pay. By the time I left that job, I was making the equivalent of $1.60 per hour.

The night crew at F. W. Dodge consisted of envelope stuffers who would arrive at 6 P.M. and fill the addressed envelopes with data sheets on construction in Chicago. The crews were mostly young women of Italian decent, and the workroom next to the mimeograph room was full of song, laughter and, occasionally, shouted ribald remarks. I didn't mind it a bit and especially looked forward to the monthly party where we enjoyed sandwiches brought from their homes and five-cent Cokes from the machine amid noise, dancing, and fun. It was a happy contrast to the dull grind of my college classes.

I was typically up early, caught the 7:30 train to Randolph Street, attended classes in the Central building at 19 LaSalle Street, and worked through the mid-afternoon. Evenings and some weekends were dominated by study, interrupted by the happy diversion of folk dancing with our increasingly excellent French folk dance group at Central. I found I liked the vigorous country dances of France and worked and played hard at the weekly practices. Classes, of course, were the focus of my effort. I decided to pursue physics in the sciences and economics in the social sciences.

Central was an excellent small college. Begun as a YMCA two-year college many years before to encourage young working people to extend their formal education, it had moved during the Depression to offer a full four-year curriculum of liberal arts and science subjects. The faculty was mixed, but most were University of Chicago Ph.D.s who could not get another post, a few European émigrés, and a few talented academic hangers-on who lived in any large city. The best of these people were very good indeed, and I sought them out: E. J. Kunst, Martin Bronfenbrenner, and Robert Burns in economics, Harry Sell, McKee Rosen, Glenn Wiltsey, and Wayne Lees in the social sciences, and William Laumann and Jay Weinbaum in history, as well as Virgil Lohr in physics. In French, I had Joseph Creanza, a mite of a man with enormous energy and a wonderful joie de vivre, who brought me to fluency in three years. Later in life he became dean of the School of Music at Roosevelt University. He also arranged for me to work in a French language summer school for girls on Vancouver Island for the summer of 1941, which was my first experience outside the middle west and a great maturing exercise.

My grades were typically straight As, which made it possible to keep my scholarship through four years. The school's president, Edward J. Sparling, was ambitious, and after the war, along with a core of the best faculty members, left the school to form Roosevelt University in the beautiful Auditorium Theater building on Michigan Avenue. It was a great coup and a great achievement on their part. Roosevelt prospers to the present day, a first-rate institution, and I have followed its progress with pride. The university remembers its own humble beginnings and that of many of its students. I have been reminded by provosts and presidents there since then that I had a reputation for intelligence and drive, and they remarked that I did not own an outer coat in my first two winters at the school. I actually did have one, but seldom wore it because it was my old Bowen jacket and looked tacky, I thought, in a college setting. I will always be grateful to Central for taking me in and giving me a strong undergraduate academic education in perfectly dismal surroundings.

The shadow of the war in Europe and in China, where its war with Japan had begun in 1937, hung over the United States in all those years. It affected the student atmosphere in major ways. The Selective Service Act—the Draft Act—was narrowly passed in 1940 by a single vote and became the major issue in the debates that took place in the student bodies of the Midwest. The leadership of the national college student group, generally regarded as Communist-dominated, was stridently against the war until the invasion of the Soviet Union by Hitler in 1941.

I had an early glimpse of some draftees, and it was my first look at real soldiers. I had taken the Great Northern train from Chicago to Seattle in June of 1941 to join the French language camp on Vancouver Island for the summer. I traveled for three days and two nights to reach Vancouver on the train, one of the great "streamliners" that constituted cross-country travel in the thirties before the age of the airplane. My companions in the coach in which I rode included several soldiers from the 3d Division on their way to Ft. Lewis, Washington and they welcomed me to their discussions. They had been drafted in the fall of 1940 and now were returning, after furlough, to their division with the extension of the one-year draft bill. Much talk was heard about OHIO, the slogan that appeared on many barns and bridges on the railroad right-of-way. It meant, they said, "Over the hill in October," and yet these soldiers, mostly single, were upbeat and positive about the need to strengthen the U.S. Army. I often wondered how those men fared in the years that followed, but did not foresee that I would meet a lot of the men of the 3d Division in the fall of 1944 in the south of France.

At the French camp—actually a well-appointed prep school facility on the shores of a large Vancouver Island lake during the regular academic year—I met and came to know all of the staff and students. The latter were mostly Canadian prep school and college girls who were learning, or perfecting, their French at several levels. I served as a waiter, porter, and general boy along with two other young men. One, Erwin Nalos, a Czech from a family that had emigrated from Prague after Hitler took over, told me tales of the German occupation of his country, and I learned more from him than I had from any modern history course on the subject. I also began to polish my French, and since it was an offense to use a word of English while on duty, I was able to concentrate on the subject matter. We were discouraged from socializing with the students, but no one paid much attention to that rule, and I developed close associations with two of the girls. It was all great fun and I was sorry to see the summer end.

On December 7, 1941, everything changed. I heard the news of the bombing of Pearl Harbor on the radio on a Sunday afternoon after church. The debacle at Pearl was mind-numbing for all of us, but it had the instant effect of coalescing the country, and after that event no anti-war talk was heard.

The tone of America's neighborhoods changed over the next several months. Almost every house that had been home to a young man soon had the blue-starred serviceman's flag in the window. I soon learned that Jack Jenkins, my old friend and locker mate who had enlisted in the navy after graduation and was stationed at Clark Field in the Philippines, was missing.

I was intent on getting into the service. That seemed to dominate the thinking of many young men, and, like most, I was both intensely interested and somewhat uneasy. Within weeks after Pearl Harbor, I decided to join the Navy Air Corps, and I applied for the Navy V–5 Program with what I thought were great references from my professors. I took the physical exam at Navy Pier on a cold winter day in Chicago and was thunderstruck to learn that I had severe astigmatism and that I had failed the exam. I walked to the train station from Navy Pier feeling dejected. I decided to stay committed to my classes and try to finish my degree before going into the army. To help that process, I joined the Army Enlisted Reserve Corps, which somewhat ambiguously promised to let its enlistees remain in school "until needed." It did not take much intelligence to see that that was an uncertain promise.

I stayed at Central through the summer and fall of 1942, studying and, at the same time, following the progress of the war in the Pacific and in Europe with intense fascination. In October 1942, American forces landed in North Africa and began an uneven campaign to link with the British 8th Army and force the surrender of the German and Italian armies in North Africa. Back at home, in early fall it was clear that I would have the credits to graduate in January 1943 in advance of my June class. I completed my degree in economics and political science, first in my class at Central, and now almost every man in the class was shipping out in one way or another. I quickly got my call-up to active duty in March 1943. I filled in the six weeks after graduation preparing income tax forms for an enterprising accounting firm, dating Marie, my folk dancing partner, and getting ready to go. It was a rather heady time, but I was glad, at age twenty, when the time came to board the train for Camp Grant in the company of fifteen other college call-ups, to find out, at last, what it was like to go to war.

My first few days in the army were all confusion and noise: uniforms, tests, shots, orientation, and moving from one meaningless place to another. The transfer into the barren life of the barracks with never-ending ordering about by yelling noncoms came as a shock. After another few days, I learned I had scored 150 points in the Army General Classification Test. "Your score is the highest in the last six weeks, and you will probably get an interesting assignment," said a major who went over the records when the first few days of indoctrination were complete. He was wrong.

The following day, along with several hundred others, I left on an early morning troop train for obvious points south. Except for that general direction, no one could or would tell us where we were headed. But twenty-four hours later, we unloaded on a sandy rail siding at Camp Robinson, named for the late Majority Leader of the Senate, Joseph T. Robinson, outside Little Rock, Arkansas. We, and eventually another trainload or two, were part of a training infantry regiment forming in a so-called new section of Camp Robinson. The new rough wood barrack huts were still being constructed, and it was a cold April in Arkansas— still cold enough to need fires in the oil drum stoves that heated the thirty-man, two-squad huts.

We were half of the third platoon of D Company of the training battalion, and we were, in turn, part of a four-battalion infantry replacement regiment, roughly 5,000 men, to be trained in seventeen weeks as infantrymen. Nine months later, most of them would be in combat in Italy. The company was largely drawn from Arkansas and neighboring states, but we had small contingents from Pennsylvania, Michigan, and Illinois, and a few of us from Chicago. I think we Northerners felt outnumbered. The "hillbillies" seemed at first to hang together, and the sound of country music, largely new to us in those days, filled the huts in the late evening. Later, we were to become a surprisingly cohesive unit. The barracks corporal was a Michigan National Guardsman, but the other noncoms were all Southerners.

We quickly learned the schedule: up at 5 A.M., awakened to the screech of whistles, formations at 5:15, breakfast mess at 5:30, huts cleaned and formations ready to go at 6:30; in the field, steady exercises through the day, with noon mess typically in the field, back at camp at 4:30, evening mess at 5 o'clock, and lights out at 9 P.M.

I disliked it intensely at first. The physical demand and constant pressure were severe but became bearable after the first week. We got used to our new M–1 rifles and the combat gear. What made it difficult was the lack of communication, the generally overbearing treatment of the cadre, and the stupefaction of the ranks. The pressure got to a fair number of the trainees. Dick Hetke, my friend from Loyola in Chicago, went AWOL after three weeks and disappeared. I never learned what happened to him. A few were discharged for real or imagined physical disabilities. A soldier in Company E smuggled a live round of ammunition during range exercises and killed himself with his rifle when his hut was deserted on a Saturday night. The Arkansas terrain and weather didn't help; a cold and wet spring turned suddenly hot and dusty as May and June came on. The piney woods swarmed with chiggers and mosquitoes, and the sand hills were full of fleas. The training officers were a mixed bag—a portent of things to come.

The company commander was a pompous strutter who enjoyed criticizing his lieutenants in the presence of the men. The platoon commanders were largely ROTC commissioned, and all but one were graduates of Southern colleges. I was much impressed by the best of them; they were tough, quiet-voiced, slow to anger, but consistent. They turned out to be typical of the Southern military breed on whom the nation had often depended. The leader of our platoon, Lieutenant Pezeley, was a rare Northerner among the officer cadre. He was an excellent officer who came from Utah and had graduated from the University of Michigan ROTC. In general, however, officers were distant from the trainees. Most direction of the troops was left to the noncommissioned cadre, with their mixed set of talents.

My attitude toward the whole process began to change. By the midpoint of the training cycle, I decided I could endure soldiering—I even liked it. I had been pulled out of the marching platoon one day and promoted to squad leader, with my predecessor fired on the spot for some unknown error. I developed confidence in my ability to keep up, and I found I enjoyed being in front of the squad rather than in the dusty rear. I also enjoyed being freed up from details like KP.

The training ground on. The week ended usually at noon on Saturday, with laggard squads doing extra work far into the afternoon. Every few weeks one got an overnight pass to Little Rock, and since there were few places that a soldier could stay in that crowded, monotonous town, most returned on the midnight bus. Also, not much could be done on $21 per month, since much of that was taken out for insurance and other deductions. Bars did land-office business, but since I seldom drank anything in those days, and then only beer, trips to Little Rock held no allure. The lucky few were those who had a date in town, but only the Arkansas boys seemed to manage that. The perils of VD were preached constantly, and the few dens of potential sin were patrolled, one was told, by heavy bands of MPs.

Little news of national events drifted into camp. I followed the progress of the North Africa and Sicily campaigns by means of old newspapers. The most memorable event was when, expecting the usual weekend respite, the whole regiment was ordered out on the road in class A uniforms. After a few miles of marching in the light rain, the companies and battalions were formed in single ranks along both sides of the road and spaced over several miles, each soldier at arm's length from his next neighbor. We were lining the state road, which wound through the camp for miles, obviously awaiting some important drive-through.

After an hour's wait in the light but steady rain, we learned the identity of our reviewer. A fast-moving procession of army command cars followed by a big black Cadillac with American flags on the fenders came moving through. Troops at attention, the cars sped by. In the Cadillac I recognized, or perhaps thought I did, the man holding his hat in half salute peering out. "Roosevelt" was the whisper, passed along hoarsely. The camp news later confirmed it. The march back to camp, still in the rain, was a glum anticlimax. My thought at the time was, couldn't someone have had a better morale-builder of an idea than speeding FDR past watching wet troops? My generally negative impression of the high brass was not improved but still, I, for one, was glad that the event had taken place. It did seem to indicate that Camp Robinson, Arkansas, was not the god-forsaken place it appeared to be if Roosevelt would take the time to visit. But then, I was still highly impressionable.

The end of the training cycle suddenly loomed before us in August 1943. By this time I thought I was a fairly good soldier. I could lead a mortar squad or a rifle squad, and I felt a certain confidence about it. It is hard to explain the satisfaction one feels moving down a dusty road in rolling step with men you have come to know and trust, with full equipment and with a great sense of confidence of being among the best soldiers around. I thought the army should have built on that spirit at that point, but, of course, it didn't have that in mind. Hot as hell, sandy, and buggy, we heard only rumors about what would happen to our training battalion.

I was ordered to go to the company commander's office, and found him and the platoon lieutenant. It was the first time I had had a direct meeting with the captain in seventeen weeks. The gist of his rapid-fire comment was that I deserved to go to O.C.S., but there was no O.C.S. quota for the regiment at this point. O.C.S. was full, he said. He was willing to propose me for a West Point appointment as the entry from our regiment, or to send me to noncom school. Finally there was a program, just announced, called the "Army Specialized Training Program," where I would go back to college for engineering or language study. That appealed to me, and in less than a minute, I had made a decision that set the course for the rest of my years in the army. One week later, I and six others from the company headed off to Stillwater, Oklahoma, and to Oklahoma A&M.

I didn't hear what happened to the old company and battalion for many weeks until, finally, a letter arrived from one of my old buddies. The battalion had been shipped out, intact, to Camp Fannin, Texas, then on to Camp Bowie, Texas, and, after further brief training, sent out as replacement units to the 34th Division. Later, I heard they joined the division in Italy and made the landings at Salerno that fall. It wasn't until three years later that I ran into Al Glielmi, once in my squad at Robinson and now selling insurance in Chicago. He told me that the old unit had been split up with complete squads joining the 34th, and had seen violent times at Salerno beginning that fall and then through the Italian campaign. He believed that almost all of the originals in our platoon were casualties out of Italy. He had ended up an infantry captain, he said, largely by luck. I have never heard anything else of that old group, but I can still see my squad in my mind's eye and wonder how they all fared. They were good men.

My experiences that fall were quite different, and I occasionally ponder the luck of the draw in the army during the war. After some testing and sorting at Oklahoma A&M, we were divided into various small groups and sent off to universities across the country. I was sent to Indiana University to study German in the Area and Languages Program of the ASTP. I was the only one of the original Camp Robinson group to go to Indiana, and I quickly lost touch with the others of us who had left Robinson together. It was typical of the service, I suppose, that one could have an intense experience and know closely a group of men in what became a tightly knit unit and then, in one quick exchange of orders, be shifted and form an entirely new group. To be involved in such a rapid reassignment and rebuilding of a group was a common experience, one I shared several times.

After an all-too-short three-day pass in Chicago to see my folks and my girl, I reported to Bloomington, Indiana. The university, like all others during the war, was striving valiantly to keep its facilities occupied productively, and at the same time respond to the war needs of the country. I saw Herman Wells, the rotund president of Indiana, more often at the university than I saw my CO at Camp Robinson. The university had army and navy units on its campus and was trying to coordinate and conduct its academic programs with a depleted staff, few male civilian students, and large numbers of female students.

Our area and language unit of sixty men was housed in the requisitioned Phi Kappa Psi House, where we ate, slept, and studied for the next five months. We were encouraged to keep to ourselves and not to mix with other soldiers during the working week. Except for company formations at 6 each morning in front of Memorial Hall, we were kept isolated. German was spoken exclusively after the first week. Penalties of no pass or confinement to the house were meted out to anyone who spoke a word of English. Of course, that was an empty threat and few people were ever turned in, but the tone of the order was respected to a large extent. Our instructors were refugee academics, with one or two regular Indiana instructors. On weekends after 1 P.M. on Saturday and until 5 on Sunday, we were free, and there was some semblance of campus life at dances and performances and quick and happy dating, largely with the Navy Waves on campus. It was a satisfactory life after the rigors of an infantry camp.

I had a four-day pass at Christmas and quickly hitchhiked north to Chicago—the only means of transportation available—where I had happy reunion with the family. Marie and I made promises that did not survive the snow's melting that spring, a common occurrence in a war-

paced world. I returned to Indiana and took final examinations, standing fourth in the class, and was given academic credits in German, geography, and history, none of which I would ever need for an academic degree. We did learn a lot of German. I felt I could interrogate prisoners and talk to the natives with some facility, but I knew I certainly couldn't pass as a native anywhere in Germany. Some of the Jewish Americans in the unit who had spoken German or Yiddish at home had a great advantage over the rest of us, and I envied their easy accents.

I also learned a lot about the geography of Germany, including the layout of several cities. I always thought I could have found my way around in several places. Ludwigshafen was one such place but when I finally reached there, the city was so flattened that there were few cleared streets to walk. In mid-January, we learned the next step. The top twenty ranked soldiers were assigned to a newly formed civil affairs unit and sent off to a pre-embarkation camp in Pennsylvania. The rest, it later turned out, went off to Camp Ritchie and an intelligence school as intelligence noncoms.

Soon on our way overseas, the unit went through the Boston embarkation port. It was my first time in New England and I was impressed even in those few days. We trained and waited at a camp called Myles Standish. Nothing remains now of the bustling barracks and grounds, which has all reverted back to scrub New England woods as a state park. We were given ten-hour passes to go into Boston, which struck me as an opportunity for potential AWOLs. I much enjoyed walking around the cold city, and I especially enjoyed lively Scollay Square, now replaced by the barren Government Center, and the view of the frozen Charles River before returning to camp. I did not see MIT across the river on that winter day, but even if I had, I could not possibly have guessed that my future life lay there.

Two nights later we boarded troop trains for the short transport directly to the piers of Boston, boarding the ship with all the efficiency of the army system and getting our last glimpse of the United States. At the gangplanks were Red Cross women handing out small boxes of stationery and playing cards as we climbed onto the ship and into the holds. If ever a volunteer wonders whether the drab practice of passing out something as dull as playing cards to departing soldiers is important, let me assure her that it is. Theirs were the only friendly faces we saw in those last hours in Boston. Our ship, a converted passenger liner renamed the *General Edmund Alexander,* was part of a huge convoy with much naval presence. I was glad to see it the next morning, catching a brief glimpse from the deck on a cold, gray day, as the convoy got under way in rather rough seas into the north Atlantic. March 1944 was still a difficult time in the U-boat war, and we sailed along with many other ships through ominous rolling waters.

My deck was the fourth below the promenade, and with our four-decker bunks, there was little room to move, much less walk around. Anyone with claustrophobia could not have survived in the fourth and lowest deck of the *Alexander.* Ten days later, however, we steamed into much calmer seas, saw the coast at last, and were told over the speaker system that we were going to dock in Greenock, the port of Glasgow in Scotland. The troops on board the ship, which included one full infantry battalion, were loaded onto trucks, and we climbed aboard our own trucks. Once beyond the bombing damage of the Glasgow dock area, I thought the countryside was quite attractive. Ours was not the only convoy on the road. To my delight, there were early signs of spring in northern England, and I was glad to see them after the winter in the Middle West. We ended up in Stockport, an undistinguished suburb of Manchester, and spent the night sleeping in a large barnlike structure on the edge of a small park.

We were still a formation of only twenty men under the command of a master sergeant who told us, next morning, that we would be billeted in civilian homes in the area and would join our company later in the afternoon. Shades of the Declaration of Independence! I could hardly believe that we were going to be bedded down in civilian houses in the area, but that is exactly what happened. The British were still using the system that the American colonists complained about in 1775. I and two other soldiers were called out in time, and followed in full military step behind an English bobby, high helmet and all, down one of the winding streets of Stockport. In order, we peeled off one by one with him, and knocking at the doors, smartly, he would address the housewife, "Our record shows one space, is that correct, madam?" "Yes," the answer came from the woman of the house, half hidden behind her door.

And so I met Mrs. Percy Sharp, who looked at me, apprehensively, and, with a tentative smile said, "Come in, won't you." The Sharps lived in a small house with two bedrooms upstairs and one down. The front bedroom on the second floor, empty except for a British Army cot that looked like it had gone into service during the Crimean War, was my home for the next six weeks. Mr. Sharp was quiet, gaunt, and somewhat disabled by his World War I service in Gallipoli, but still working at a local food factory about half time. Mrs. Sharp was a cheerful, reserved English lady who later confided to me that the rumor in Stockport was that they would billet American Negro soldiers.

She introduced me to her daughter Muriel that evening after my return from the company formation. Muriel was a pleasant young woman of about twenty, who worked in a war plant and left each morning early and arrived home in the late afternoon. She got my attention that evening by asking if I had an alarm clock. When I told her that I did not, she responded, "Then, I can knock you up every morning."

Her husband, whose photo was on the mantel, was an RAF corporal somewhere in the Middle East. She had not seen him for about a year. Mr. Sharp, whom I came to know in the days that followed, was unsure of himself about meeting an American, but in time we both came to enjoy our late evening conversations. When I was pulled out in May, he told me, with a quiet catch in his voice, that he would have liked to have a son like me. I think he was fortunate to have a fine wife and daughter.

Our unit finally came together: a detachment of the 2678th Regiment, First European Civil Affairs Division, with some earlier identifications along the way. Eventually, we were to become Company L, First Regiment of the First European Civil Affairs Division. The unit included about thirty officers and thirty enlisted men. The officers were mostly specialists of some kind, public health, police and security, law, food and agriculture, engineering, transportation, utilities, and other areas useful to running a city. The enlisted men included our Indiana group plus a few others and some MPs from divisions now in the U.K., as well as several enlisted medics. It seemed like a good group. We trained every day, six days each week, from dawn to dusk, with occasional night exercises. We were issued our vehicles: jeeps, three-quarter-ton and two-and-a-half-ton trucks. We were also issued six brand-new olive-drab Indian motorcycles. The powerful cycles were not made for English roads. One was assigned to me, and I learned to drive it with some uneasiness. Since we did a lot of small convoy exercises, the motorcycles typically served as advance scouts or messenger vehicles between convoy sections. The narrow roads and "wrong way" English drivers made such exercises sporty, especially at night. After a warrant officer broke his leg after crashing into a tree and two other cycles were damaged, the six cycles were reassigned somewhere, and we went back to jeeps. We also were issued weapons. Mine was a Thompson submachine gun which was notoriously inaccurate in distance firing, but it looked formidable and I kept it for the next several months.

Duty typically ended after mess at about 7 P.M., and I walked home to the Sharps. At nine, Mrs. Sharp would serve tea and we visited while we listened to the BBC. It was a happy way to end the day. Our Saturday nights and Sundays were free, and I joined in the social doings at a local church in the company of Muriel. Occasionally, returning home at night, we stopped at a blacked-out fish and chips shop. We felt an ominous excitement on those darkened roads. I enthusiastically went to the movies with a girl who lived on the block. She seemed mature and eager to meet a "Yank." When Mrs. Sharp whispered to me that I ought to know that she was just fifteen, I quickly retreated. I would have sworn that she was a least four years older than that, and I believe that she would have sworn the same. I soon found older company.

The spring in Manchester was lovely in 1944, but our unit packed up on six hours' notice one early May morning and we headed south for Shrivenham, outside Swindon and London. Several British officers, specialists in various areas, were assigned to our unit. By this time the unit was functioning quite well, and we assumed that France was not far off.

Shrivenham was a former college of some sort, but it had served as housing for several military units in the years before we arrived, and the buildings showed it. We now settled into a state of readiness for the invasion that was on everyone's mind. We had a few weekends free in those late May days, and my new buddy, Bill Dufty, who had worked as a union staff member with the UAW in Detroit, and I would head for London when we could. Dufty had some kind of UAW introduction to Aneurin Bevan, the Labour Party leader, and Jenny Lee, his wife, also a notable M.P. from Wales. They lived in a large apartment on Sloane Square in London, and that apartment was a haven for all kinds of labor and political types.

Jenny Lee was one of those amazing British hostesses who could accommodate any number of visitors with equanimity. We were made wel-

First European Civil Affairs Regiment, officers and enlisted men of Detachment A1 L1, including seven British officers. HWJ is in the top row, fifth from the right. May 1944, just before D day, Shrivenham, England

come and told we could stay as long and as often as we were on leave in London. The party never ended, it seemed, and I remember that first weekend, blind with fatigue, going to bed at 3 A.M. in a back room with the debate still going on, hot and heavy, in the large blacked-out drawing room. Everything from government policy on the colonies to military strategy after the invasion was on the agenda.

The Welsh accent and the musical voices were all new to us. So was the drinking. Up to that point, I had never seen such drinking, but the Welsh politicians were bottomless when it came to alcohol. Nye Bevan and Jenny Lee were in and out, of course. Bevan, who had a voice like a musical instrument, worked with little sleep, as far as I could see, and went back and forth to Westminster several times that weekend. When Dufty and I returned a week later, it seemed as though the conversation was still going on except that several new faces were present.

Back at the unit in late May, it was clear that something big was about to happen. For one thing, our unit and every other one in the area was confined to quarters. No one could get in or out of the immediate area.

We were ordered to prepare our vehicles for beach landings and sea water immersion and spent hours putting putty and cosmoline around all the vents and ports of the vehicle, and a high pipe extension on each exhaust pipe. Even to me, the notion of driving a jeep submerged in several feet of water seemed absurd, but that is what our motor pool lieutenant was talking about. We loaded up the gear that we intended to take into France and then waited. Before dawn on the morning of June 6, I was aware of the heavy droning of an aircraft fleet far larger than the usual. At dawn, we could see continuous formations of aircraft, all with broad white stripes on their wings. Two- and four-engine bombers, fighters and gliders being pulled by DC-3s, all roaring east from the air strips that dotted the countryside around us, all heading for a level of activity that no one had ever seen before.

At dawn, the unit ate a hurried mess and assumed—wrongly, it turned out—that we would leave for the embarkation ports. At midday, a captain came by and distributed Ike's invasion letter, which we learned was given to all troops designated for the landing, one to each man. That afternoon, our sister unit got orders to load up and leave, eventually landing on Utah Beach on D day plus eight. We stood in reserve for that unit and, although we didn't know it then, we were destined for the south of France. We were held in reserve in case the first group took major casualties and needed replacements.

We then waited and wondered. Typically, neither the commanding officer nor his deputy ever uttered a word of explanation to the enlisted men. Nor did any other officer come to see us during that time. In later months, I marveled at the blindness shown by these highly educated and dedicated men. Communication, building cohesion, listening to their people, never occurred to those officers. This continued in the months ahead. I assumed it happened to all units, and I now think it was the height of bad leadership to exclude the men—and probably the junior officers too—from any stream of communication. Such isolation bred rumors, which, in turn, bred uneasiness. That was the army's practice, and it lost immense amounts of cohesion and commitment from the troops.

Although our half of the unit was awarded the Battle Star for Normandy along with our sister group, we never saw the beaches and participated only by proxy with our twins in Company A.

We waited, the quarantine was finally lifted, and a week later Dufty and I were back in London. We saw the Bevans again, ducked the V–1s, which were now dropping like ominous and deadly flies in London, and took up with new friends from other units similarly waiting. The news from the Normandy beaches was mixed, and that was all anyone ever talked about. The landing forces were still there but making slow progress. One weekend I checked into enlisted men's billets behind the Regent Palace Hotel for two nights and returned, after a day of roaming London, to find the hotel cordoned off. It had taken a V–1 hit that had demolished a section of the hotel.

Having a drink with some Canadian pilot officers, I asked one, Jack MacElhone, if he would write to my mother and tell her that he had seen me, since our mail was still embargoed and the Canadians had no such stricture. My mother, I later learned, received a nice note from him; the next week I learned from his buddies that his plane had been hit and was down in France.

By the end of June, our unit finally loaded up and moved, not to the embarkation ports for France, but rather to Liverpool, where we boarded the battered and worn *Empress of England*. We sailed south in a small convoy through Gibraltar, watching Spanish fishing boats that we assumed were noting our passage. (Months later, the British Navy announced that the *Empress of England* had been sunk by a submarine.) It was rumored that we would land in Oran, Algeria, there to prepare for entry into Italy or Southern France, and that is exactly what we did. We landed in Oran, traveled by truck to Algiers, where we took up a camp site, then killed a lot of time and saw some of the old wreckage of the North African battles of months before.

Finally, we were loaded into a large landing ship for debarkation in Southern France as part of the Seventh Army. Our ship left Algiers in the company of several other combat-ready ships, and we quickly learned that our shipmates, not exactly friendly, were an infantry company of French Moroccan soldiers. They were under the command of a continually drunk French infantry captain, and they were bound as reinforcements for one of the French divisions coming from Italy and also destined for the beaches of Southern France. Our small group was finally told that we were heading for St. Tropez and the civil affairs operations in Southern France. This time we earned the Battle Star, but the invasion of Southern France was relatively mild compared to the Normandy invasion. For the men of the 3d and 45th Divisions who made the combat assaults preceding us, however, it was a grueling and bloody campaign. Both divisions, along with the 36th, soon headed west and north, ending their war nine months later in Germany. The 3d, from the time it entered combat in Southern France, was to endure 28,000 casualties, a turnover of more than 200 percent in its ranks. The other two divisions were close behind in these grisly percentages.

The civil affairs people were not combat soldiers, however, and we found ourselves eventually following the combat units across the southern rim of France. The German troops fought hard along the coast and in the interior but were constantly retreating to the west and north. The air was dominated by the Americans, and offshore a sizable and visible fleet of warships occasionally threw shells far inland. Debris, wreckage of vehicles, houses, and bridges, and occasionally bodies were all over the area. Toulon, which the French took on August 28 with a loss of 2700 casualties, was a smoking ruin. The wreckage of German transport and ordnance was everywhere.

Marseilles, the major city on the delta on the Rhone, was a blown-up port full of sunken ships and exploded quays. The remnants of German units were still surrendering. There, the civil affairs units did have plenty to do, reestablishing a functioning city, its political network, its water, transportation, food supply, and safety. The politicians and civil servants, split by deadly arguments over their presumed collaboration with the Germans, seemed stunned. The number one goal was to open the port so allied ships could reenter and unload troops and supplies. Within a few weeks there was some improvement, but the city around the port remained a partially gutted and malfunctioning place for the rest of the war. A quick run against the military traffic back to Cannes and I saw that still attractive town, including the Carleton Hotel, vacated by the Germans not long before. But the civil affairs function was assigned to others and I returned to duty in Marseilles.

Today, there is no sign of the battles or even the ruins of the huge concrete fortifications and emplacements that dotted the Mediterranean coast. Many events still seem vivid to me, crowding one another with a sequence of days and times completely jumbled. Some, I suppose, I have

HWJ, early September 1944, Marseilles, France

tried to forget. One I remember well. We were showing an American presence by running irregularly timed jeep patrols around several streets and roads in Marseilles. The purpose no doubt was to establish a sense of order and control for the civilian population. Of course, an air of lawlessness still existed in the city. One night I was scheduled to ride in a jeep patrol, as usual, but at the last minute a sergeant just transferred from Italy, was assigned in my place, sitting in the rear of the jeep with two soldiers riding in front. He was killed by a rifle bullet in the back of the head an hour later, and we buried him at the new raw earth American cemetery just outside the city. He was from St. Paul and married, and that was all I knew of him; but he seemed close to me that day.

The city of Marseilles, apart from the litter and wreckage of the port, returned to some semblance of order rather quickly. Civil affairs was shortly placed under the command of Delta Base Headquarters, headed by a one-star general who soon after ordered in more military police companies to keep reasonable order. The civil affairs unit was soon fanned out over the major towns around Marseilles to get civilian institutions and functions in place.

General Charles de Gaulle, fresh from his triumphal entry into Paris, came to Marseilles to establish his authority over the city and the region. He was accompanied by a large contingent of his loyal supporters as he strolled into the main plaza of the port. A few American units were represented, but I got a good look at "le general" as he moved imperiously around the square. He was impressive, no doubt about it.

I hoped I might be assigned to a town away from Marseilles. I had a good reason for wanting to leave. The port battalions soon occupied the ruined port structures and began the round-the-clock task of clearing lanes for ships, loading the red ball express trucks, and clearing the exits to the city. The big problem was supplying the advancing troops toward the north. An enormous black market soon was functioning, with largely port battalion soldiers and French Arab troops the ready conduits for food and gasoline to the starved civilian population. It was not a wholesome situation. A few of us soon developed ready and welcome entrance to the noncom haunts of the port. Liquor, cigarettes, and women were the currency of the port, and few officers, unless in the company of much advertised military police, showed their faces in those port areas, especially at night. I was acceptable because of some friendships with port battalion sergeants with whom civil affairs worked, but the atmosphere was far from comfortable. It would be hard to remain there without some complicity in the black market.

In the meantime, the American combat divisions were making progress north of Lyon to Dijon, and after linking with the army units heading from Normandy, Falaise, and Paris, they pushed on to the Rhine. It seemed possible, in those balmy September days, that the war would end by Christmas. The Allies were soon to be disabused of that idea by stiffening German counterattacks and a strong defense.

In early September, I was assigned as interpreter to a small reconnaissance unit that was going to cross the Rhone and survey the departments of Languedoc-Roussillon. The detachment was headed by a Captain William von Seggern, an agricultural specialist who had just come up from Italy and service with the military government there, and whom I had never seen before. Von Seggern, an unlikely name for an American in civil affairs, I thought, turned out to be a taciturn Nebraskan, full of quiet wit and a steady dislike for headquarters. I would work under him and with him for the next nine months.

The route of U.S. military operations had sped northeast and no American military units had crossed the Rhone into the southwest quarter of France. One French armored battalion from De Lattre de Tassigny's division had made an early quick sweep across the river, but the Germans were not seeking a fight at that point and were either surrendering or, mostly, succeeding in moving north to join their retreating army. The bridges across the Rhone had all been destroyed by retreating Germans or by allied bombing at the times of the landings. Our detachment was supposed to cross the Rhone at Tarascon and Beaucaire, where a ferry crossing existed. After that, we were on our own, with instructions to visit the several major towns of the region and make contact with whatever civilian leadership was replacing the Vichy French prefects, mayors, and other officials. We were not to go as far as Toulouse, which would later be the goal of another detachment. Bordeaux, further west, remained in German hands, as it would until almost the end of the war.

The makeshift ferry at Tarascon, essentially a small barge powered by a large and noisy outboard motor, ran back and forth on an irregular schedule by a cable moored at an angle across the wide river, which was running slowly at that point in the season. Since there was little motor traffic, we quickly commandeered the ferry, loaded our two vehicles, and started across toward the bluffs on the Beaucaire side. A hundred yards out we heard rifle shots and the whine of ricochets aimed at us from a copse of trees on a hill on the other side. The range was a long one and there was little danger, but the operator of the small craft soon got down on the deck behind his cargo of sacks and boxes and motioned to us to do likewise. Von Seggern calmly lit a cigarette and said quietly, "That SOB can't hit us. Let's show this guy how Americans act under fire." Looking back later, I thought we were kind of silly, but the French must have thought we were crazy. I never did get a line on who was firing at us, but it was a pair of military rifles at least three hundred yards away and was not serious. It was probably coming from retreating militia members who, facing a hopeless future, were venting their anxiety and anger. I was glad to have us tie up on the dock at Beaucaire.

We then headed north and west for the major cities of the region: Arles, Nîmes, Montpellier, Béziers, Narbonne, Perpignan, and Carcassonne. Along the way we entered many villages and towns, and the pattern was always the same. We were the first American troops to enter most of these places, and when we drove up to the prefecture we generally got a big and enthusiastic greeting from the survivors of the republic and the "resistance heroes" who had come out of the hills to take over the villages, along with a couple of military types who were eager to cooperate with the Americans. The food and medical supplies needed in these places were enormous, but usually the first order of the day had been to enact some kind of vengeance on the members of the population who had collaborated with the Germans and the Vichy French. Most often, within ten days or two weeks after the Germans had pulled out and headed north, the quick trials of the Milice chiefs had already been held, and the guilty had been executed or imprisoned. In Montpellier alone, over ninety were tried and found guilty, and several were executed. The total number of executions in all of France at this time is still not precisely known, but the best estimate is that some 400 collaborators were executed in summary fashion in the weeks following the invasions of Normandy and the south of France. The former Vichy representatives had much for which to answer. Among other collaboration activities, they had presided over the systematic roundup of Jews and others for one-way transport to the concentration camps. The same grim events had unrolled in most of the towns and cities of the region.

In many places brief battles occurred between the retreating German troops and the French resistance forces. People were still being jailed, but the drumhead justice had come to a halt and some kind of judicial process was coming into effect in most places. We strongly pressed for the process. A bigger question was who among the leaders vying for power would take office. The Communists in the south of France, many with experience and bitter memories of the Spanish Right during the Spanish Civil War, had been the most active and most effective members of the French Resistance. The hundreds of "D-day Maquis" also wanted a part. The French Army of the Vichy government expected a major role as well.

HWJ at the entrance of an abandoned German dugout near Montpellier, France, September 1944

The Catholic Church had by and large cooperated with the occupation and with Vichy and now was regarded with suspicion, although eventually it returned to its accustomed place of influence. The Huguenots, always important in southwest France, had a better record and had provided refuge and leadership for the Maquis, but their numbers were small. The new press was largely Communist controlled, and newspapers were springing up all over. A third large group were the followers and emissaries of de Gaulle, who wanted to run the departments of the region. These latter, in time, succeeded, but it was an up and down struggle for some months in many places. The Maquis were either incorporated into the army or they melted back into the civilian population. The Communists were the most powerful and most disciplined of the minorities seeking power. The American Army's official position was to let the people decide, but clearly we were supporting the Gaullists.

Our reception in Montpellier, the capital of the region, was especially warm. A large crowd of people congregated in the central square—La Place de la Comedie, called, informally, "l'Oeuf" because of its oval shape—as we rolled in; upon seeing we were Americans, many broke into tears and shouting. I remember one curious incident. A young man in civilian clothes pushed close to us and said, "Hi, fellas. Am I glad to see you." He was an American, Amédée Vandeputte, who had been born in France, had emigrated to the States as a young boy, and had lived in Rhode Island until the French Republic had called him back to army service at the start of the 1939 war. He had been captured with the fall of France, escaped to southern France, and eventually married a young woman from a well-known Montpellier family. He had spent several years dodging the Germans and the Vichy police and now wanted to get back to the States. He volunteered to help us, and we later hired him as an interpreter, in which role he served the detachment well. After the war he was able to return to America with his family, and settled again in the United States.

That evening, following a day of meeting the various city departments and hearing their problems, we had dinner with the local leaders of the French Army and some civilians at the Hotel du Midi. After dinner, I was introduced to a group of young men and women who had waited for us in the hotel lobby. They were all in their early and mid-twenties and insisted that we join them at a nearby apartment for drinks. Von Seggern looked at me without a smile and said, "You go ahead, but get in before dawn. We're leaving early." I barely made the dawn curfew. They were full of questions about America, and I enjoyed answering them. One student produced a collection of prewar records, mostly Dorsey and Goodman, and played them on an old windup Victrola. The records were scratchy with wear, but they created a marvelous atmosphere. I danced a lot with one young woman who introduced me to the tango and its intricate, moody melodies. I never hear "La Cumparsita" without thinking of that evening. She said that they hoped they would see me again.

In the next days, we traveled through the area and met dozens of enthusiastic leaders as well as the average men and women on the street, eager to get their lives going again. In Béziers, we toured the gloomy cathedral that had been the site of the massacre of the Protestants and the Catharists in 1200, and in Carcassonne, we stayed in the beautiful walled city, open again after years of occupation. Years later on a visit to France, I found my name in the Livre d'Or at the Hotel de la Cité in which the authorities had insisted von Seggern and I sign our names, dated 1944. The

At the edge of a minefield, Palevas, south of Montpellier, 1944

French manager was at first incredulous to see an actual participant in "La Libération."

Everywhere, people were expecting to see the Americans, and, clearly, they were expecting things to get better immediately. We had to tell them that food was still going to be scarce for some time.

Further south, we entered the great Catalan city of Perpignan where we were guests that evening at a grand dinner in the city hall. Our host was Jacques Violet, the leading citizen of the department, who had followed a difficult path of noncollaboration with the Germans and somehow survived. The dinner to which we contributed two cases of rations lasted three hours, and I was hard pressed in translating all that was said by the Frenchmen to von Seggern and to me. The next day von Seggern told me, wryly, that he knew I was getting tired when I peeled the apple in the fruit course and threw the peelings over my shoulder onto the floor. The next day, south of Perpignan, we entered the last two small fishing ports on the French coast. The tiny ports of Cerbere and Port Vendres were full of wreckage, demolished docks, and ruined warehouses. Clearly, the only possibility of establishing a working port west of Marseilles was at Sète, which had also suffered some damage. We surveyed the area and concluded that it would be difficult to reopen any port for many weeks. Beyond Port Vendres was the Spanish border, with a well-armed Spanish border guard staring at us menacingly. We had the sense that they would have preferred to see Germans, and guessed that not a few German vehicles had passed through to safe haven in the preceding days.

West of Perpignan, we were directed to Prades, a Pyrenees mountain town where Pablo Casals was said to be ready to see Americans after a self-imposed exile during the years since the Fascist victory in the Spanish Civil War. Months later, he gave his first public concert since fleeing Fascist Spain in Montpellier at the Opéra. It was an unforgettable, intensely moving performance. He signed the program for me; years later I gave it to Yo Yo Ma, who had expressed his admiration for Casals during a Bach recital at the home of some friends. It seemed to me that Yo Yo deserved to have the autograph of his idol, and I thought it was a fine place for that modest document to find its home.

When we returned from our reconnaissance after ten days or so, the headquarters colonel seemed unimpressed by von Seggern's report, and I went back to routines in Marseilles. These were interrupted at one point by a cheery visit from a young lieutenant who was on the staff of the general commanding the region of Montpellier. The lieutenant's name was Hubert Boutry, and he had attended the party in Montpellier. He said he hoped we would return to the old area and his view had been seconded by his female friends. I doubted that that was likely but did get him outfitted with a few pieces of American uniform, which he badly needed. We did see him later in Montpellier, and we became good friends. Much later, he was among the French officers killed in French Indochina in their ill-fated colonial war.

In Marseilles, I was expecting to get orders to move to Dijon or further north, and I did not look forward to it with great excitement. A short time later, von Seggern looked for me and said he had orders to set up a civil affairs unit in Montpellier, and to be the American Army representative for the five departments of Languedoc-Roussillon. The unit eventually consisted of von Seggern and two other officers, four enlisted men including me, and a few later additions including Red Cross personnel concerned with missing persons. We were assigned a French liaison offi-

German fortification on the Mediterranean Coast, 1944, with James Whitehead

cer, a lieutenant with the mind-boggling name of Gilbert Colomb de Daunant, who became a great asset to the detachment. Our unit also had
responsibility for a *groupe de transport*—a company of eighty American
front-wheel drive trucks with French officers and men—to carry food
supplies and other needed materials within the region. These trucks were
a great asset for the transportation-starved region. They were maintained
under the supervision of two motor pool sergeants assigned to our unit,
Sergeants Livio and Virgil. The senior NCO was Jim Whitehead, who
had soldiered with von Seggern in North Africa and Italy. Jim was a
lighthearted Californian who had been in the army since 1940.

My chief responsibility was interpreting for the unit and acting in general liaison duties with the administrators of the various towns. Von Seggern called me the chief of staff, but I was soon dubbed "Le Maire de
Montpellier" by my humorous buddies. Two civilian interpreters—Vandeputte and René Lorteur—worked for the detachment and for me full-
time. Lorteur was a suave Parisian right out of central casting, in his
sixties, who mostly wore a threadbare pinstriped black suit and white
shirts with badly frayed collars and cuffs. He had been head of an adver-

tising agency in Paris before the war and was a slightly eccentric, lovable character who ate with us, told droll stories, and was of enormous help.

Returning to Montpellier, we now set up shop as Detachment D3 L1 of the 1st European Civil Affairs Regiment in a serious way. Montpellier, the capital of Herault and of the region of Languedoc-Roussillon, was a city still groggy from the occupation and trying desperately to regain its lifestyle. In 1940, it had reported a population of 90,000, but when we got there, the city's population had swollen to approximately 120,000, or perhaps more; the authorities were not sure. The main duty of the detachment, in the long run, was to help with the return to a normal life of the citizenry, not only in Montpellier and Herault but in the other five departments of the region with their capitals: Nîmes, Béziers, Mende, Rodez, and Perpignan. It was clear, too, that an ancillary civil affairs purpose was to keep the civilian population from being a burden to an all-out military offensive against the Germans. We worked with the new Regional Commissioner, Jacques Bounin, appointed by de Gaulle, a bright, ambitious man who had made the long march with de Gaulle from North Africa. In each department capital, we worked with a French liaison appointee and the French Army. The newly named French office holders were touchy about their prerogatives and, clearly under instructions from de Gaulle, were sensitive to the American presence. In our region, but not in others, we worked this problem through rather well, thanks to Gilbert.

As things settled down, we took office on the second floor of a comfortable building on the Rue de la Loge, one of the main streets of Montpellier. There, we did indeed fly the American flag, clearly visible as one came up the busy main commercial street. For quarters, we requisitioned a pension within walking distance of the center. It had been used by the Germans, and we moved in right behind them. Some of the luggage, uniforms, and miscellaneous paraphernalia of the Germans were still there, although the vehicles and armaments were all gone. The pension was run by the Testard family—a grand dame, Madame Testard, and her two forty-ish daughters, one of whom was married, the other a delightful, confirmed spinster whom we all called Mademoiselle.

We had duties around the area through the day and often in the evening, but we tried to make our detachment mess at six each evening. The

HWJ with a gutted German Tiger Tank, Das Reich Division, near Montpellier, September 1944

basic food was our American Army rations, but, as prepared by the French, it was greatly improved. These were supplemented by vegetables, breads, and the red wine of the region. We had occasional army visitors, some for days at a time, and when officers came through, we often reverted to an officers' mess with the enlisted men messing separately in a small dining room off the courtyard. When alone, von Seggern insisted that we all eat together, and we usually spent dinner talking over the situation. We began to get a clearer sense of the region and its problems.

I usually spent the days traveling around the area, checking on the local situation. I believe I visited every town in the region and came to know every large one. We were in the unique situation of being the only Americans, except for occasional top-brass visitors, in a large region of several hundred thousand people. Occasionally, we went on morbid missions such as checking on the remains of U.S. air crews who had crashed and perished in the area. Food supplies were short, some critically so, including flour, powdered milk, and sugar. We concentrated on food categories for children, which were scarce and expensive. Medical supplies were hard to come by, and a flourishing black market in these items had sprung up. The local marketplaces were severely hampered by spot shortages and by the supply functions controlled by Communists in some towns. Labor unions were not happy with food shortages and difficult working

With German POWs in the motor pool and Sergeant Poggioli, November 1944

conditions, especially in Alès, the mining center. The French had a way of making use of German prisoners that, while understandable, was against the Geneva Convention. Our detachment soon improved that situation. We also took direct responsibility for six German POWs who were mechanics and who worked for our truck company. They were obviously happy to be with us. Gradually, everything began to settle down and improve, although outbreaks of retribution and vengeance were real concerns for the police everywhere.

We had a fairly good relationship with the prefectures, but in many cases the police, often holdovers from the Vichy, were difficult. One morning before dawn, Francette, Vandeputte's wife, telephoned in hysterics. Her husband had been picked up at home by the police in the early hours and taken away "for questioning." "He will disappear!" she shouted over the phone. Shades of the Gestapo and the Milice—the Nazi-organized French militia!

Von Seggern and I dashed to the prison, where we assumed he was being held, and after some protests from the guards, we walked into the local commandant's office. Von Seggern, through me, asked if they were holding Vandeputte. After repeated denials, the commandant finally admitted that they were questioning Vandeputte after an informant reported he had seen him talking to a German soldier a year or so before. When we asked who had supplied the information, the commandant refused to name anyone. The commandant, a swarthy, grim-looking thug, had no intention of giving us our employee.

Finally, von Seggern said, "Tell him I want him back now, within three minutes, or he will have to pay the consequences." He also told me to uncover my .45 colt and put a round into the chamber. I did that, quickly, and for a full minute we and the commandant stared at each other. Just what we would have done if he hadn't responded, I'm not sure. But he did respond. He looked back and forth between us and called to the guard who was standing just outside the door. He ordered him to get the prisoner. Vandeputte was escorted in, looking unkempt and bleary-eyed, and we all left in a hurry, followed by dirty looks and muttered curses. A week later, the commandant was relieved of his post, and von Seggern was congratulated on the "raid" by General Zeller, head of the 16th military region, headquartered in Montpellier. The charge later melted away, but Francette, forty odd years later, told Walter Rosenblith at my sixty-fifth birthday party, "He saved my husband." "Il a sauvé mon mari."

We had a few other examples of posturing by local resistance types, but we were able to keep reasonable order simply by being there. One night, I walked, rather than rode, into the center of the city and called on friends in an apartment near the square. Few cars were on the streets at this point except for an occasional military vehicle, and the city was always deserted after ten at night. Returning late that evening, I was startled to hear a shot with the familiar whine of a ricochet on the building just above my head. I clattered ahead, looking for someone, somewhere, but soon all was quiet.

Our reception was mostly positive. I was invited by Professor Martin of the venerable University of Montpellier to lecture to his class on the American educational system. I was well received, largely, I think, because I showed up and spoke French, then took questions in English. After class, we adjourned to the local student cellars for songs and drinks. The lyrics that were sung were surprisingly salacious, but everyone joined with great gusto and hilarity. When they asked me to sing a song from our colleges in return, I could think of nothing to compare with theirs.

They then sang a few more, including one to the tune of "The Stars and Stripes Forever," with a wonderful chorus in the most scatological French. I decided that these boisterous and attractive young people were delightful, but I avoided all entanglements.

Of course, there was a social life that went beyond singing with the students. My friends from my first days in Montpellier were frequent companions in free time. I remember with great affection two close friends, Denise and Janot, who shared a terribly sad personal situation. Their husbands—medical doctors in the services—had been imprisoned in France since 1940 and had still not returned from Germany by late 1944. The two, both in their mid-twenties, had settled in the medical university town of Montpellier—where their husbands had been trained—in order to be near the headquarters of the military region. They had a waning hope that their husbands would return. The three of us became close friends. They extended my knowledge of French and my knowledge of life in France during the months we socialized in the limited circle of Montpellier. I think I was an acceptable escort, or at least was looked upon that way, as things were returning to normal again. I never heard from either after the war, nor did I seek to be in touch.

We had many friends in town and in other cities in the region. We few Americans were fairly visible in uniform, especially since we drove around the area in U.S. military vehicles. The French authorities for liaison with our unit suggested, wisely, that we might requisition some private automobiles to make travel less conspicuous. We soon discovered a large storage garage where the warehouse man showed us several hundred vehicles, mostly in storage since the massive retreats of 1940, when many people fled Paris for southern ports or melted away into the countryside and cityscapes of unoccupied France. Since there was no gasoline available for civilians after 1940 and no tires or batteries, there was no use for conventional automobiles. Some automobiles had been converted to charcoal-burning engines, but these were limited to priority drivers, such as physicians. The supervisor showed me some of the striking automobiles abandoned by movie stars and public figures. One, owned by the singer Charles Trenet, was a very attractive De La Haye with beautiful late–1930s streamlining. I thought it would be too conspicuous to drive such a car and settled for a modest Ford, which I used for the next several months until a visiting colonel, in turn, requisitioned it from me.

Our relationships with the French people were quite positive, but there was one tragic incident. While it was suitably hushed up by a cooperative police department, I often thought about what we might have done to prevent it. Virgil, a big, handsome soldier, was one of the two men supervising the maintenance of our truck fleet. He attracted women to him like honey attracts bees. One woman had followed him from Marseilles, where he had been stationed the first month after the landings. Now, he had broken off with her, and she had followed him to Montpellier in a vain attempt to win him back. In a fit of anger and remorse, she pulled out a small pistol from her purse, shot herself through the temple, and died almost immediately in our doorway. It was a terribly sad event to all of us except for Virgil, who apparently saw the incident as the solution to a problem.

By mid-November, progress in the area seemed noticeable to most people. Foodstuffs were arriving, some modest economic pickups occurred, and justice, or at least the outlines of a system, was functioning. Schools, churches, and the press were all functioning. Not that there weren't any problems. The mayor of Nîmes, who had escaped the August and September vengeance trials that ended in the executions of so many of his counterparts in other departments, was also convicted after a long, drawn-out trial. He was subsequently murdered on his way to a jail cell before sentence could be passed. This took place in Alès, perpetrated by individuals who broke through a police cordon. The actual murderer was never arrested.

Prison terms for hundreds of collaborators were now common, and I believe any review would show that the process of justice had been distorted. France is still trying to deal with its collaboration on a mammoth scale with the invaders, its seemingly willing support in rounding up Jews for deportation to Germany and, in most cases, death, and, finally, its overreaction and unjust reaction to many who were accused of collaboration.

Our area became quiet enough for von Seggern to come up with an idea. He and I, along with Gilbert, our French liaison officer, and a French sergeant driver would go to Paris to see how civil affairs matters were proceeding there. Of course, there was no real business to be done, but a week away from our base was due us and, since we knew what was going on in Lyons and Marseilles, Paris seemed to be a good destination. That decision nearly cost von Seggern, and perhaps all of us, our lives.

We drove to Paris by the Lyons route in Gilbert's large Citroën *traction avant,* with French military markings. We had a great time seeing the sights in Paris and calling on some counterparts from the old regiment who were now stationed there. Seeing Paris was a fantastic experience. The city was enjoying freedom after years of occupation and grimness. Beautiful, if shabby, full of a feverish gaiety, that great city was like all the pictures of it in our minds.

I ate and slept in comfortable noncom messes and hotels. Von Seggern would look for me in designated places, and we would pursue our review of the city. I remember sitting in on a briefing that von Seggern was given on the frosty reception that the new American Ambassador, Jefferson Caffrey, was receiving in his dealings with the de Gaulle government. After a few days of this, von Seggern became tired of the overbearing presence of the army brass and bureaucracy. In places like Paris, captains and lieutenants, and surely sergeants, did not count for much.

After covering what seemed like all of Paris, we headed back south, this time over the mountain roads of the Massif Central. We decided to drive most of the night in order to make up some time, and because of the scarcity of sleeping accommodations all along the route. Twenty miles from Rodez, we were involved in a major crash. Later on, when the details could be reconstructed, we put the facts together. On a high curve on a winding mountain road, a front wheel of the famous front-wheel drive Citroën spun off. The car crashed through a low stone wall with a horrendous noise and came to rest hanging over the precipice on a big rock, swaying gently. It was near midnight and there was no light to illuminate the wreckage. Gilbert and I were in the back seat, with von Seggern and the driver in the front. Armand, the French sergeant, was stunned but conscious. We later learned that he had tried so hard to control the car that he had broken the steering wheel.

We pulled both Armand and the unconscious von Seggern from the front seat of the teetering car. Von Seggern's field jacket was drenched with blood and his face was a bloody mask from a deep cut in his forehead. We carried the two to the edge of the road, feeling our way in the darkness. The car still hung on a large boulder at the edge, but it seemed fairly stable. Von Seggern began to come around, but when I felt his pulse, it was very weak and very rapid. I knew he was in shock, and I wrapped my jacket around him and tried to press the wound enough to control the bleeding. I asked Gilbert to reconnoiter the road to see if there was a building in sight with light showing. He and Armand, who was now functioning, went down the road a bit but came back having found nothing in the way of help. After twenty minutes that seemed like an hour, we saw a flash of a headlight coming up the road, and quickly flagged down the oncoming civilian car.

Fortunately, the car had in it two reasonably alert men and a woman who were on their way to Rodez, where they told us there was a hospital. We took over the car and with the light of their headlights and a flashlight we were able to tend to von Seggern. We got him into the car, and I sat in the back with him. The driver and his two companions produced a clean towel, which allowed us to press the wound, and they also produced an old blanket in which I was able to wrap von Seggern. Our Samaritans were very helpful in every respect, and I regret that I never got their names. Since there was a curfew still in effect, they were more than eager to cooperate.

They drove us through the mountains to Rodez and to the hospital, and as we approached it, with its light dimly glowing ahead, it was the most wonderful sight. The fair-sized hospital quickly produced a sleepy doctor and nurse. After an examination and cleaning up the wound, they reported to me that von Seggern had a severe gash in his forehead that was so deep that the frontal bone of the skull was visible. The wound was stitched and von Seggern was put into bed after some strong sedatives.

The next morning, von Seggern and I learned that the antique x-ray machine showed a fracture of the external plate of the skull and a concussion that should have kept von Seggern in bed and quiet for at least a week. Two days later, at von Seggern's insistence, they produced an ambulance that transported us back over the roads to Montpellier. It seemed an extremely long ride. A U.S. Army doctor came out from Marseilles and checked von Seggern out, and in the end, after examinations in an army hospital, he had a full recovery except for blinding headaches for some weeks and a big scar in mid-forehead for life.

Gilbert remained at the wreck site that night and the next day commandeered an automobile to take him and Armand back to Montpellier. Eventually he had the car, which was a total loss, retrieved from the roadside and brought back to Montpellier. He reported that there had been "sabotage." He said that all the lug nuts but one in the right-hand front wheel had been removed. Fifty years later, when we recalled the incident, he still insisted that it was sabotage.

Much later, von Seggern told me that he had proposed me for the Soldier's Medal for the rescue effort, but that in the absence of a second American officer witness, it had been turned down. It bothered me not at all, although in later years it struck me that it would have been a memento of a perilous situation.

In the meantime, the affairs of the region had gone on. The German offensive of the Battle of the Bulge had begun in mid-December to everyone's surprise and dismay, and shattered the hope of an early end to the war. The Bulge dominated everyone's thoughts behind the line. For a while during that grim Christmas of 1944, it looked as though Whitehead and I would be transferred to an infantry replacement depot at the request of headquarters; sergeants were apparently in short supply in the fighting army. Von Seggern must have made a strong case on behalf of the unit's needs, because January came and went without the transfer taking place.

We continued to do our own work, and as winter ended and early spring began, we began to feel that the war was approaching its end in Europe. In April, the radio brought word of President Roosevelt's sudden death. It was a stark reversal in the midst of a rush of otherwise positive news from the battle front. Lorteur, the interpreter, asked me anxiously whether the name of FDR's successor, Truman, really translated "un vrai homme." No one knew the answer.

Our detachment was ordered to report to Marseilles and our headquarters. There was a final set of reports and formations of the Southern France Civil Affairs Personnel. I was asked by Colonel Snow, now the unit commander, if I wanted to go to a shortened O.C.S., near Paris, for a commission, but with a commitment to remain in the European theater for one year after the cessation of hostilities. I had no interest in that and declined.

The whole unit was assigned to Bad Hamburg and Heidelberg in Germany to set up military government functions there. The detachment was ordered to make a final quick return to Montpellier to shut down operations. A nostalgic farewell party was held, and the major newspaper printed a glowing editorial. The mayor and the town council invited von Seggern and the sergeants to attend a town council meeting where we were thanked in a solemn ceremony. And so the history of the unit

Montpellier City Council. Left to right, James Whitehead; William von Seggern, mayor of Montpellier; HWJ; and Livio Poggioli, 1945

quickly ended. We closed the doors of our old house on rue Auguste Comte, loaded the records into a truck, and headed back to Marseilles.

Looking back on the operation of the unit in France, one has to say that its remote location had many advantages. We seldom saw the brass and the bureaucracy of the army. Indeed, we seldom saw anything of the army except when we had to cross the Rhone to go to Marseilles to pick up mail and rations. We did the work without interference, but the remoteness also put our detachment out of sight and out of mind in a certain sense. Since von Seggern did not want to call attention to us, and since the reports in the area showed a situation under control, we went our own way for many months. Years later, I saw a copy of the U.S. Army Report on Civil Affairs Operations in World War II, and it had, buried in its lengthy chapters, a revealing summary of events in the south of France in the fall of 1944. "Famine, street demonstrations . . . spelled the chief civil affairs problems in the Nice-Cannes area. In Toulouse, constant attention had to be given to reported threats of a Communist uprising. Only in Montpellier were conditions calm."

The detachment had a great deal of leeway in its operations, but we probably lost opportunities for many things dear to the hearts of the army. Von Seggern remained a captain for the rest of the war, and Whitehead remained a sergeant. I became a sergeant—a technician fourth grade—but that was the only promotion in the detachment for eight months. I never found cause to complain.

Years later, von Seggern, living in retirement in Florida, would often say that he had not done as well by the detachment and its people as he should have. Toward the end of his life, he made a trip to the Pentagon "to put the record straight" and to get me "a couple of medals," as he put it. But he failed. He wrote me a letter, after it was all over, apologizing for his "mistakes." I told him that we had all learned so much in the Montpellier experience, that it was enough to return home in good shape. We survived the war, learned a great deal, and actually did some good for a great many people—unusual in time of war.

Forty-five years later, my wife Betty and I visited Montpellier, now a dynamic city of 200,000 people, during the summer and called on the mayor in the modern, but undistinguished, town hall. It had none of the character or patina of the old one. The mayor was away, but his adjutant, a clear-eyed young woman who was a graduate in political science, received us, and said she was surprised to see an American who spoke French, especially one who spoke, she said, with the accent "of the south of France." When I described the experience of the detachment in 1944–1945 in Montpellier, she was fascinated but a bit disbelieving. She did not know there had been an American unit in Montpellier, as the records of those months were incomplete and some had been destroyed. She herself knew very little about that time. I gave her the photo showing the mayor and the council and our group at the final celebration; she was surprised to see it and delighted to have it. A month later, I got a letter from the mayor, expressing pleasure at our brief visit to Montpellier, and our earlier "visit" in 1944–1945. He wrote that we were following the footsteps of Jefferson, who had come to Montpellier for a brief visit. The mayor seemed unclear on the U.S. Civil Affairs units. I may never return to Montpellier, but I will always remember it very fondly.

Our time in southern France came to a close just before V-E Day, May 8, 1945, and by that time the entire unit had convoyed back to Heidelberg and Bad Hamburg in Germany to take up duties there. V-E Day celebrations were prolonged, with much liquor and aimless enthusiasm. The old detachment, small as it was, was quickly broken up. Von Seggern went off to Stuttgart, and I was assigned to the Food and Agriculture section in Frankfurt, Eisenhower's headquarters for the American Army in Germany. The buildings were the former headquarters of I. G. Farben, and they alone were undamaged, amid the mountains of rubble around them. Occasionally, we would see Ike, the best liked by far of all the well-known generals of the European Theater, striding into the headquarters, flashing his famous grin.

I was assigned a tiny office with three GIs, two of them WACs, to set up a statistical unit for grain crop production in Bavaria. It was a ridiculously confused organization. One memory sticks in my mind. The laboring Germans were being rationed at 1000 calories per day, with less for non-laboring Germans. Of course, that amount of energy is not enough to keep a working person going, and people frequently fainted in the fields. The goal was to extract as much work from the working population for as little food outlay as possible. Most of the people working on the problem were army personnel who knew very little about their new trades, and we passed most of the days rearranging numbers without any really constructive ideas for dealing with the situation.

I was billeted in a small apartment from which the previous occupants had been ousted. Once each week, the former owner, a sour, scared German housefrau, would be permitted to return to clean up her old house. She was frightened and unhappy, and forbidden to remove any of her own belongings from the house. I found it sad to be living among the ruins of other lives, with pictures of soldiers and other relatives on the wall and banal reminders of another world.

Since I had a lot of free time, I tracked down a few old buddies in other towns. Bob Emanuel, from Indiana University, was now a G–2 sergeant in Frankfurt. He had a jeep assigned to him, and together we traveled a bit of the surrounding country. There were displaced persons everywhere searching for new homes. There were German prisoners of war, sullen and dejected, being moved to various destinations. Fraternization with German civilians was forbidden but in those early days that didn't stop many people.

The news of the death camps was now out in all its gory detail, and most soldiers were surprised at the extent and grimness of that news. The existence of the camps was not widely known until late in the war. The displaced persons' issue, however, was familiar to everyone. We had seen many, and in Montpellier trainloads of them needed to be put up someplace in the area. During the darkest days of January, the French authorities had used, briefly, the abandoned and infamous Rives-Saltes Camp, south of Narbonne, which had housed imprisoned Jewish detainees in 1942 and 1943. In 1945, at least, American rations and supplies were available.

The Germans who were bombed out of their cities added to the hordes of hungry, homeless, and desperate refugees. Looking at the flattened cities, the destroyed countryside, the ruined lives, one had deeply mixed feelings: a great sense of relief that the war was over, and at the same time a feeling of deep sadness about all those ruined lives around us. Old photographs of the German cities barely capture the massive scale of disaster, the overwhelming stench, and the sense of a civilization gone to dust.

The news of the A-bomb dropping in Hiroshima was the most stunning single piece of news I heard during the war. Imagining what the new device portended was mind-numbing. There was no doubt, however, as to the reaction of the armies. V-J Day, August 15, 1945, had removed the dread that accompanied every soldier who thought about the war in the Pacific. Divisions and regiments of all kinds were being formed to go to Asia, and many had already left. While my point total was high enough to delay immediate deployment, no one who had spent time in Europe relished the idea of the war grinding on, and that is what we all expected. Now, in these days when the revisionist historians are writing that the war would have ended quickly anyway, and that the bomb should not have been dropped, I wonder if they have fully considered the price of an invasion of the Japanese mainland in terms of both American and Japanese casualties. Surely, most servicemen who participated in the war have no doubt about Truman's decision from all points of view except for the victims of the blast itself. That inexpressibly awful result must take its place with all the tragedies of death and destruction that visited humankind since September 1939. Now, suddenly, it seemed that it was all over.

When the dust of V-J Day settled, I assumed I would have a few months of military government assignment and then quickly qualify for shipment home. But a different fate intervened. I happened to check the bulletin board at our food and agriculture headquarters one morning in late August, the only way one could keep up with the rapid news of reorganization and redeployment. There, I saw the notice of postgraduate fellowships available at several British and French universities. Deadlines were immediate, and I quickly applied. I learned of my acceptance within a few days, and I quickly packed my somewhat worn belongings in my duffel bag and headed for the airport and the U.K.

France and Montpellier provided a great source of learning for me. Montpellier was not a beautiful city, but was an intensely fascinating one. Its real roots were in the France of the Middle Ages and the Protestant revolution. Its university dated to the twelfth century, and its sense of serious academic work seemed palpable to me in those winding lanes within the old university walls. The great equestrian statue of Louis XIV in the park called the Peyrou and the victory arch on the main promenade of Montpellier were an attempt at provincial grandeur. But more impressive still on that site was the faded slogan painted on the base of the Louis XIV statue, "Je n'aurais jamais collaborer."

The surrounding countryside in Languedoc-Roussillon was rough-hewn in many ways but it was blessed by the sun of the south of France on rock and vineyard. It had the character of a Cézanne painting: field after field, rugged streams, fierce villages. To the south of the city was the short road to the Mediterranean, inaccessible to everyone since the German occupation, when the area was fortified and the beaches mined. At the gutted village of Palavas, there was a short stretch of beach that was mine-free, thanks to the labor of German POWs, and a few of us could swim there until late in the fall and again beginning early in the spring. Today, of course, the whole place has changed, with new clusters of high-rise buildings all along the coast. The city now has grand new buildings and roads in a new university town. But the old Montpellier will always be a moving memory for me, even though the lovely and lonely city I knew is gone.

The greatest school, of course, was the army itself. I have reflected occasionally on my experience in its ranks. I was no great soldier by any definition and my experiences were modest. If Richard Dana could say of his two years before the mast that the sailing ship was his Harvard College, then the army was mine. Soldiering is a dumbing-down process and war is a grim and dirty business. But it is an opportunity, too, unlike any other in life. I ran across Oliver Wendell Holmes, Jr.'s quote from a speech at a Memorial Day celebration in 1884. Holmes, a three-times wounded veteran of the Civil War, said in a famous passage, "The generation that carried on the war has been set apart by its experience. Through our great, good fortune, in our youth our hearts were touched with fire. It was given to us to learn at the outset, that life is a profound and passionate thing."

So it was for me. Apart from the momentous ends that were at stake, I learned a great deal about life, and I learned much about the man on the bottom rung. I learned a deep respect for the common soldier, and I learned that great results are possible from a closely knit group of people. Mostly, I learned a lot about myself. I learned to live under fearsome pressure, and I learned something about compassion in the midst of disaster. Those are fundamental lessons and, overall, it nourished one's soul to participate in these great events. I have sometimes felt sorry for my contemporaries who were not part of the uniformed services. I have detected a note of embarrassment among some of them. One thing is certain; no one who served in that war can ever forget it. As time goes on, some essence of that memory gets even stronger.

I remember as a little boy going with my father and brother each year to the Memorial Day parade on Michigan Avenue in Chicago. It was a big event for us. We would arrive early and, if we were lucky, found a seat on the curb to watch the parade go by. There were usually a few units of the Illinois National Guard, the 33d Division, wearing the familiar black and yellow patch, leading the parade. Close behind were the uneven ranks of many American Legion and V.F.W. veterans, looking, even to a little boy, overblown and unruly. A few ranks of Spanish American War veterans then followed, looking unsteady and marching a bit uncertainly in their strange-looking khaki. The biggest cheers were for the very few Civil War veterans, looking like frail birds and sitting in the rear seats of big open cars. They must have been, then, in their late eighties and early nineties, and there were only a few of them left. They looked ancient to us, and soon they were gone.

In another twenty years or so, the World War II veterans, now still so numerous, will also be gone. Many already look a little bit frail to me, especially when one thinks of the way we all looked in 1942 and 1943. And their spouses, who looked so young and gay and marvelous in those years, have now a look of age about them and move with a slower step. Soon they, too, will all be gone. Perhaps those little boys and girls in my grandsons' generation will find it interesting to read about us as we head down the parade boulevard, already in ragged lines and disappearing over the rise.

At the University of Chicago, 1950

3

The University of Chicago after the War: Student and Faculty Member

My discharge from the army on February 6, 1946, marked the new beginning of my life. Like many soldiers, I felt there was a good chance I would not survive the war. This was not a particularly morbid notion, and I knew many who had the same idea. It did not weigh me down; it simply seemed realistic. I had trained as an infantry soldier, and although my European army experience was largely in noninfantry duty, my army specialization as a rifleman was always there.

On that cold February day in 1946, as I boarded an army train on the siding at Camp Grant, a discharged veteran carrying a shoulder duffel and heading for Chicago and home, I felt for the first time that my life was in front of me. I had to begin to make the fateful decisions of where to go and what to do next, having spent my twenty-first, twenty-second, and twenty-third birthdays in the army. Almost exactly three years had been lost. Of course, I knew it had not really been wasted. We had all been part of a great army that had fought the last "good war." I knew, too, that I had matured. When I went into the service, I was still a boy in many ways, but I was now a man, fit, and with no psychological hang-ups, as far as I knew, and no encumbrances. How I valued that sense of freedom!

I had thought about the matter, of course. With great good fortune, I had spent the previous months at Glasgow University in Scotland on a U.S. Army fellowship. The army had initiated, among many other programs for "high point" soldiers, study assignments at several universities—mostly British but with a few in France—for soldiers who had completed an undergraduate degree. I applied for a Glasgow University fellowship in August 1945, largely because Adam Smith, whose writings had made a big impression on me as an undergraduate before the war, had been a professor of moral philosophy and political economy at Glasgow.

I had tentatively decided that graduate study in economics was a lot more relevant to the immense problems of postwar America than any other field I might be qualified to enter. That thought had jelled during discussions with the British political leaders Aneurin Bevan and Jenny Lee, his wife, during chance weekends in London as we all waited for the invasion of Europe to begin. Later, a letter exchange with Robert K. Burns, then a professor at the University of Chicago, reinforced this decision. In my undergraduate days at Central College in Chicago, I had taken courses with Burns in economics and statistics, and I had been greatly impressed with his vitality, his interest in his students, and, most of all, his eclectic interest in contemporary problems. I had read during the war that Burns had been appointed head of the Midwest Regional War Labor Board, and had heard that when the WLB and the Newspaper Labor Board had shut down as the war ended, Burns had been appointed to a professorship at the University of Chicago. I had written to him cold from Glasgow, and he had replied promptly in the exuberant style I came to know. He said he remembered me well and urged me to see him on my return to Chicago. He and a colleague, Fred Harbison, were trying to establish a new industrial relations center at the University of Chicago. I wrote to him that I hoped to see him at the university after I was discharged.

Glasgow was an experience of vital importance to me. I had come to it as if it were an oasis. Soon after the war ended, with a fellowship awarded to me in less than ten days, I had orders to catch an army flight out of Frankfurt for London. I climbed aboard a battered DC-3 with one other soldier. The pilot and his copilot looked no older than teenagers wearing the usual "50-mission crush" on their hats. We soon landed in London in a steady rain. I caught the Royal Scot, tipped the porter to get a berth, and arrived at Glasgow station on a foggy and damp October morning.

Enrolling at the university, I had a choice of three courses. I picked political economy as a concentration, then French literature and Scottish history. The faculty did not expect much from the few Americans who suddenly matriculated, and neither did our fellow U.K. students. In September 1945 the university student body was composed entirely of female students and physically disqualified civilian men; few United Kingdom men had yet returned from the war. The ten Americans who appeared on campus were a mixed lot. I came to know most of them, but lost track of all but two: George Johanson, a paratrooper from Nebraska who much later became the mayor of his Nebraska city, and Charles Brossman, a bright medical corpsman from Pittsburgh with whom I corresponded for years after the war.

The main impact of the Glasgow experience was that, after more than two years of thinking only as far ahead as tomorrow and the next hill, I suddenly could think about intellectual issues and a long-term future. I stood well in the political economy course. I thought, however, that Professor MacFie, although kind to the two Americans in his class, was unworldly, mired in the perfect world of Alfred Marshall, and grappling with a business cycle he did not begin to understand. The Scottish history class was insular, but delightful. French literature was a complete surprise and a pleasant sojourn into Molière, Voltaire, and Racine. Not having to think about soldiering was pure joy.

On Sunday afternoons, we were invited often to join the McGregors, the owner-editors of the *Glasgow Herald,* for tea and sherry and discussion at their home. Several evenings each week I saw Molly, a fellow student. We attended countless productions of the newly revitalized theater in Glasgow. On weekends, I entered interminable discussions in the Commons with our fellow students, bicycled in the Trossacks, or went to Skye with Molly to see the countryside. What a change from soldiering! I was drawing sergeant's combat pay plus an allowance for food and lodging. There were no formations, no duties, and no army, although I was still in uniform. Still, there was that persistent question, "What are you going to do when you get out?"

I applied for the U.S. Foreign Service examinations, which were offered for the first time since before the war to active duty personnel. The foreign service had been on my list of interests since I had entered college six years earlier. The entrance examinations were long and difficult, and had a reputation for having a decided slant toward Ivy League preparation. The examinations were scheduled for November in London, and I quickly obtained orders to go to London to participate. By that time, I had six weeks of reading, thinking, and acting the student, and I felt ready. The group that assembled consisted of at least 250 men from all services and branches—both officers and enlisted men. After the several hours of written examinations, I knew that I had passed. While in London, I was invited by Aneurin Bevan and Jenny Lee to join them for dinner. Bevan, now a minister in the Attlee government, expressed delight that I had emerged from my time on the continent unscathed, and he was surprised to learn that I was studying in Glasgow. I remember how much his kind encouragement meant to me at the time. Months afterward, in the United States, I learned that I had indeed passed the written examination and was to be scheduled for the orals. But the orals were not scheduled in 1946, and by the time they were called, I had lost interest in the foreign service in favor of completing my academic work. It turned out to be just as well, since I, along with two others I knew, failed the orals when they were finally convened.

I enjoyed that autumn in Glasgow more than any season for many years. It was satisfying to attend class, read, and discuss, and during this time I decided I would return to a university for graduate study.

But the fall and winter of 1945 were especially difficult for many. The winter was severe, and rationing was still enforced. The American students had ration books like everyone else, but the food was dull and monotonous. We were even issued whiskey ration cards. Most of my time there I had rooms in a rooming house for students. A penny-operated gas heater kept the room from freezing on cold nights, but not much more. The student body was serious but had periods of explosive great fun. The great event of the autumn was "Daft Friday," when all classes were cut, hilarity reigned through the night, and enormous quantities of beer were drunk (whiskey still being rationed and expensive). The other traditional event was the speech by the university chancellor to the entire student body. He had barely begun his rather formal paper when the students began to throw all kinds of old vegetables and fruit at the stage and at the speaker. The chancellor was not surprised, for that was standard procedure in those rowdy days. He took it in good grace but left the stage quickly.

Another event was the much publicized theft by either Glasgow or Edinburgh students of the Stone of Scone from the Coronation Chair in Westminster Abbey. The stone turned up undamaged after several days of search, but the perpetrators were never caught. It was a preview of the creative student pranks, called *hacks,* that I later came to know so well at MIT.

The city of Glasgow was a rough and battered city in 1945 and 1946. It was threadbare and careworn, but it had charms nonetheless, and after six years of war it was eager to come alive. I left the university the first week of January in 1946 with a certificate and with regret at the sudden receipt of orders to report to the embarkation facilities in Southampton, England, for shipment to the States. Sir Hector Hetherington, the severe vice chancellor of the university, met briefly with the American students and said he was pleased with our progress. He seemed surprised as well. I said good-bye to Molly with sad finality. At Southampton, the soldiers reported individually, since most units were being dissolved and reassembled in some fashion for transportation home to demobilize in a rush. The same process was going on all over the world and it described the unraveling of a once-great army. I was assigned to a not-unpleasant barracks, and soon was on the roster of some phantom unit that was assigned a date in mid-January 1946 for the voyage home.

We held a Christmas celebration in Glasgow, but the students, including Molly, had left for Christmas vacation, and the holiday was spartan. In Southampton, there were remnants of Christmas in a macabre form. We were each given three or four random packages, sent from the States and addressed to soldiers who had already left for home, I suppose, or were either missing in action or late casualties of the campaigns. I didn't relish the idea of opening packages not meant for me, but I must admit that new socks, books, and candy were welcome fare. We were also required to turn in all but one firearm taken from the Germans under threat of confiscation of all such weapons, as well as all U.S. firearms. I kept a German P38 pistol that I had taken in France and turned in a perfectly nice chromed Browning automatic pistol that I am sure some stateside officer quickly grabbed. I still have the P38 and occasionally wonder what happened to its original owner.

In the two weeks in the south of England I had some time to think about my next steps. I was determined to enter the University of Chicago Labor Economics program in the Department of Economics. It seemed to me that the personnel field—the management side of the labor coin—and industrial relations were fascinating and high-demand areas. Robert Burns had given me a sliver of hope, and I felt I had one possibility at least. There had been no mail from home, of course, during all that time and while communication was open and censorship had ended, no transatlantic telephones were available in those days. The vessel to which we were assigned, *Alhambra Victory,* departed on schedule on January 18, but it returned to port after one day out for generator repairs. Understandably, there were groans from the troops on board, but eventually we were underway once again. It was my fourth troopship since 1944, and by far the best of a bad lot.

The ships now traveled without convoy formations. Lights blazed on deck at night and sealed portholes were opened. It was an easy voyage—fixed cots on cargo decks, plentiful army food, and no duties. There was none of the typical grousing. Gambling, including big-money crap games, and reading were the principal pastimes. I remember one sergeant who bet all his accumulated winnings, several thousand dollars, in one dramatic roll of the dice. He lost and shrugged his shoulders: "Easy come, easy go."

We arrived in New York and, contrary to the usual impression, there were no bands, no greetings, no parades. The arrival of yet another shipload of returning soldiers was hardly newsworthy. A "Welcome Home" sign plus the ubiquitous Red Cross donuts and coffee greeted us as we boarded troop coaches for Fort Dix. After a day of sorting out, I boarded another train for Chicago and Camp Grant. I had entered Camp Grant in March 1943, and on my return on February 4, 1946, it was absolutely beautiful under several inches of new snow.

Here the demobilization process took place, surprisingly quickly and efficiently. Torn and worn uniform parts were replaced. A German POW quickly stitched a "ruptured duck" on the uniform jacket, the insignia of the honorably discharged soldier. A quick physical examination—much more cursory than the entrance physical—a short interview with a medical officer, and a discharge certificate, signed in my case by an air corps major! What a comedown! I quickly telephoned my mother and father. I learned that my brother Kenneth had been home from the navy for two months, and that Arthur Harvey, my brother-in-law, returned home from the army a few weeks before. I had not talked to my parents since January 1944, and they sounded just fine. I was able to tell them my approximate arrival on the evening of February 6, and the train to Chicago pulled into the station on schedule. The crowd of civilians waiting at the station gate was almost unmanageable with joy as the soldiers pushed through the iron grating gate, and suddenly there were my sister, Evelyn, and Richard, my younger brother. To my surprise, on one day's notice the folks had assembled some relatives for a late evening party, and it was a wonderful homecoming.

Now I came back to the question of what I was going to do. I had alternatives to graduate school. I was not sure that I would do well at the university were I to be accepted. Was I thinking straight? I spent a day or two getting used to the neighborhood and buying a couple of suits and other civilian clothing. I wondered if I should call my old girl, Marie; she had sent me a "Dear John" letter soon after I had gone overseas, for which I certainly did not blame her. Finally, I decided my first priority was to see where I stood at the University of Chicago.

I had a productive interview with Robert Burns and his partner, Frederick Harbison. I also talked to H. Gregg Lewis, the economics department registration officer, and Harry Millis, the senior professor in the field of labor.

Yes, they would take me, but with no advanced credit against the Chicago requirements for the M.A. and the Ph.D. Three years in the army and a term at Glasgow had counted for nothing at Chicago. It was clear that I could easily pass the language requirement for the Ph.D. Although I was unsure whether I would seek the doctorate, I was now certain that I should enter the university. I had the feeling of having lost three years of my best time, and I was eager to get at the real world. Chicago was flexible and proposed that I enter.

After a period of waiting, I was delighted to learn that I had been formally accepted by the university for the spring quarter. The GI Bill, a remarkable national investment, was marvelous for the returning vet. It paid tuition, a book allowance, and for me—a single man—$75 each month as a living subsidy. It also required some waiting, which all veterans hated.

In one line I stood behind one of the many veterans among the registrants and during the half-hour wait, I learned my new colleague was John R. Coleman—Jack Coleman—from Canada. Drawn to the university, he also would study economics and labor economics, because his wife, Mary, was the daughter of a University of Chicago professor of the Old Testament. We became the closest of friends—eventually, I practically lived with them in their apartment. Coleman was a delight—bright, humorous, and full of fun, but with a deeply serious streak. He had spent his war years in the Canadian Navy and had the cynicism and confused ambition of most of the other vets. He was to remain a good friend long after our Chicago days.

Classes began with a particularly charged atmosphere of expectation and energy. I was accepted for labor and industrial relations with Fred Harbison, labor legislation with Paul Douglas, price theory with Milton Friedman, and later for philosophy with Frank Knight, economic history with John U. Nef, and government finance with Simeon Leland. Friedman was teaching his first course in Chicago after his arrival from Columbia, and the class of about twenty or so was increasingly impressed by his lucidity, his careful preparation, and his relentless logic. There were many in that class who went on in academics, including Albert Rees, Norman Ture, Kenneth McCaffree, James Buchanan, Sidney Rolfe, and John Coleman. It was a tough but exhilarating class. I managed a B in his first course, but that was in a sea of Cs and very few As. Buchanan, later a Nobel Laureate, and Rees, later head of the departments at Chicago and Princeton, and still later president of the Sloan Foundation, probably were the As.

The University of Chicago's stars of the twenties and thirties were still there, but they were waning, and a great new group was emerging. That was true in all of the social science departments, and probably in the physical sciences as well. I quickly found the labor and industrial relations field to be my dish. In addition to Harbison, Burns, and Millis, there were Avery P. Leiserson, Paul Douglas, Robert Dubin, Carl Rogers, William F. Whyte, and several younger men. A constant flow of compelling speakers met with the graduate students in informal discussions at the Friday afternoon teas. I was appointed a reader in the second quarter for Burns and Harbison and appointed research assistant in the third quarter. I also worked for Paul Douglas, who made a tremendous impression on me.

Douglas had been a theory star in the early thirties, but had moved toward policy questions as the decade came to a close. A Quaker, he held the antiwar sentiments of that group until 1940 when France fell and the German Army dominated Europe. He must have had an epiphany, for by early 1941 he was taking a public stand supporting aid to the British. I heard him then in a debate on compulsory military service in which he took the prodraft position. The audience, largely members of a left-leaning student organization, was vociferously against him. I was deeply impressed by his sincerity and his passion and, inevitably, had found myself coming to his position. Douglas had enlisted as a private in the Marine Corps soon after Pearl Harbor, but was quickly commissioned although he was fifty years old. He went through the war, earning promotion and a wound that permanently crippled his left hand.

Douglas told me something in one of our many brief sessions that influenced me for the rest of my life. He had two large photographs framed on the wall behind his desk. Both were of sculptured Roman figures: one a figure in repose, thinking; the other, a gladiator of some kind, without weapons but in a wrestling crouch. He saw me looking at the photographs and said that they described his personal philosophy: He had a need to contemplate and think, but he also had a strong need to take action and take up a fight. I wish I had copies of those great sepia photos; the two poles of contemplation and action seemed to describe my own attitude toward life more and more. Douglas later demonstrated his personal philosophy in a dramatic way. In the spring of 1948, the Democratic Party leadership in Illinois must have concluded that the campaigns for governor and senator against the incumbents, Dwight Green and C. Wayland "Curly" Brooks, would be hopeless, and, expecting a defeat, had nominated two relative unknowns: Adlai Stevenson for governor and Paul Douglas for senator. In an upset election campaign—typically-rough-and-tumble Chicago style—both unexpectedly won by large margins. I will always remember my profoundly positive impression of both men for whom I worked in the campaign and came to know. Douglas began his career as a first-rate senator and served for three terms. I saw him occasionally and often thought of his philosophy of contemplation and action, and I concluded that he had found the best possible place to exercise his view of life. Stevenson became an effective governor, and in 1952 was nominated as Democratic candidate for president. With his sharp mind and elegant style, he made the most intelligent and compelling speeches I had ever heard, although he seemed to me then, and later, indecisive in critical moments.

Robert Burns and Fred Harbison were my principal influences. They were quite different types. To many of his colleagues, Bob Burns seemed superficial, but, at his best, he was an academic entrepreneur with great style. He had ideas, great marketing skills, and a facile and flexible manner, and he could work doggedly and effectively at several things simultaneously. A strong communicator, he had lofty goals and the help of some good sponsors. In the end, he was unable to juggle all his projects and, as a result, made some major mistakes. But he was a generous, decent man, who deserved more respect than he received.

Fred Harbison was a serious professor of an older school. He combined a wonderfully warm heart with an inventive theoretical mind. Years later he left Chicago to go to the Industrial Relations Center at Princeton, his alma mater. Burns and Harbison were a formidable pair who were interested in the application of theory to actual work situations. They were an asset to the Department of Economics and the Social Science Division at the university but rarely appreciated by their theory colleagues. Chicago was not a place for people interested in applications in those days. Burns and Harbison probably should have been in the Business School at the university, but that place had not yet had its postwar rebirth; its most distinguished professors were close to retirement, and the new stars were not yet recognized. People like Eli Shapiro, Ezra Solomon, and John Jeuck were not yet in power, and in time all three left Chicago for other places: Shapiro for MIT, Solomon for Stanford, and Jeuck for Harvard. People like Raleigh Stone wanted to follow the pattern of the economics department. In short, there was a fatal gulf between the school and the department, and the lack of cohesiveness between the fields made the Industrial Relations Center the only interdisciplinary place for management economics. The center generated its own funds from "member companies," developed its own facilities, hired its own people, and moved aggressively in developing training programs for management and labor. As my academic work progressed, I found myself spending more and more time there.

I learned a great deal at the Industrial Relations Center besides the academic content of the program, such as how to develop a program that could be communicated to all kinds of constituents, about managing a staff of intellectuals (far different from ordering soldiers around), and about developing organizational cohesiveness. I also learned something about university organization. The university's president, Robert Hutchins, was famous, but he was rarely seen on the campus during my years there. Later, as a member of the faculty, I saw him once a year at a faculty reception. He seldom showed himself to the student body; his feelings for the veteran students bordered on disdain. I did not know then about his negative position on the GI Bill, much quoted later, but he was an invisible administrator and showed little interest in his students. The GI Bill, as I observed it in operation in Chicago and from later evidence all over the country, was enormously successful, but few academic leaders were heard in support of it at the time. Years later I came to know Hutchins, then residing in California as a program officer of the Ford Foundation, and I found him an enormously gifted conversationalist, but in his waning Chicago days he was aloof from most of the faculty and students.

As time went on, the question of whether to go forward for the doctorate became pressing. I decided to complete the master's, which I would conclude by the end of the summer term of 1947, and then get some hands-on experience before continuing. The department was and remained wonderfully cooperative. In the meantime, I was offered a job, to begin at my convenience, by R. N. McMurry and Company, a Chicago consultant with a good reputation specializing in psychological testing, selection procedures, industrial relations counseling, and training. McMurry was a well-known psychologist who knew Bob Burns, and he had hired another of the center's graduates the year before. I thought a year or two at McMurry would extend my knowledge of personnel management subjects, and I decided to accept. I started the day after Labor Day in September 1947 at $250 per month.

At McMurry, I learned a great deal at close hand about the disciplines required to assess performance among job applicants. It was invaluable training that I used often in later years. I also learned a lot about client relationships and developed close working relationships with my colleagues. For the most part, however, the work was not challenging. I quickly concluded that the organization would not keep me interested very long. Although I still was not sure what I was going to do for a career, I knew that McMurry was not the place to do it.

But a very important event did occur. I met Betty Weed, a supervisor at Carson Pirie Scott and Company, the Chicago department store to which I had been assigned to develop a wage and salary program. The program turned out well, but Betty's and my program turned out even better. We began to go out together, and although I was not fully aware of it, I was becoming deeply attached to her. When I decided to leave McMurry at the end of 1948, we were very close.

In the meantime, Robert Burns and Fred Harbison asked me to meet them at the Industrial Relations Center to discuss a new post. Bob Burns proposed that I rejoin as a research associate and director of management programs, and jointly teach his courses. He wanted to build a staff, develop supervisory and middle management training programs, and market the materials through his partnership with Science Research Associates and Lyle Spencer. It was a big idea, and I liked it. McMurry tried to persuade me to stay with a substantial pay increase. Although the Chicago salary was lower, there was a chance to build something and I returned to Chicago.

The University of Chicago had changed in a year and a half. The Business School, with a new dean, was beginning to stir, and a likely path for myself was materializing. In the meantime, the Industrial Relations Center had acquired a new home, the old Taft House on the Midway. We began to attract the best people in the field from the Graduate School, including Richard Thornbury, Ted Alfred, Roger Allen, Bob Coughlin, and, in time, L. C. Michelon, David Moore, Melanie Baehr, Nicholas von Hoffman, as well as a number of industrial clients in several areas and industries, including the Campbell Soup Company, A. B. Dick & Company, and Republic Steel Company. I felt that the University of Chicago's Industrial Relations Center was becoming one of the very best in the field. On January 1, 1950, I was appointed assistant professor of Industrial Relations, jointly in the Division of Social Sciences and the

Teaching at the Campbell Soup Company, Chicago, 1951

School of Business, at $3,000 per year, to go to $3,600 in the next quarter.

The casualty was my expectation of a doctoral program. My job was full-time, but even without that pressure, Chicago frowned on assistant professors as candidates for the degree. Finishing a thesis was one thing, taking qualifying examinations was another. Although I had an encouraging talk with Gregg Lewis, I knew it would not work, and I soon lost my initial guilt feelings about it.

In the late summer of 1949, with some well-timed encouragement from all sides, Betty and I decided to get married. The ceremony took place on February 18, 1950, and after a honeymoon in New Orleans, we settled into a new apartment building at 56th and Dorchester Avenue. The commute to the Loop for her job at Carson's became increasingly difficult, and she soon took up a job in the personnel office at the University of Chicago's Institute of Metals, a postwar outgrowth of the Fermi atomic project and its associated activity. The university was a bustling place, although the World War II veterans were beginning to leave. The work at the Industrial Relations Center Center was rewarding but demanding, requiring much travel to places like Cleveland, Minneapolis, and Pittsburgh. We enjoyed the University of Chicago campus and its neighborhood, but the progressive decay of the South Side began to be a problem.

The university group, mostly young and newly married, had a great social relationship. We developed enduring friendships with the Alfreds, the Moores, Tom O'Farrell, and many others. The last years of the Truman administration, however, were not so great. The North Koreans had invaded South Korea, and suddenly there was a full-scale war going on in that far-off part of the world, with large-scale operations resulting in large-scale casualties. Douglas MacArthur, the World War II legend and by then the U.S. and U.N. Commander in Korea, made an unpardonable blunder in disobeying the commander in chief and was recalled and retired. For the moment it seemed that he could be a viable political candidate for the 1952 elections. I remember well his motorcade passing our office on the Midway with him, corncob pipe and all, in an open car, despite the February weather. His campaign fizzled, however, and Dwight Eisenhower began to be talked of as a candidate. We were torn as Adlai Stevenson and Ike began to appear as the likely candidates of the two parties. We liked them both.

Then, in 1952, almost out of the blue, came a proposal from General Mills in Minneapolis. We had had a small Industrial Relations Center project in Minneapolis and another in St. Paul, and I had met D. E. Balch, vice president for personnel at General Mills. He now proposed that I take an academic year's leave to work as his assistant. The company had a program for such "fellows" from the University of Minnesota, and Balch thought that a Chicago candidate would broaden their horizons. I had been wondering how I could learn what it was like actually to manage instead of just simulating the process. This seemed an ideal opportunity. Betty and I decided to accept, and Robert Burns reluctantly agreed to let me go on leave from the university. In April, we moved to a rented half-house on the south side of Minneapolis. The plan was complicated by Betty's news that she was pregnant, with the baby due in October! We had, nonetheless, decided to move, and, not without some trepidation, we did.

Minneapolis was, and is, a vigorous and scenic city, surrounded by lakes and boasting many civic amenities. In comparison with Chicago, it had a small-town atmosphere. Most of all, it was full of friendly people, eager to hold out a welcoming hand. Nearby Abbott Hospital seemed adequate, and Betty uncomplainingly dealt with the brand-new situation. I found myself with a widening portfolio at General Mills, from wage and salary administration to supervisory training, to organizing decentralized industrial relations staffs. It was a relatively disorganized company in those postwar years. General Mills knew flour milling and cereal production very well, but after the war it had diversified into many new areas, from appliances and chemicals to other food products, and in doing so had developed major organizational problems. Dewey Balch liked having me accompany him to his top management presentations, and I quickly came to know Charles Bell, the CEO, and the divisional heads.

Stephen arrived safely on October 9, 1952, and our lives changed dramatically overnight. Our little house was sparsely furnished, but we now had a family with a baby boy and a big red setter. Time passed quickly, and the university and Burns reminded me that I was expected back for the start of the winter quarter after Christmas 1952.

General Mills and Dewey Balch wanted me to stay. I was being paid at the remarkable rate of $8,000 a year, but they began to talk about a raise and a promotion to a better job. Charles Bell summoned me. He was thinking of appointing an assistant to the president, and I would be a leading candidate. I was not tempted, but we both well remember Betty's father's gentle advice: he would accept the General Mills job were he in our place; it offered a sure career at a stable company, solid salary and benefits, and a very good city in which to live and raise a family. Speaking from the background of the depression, he urged me to consider our family future if we were to go to an unsure post in Chicago, presumably at a much lower salary. He was disappointed, I know, when we decided to return to Chicago.

In Chicago I had to re-establish myself after a nine-month absence. We had rented an inadequate apartment on our return, and it was a miserable Chicago winter. But spring did come and, with it, new plans. We found a house in Palos Heights, and with loans for the down payment from both sets of parents (repaid within one year) we bought it for $20,500:

Quetico Provincial Park, Canada, 1951

a three-bedroom, one-bath ranch house. The job still interested me, I was being paid somewhat more, and we liked our new neighborhood. The Smiths and the O'Reillys, our neighbors, became our good friends. Dr. "Bud" O'Reilly, our next-door neighbor, had to deliver Laura, our second child, at a hospital nearer to our home than the university's Billings Hospital because she arrived two weeks early, on April 6, 1954. In Pittsburgh participating in meetings, I felt terrible about not being there, and vowed I would never let Betty down again.

We liked our new house, and I endured the long commute, but we were restive. Finally, I could see that the Industrial Relations Center was not going to be a solid base from which to move forward at the university. It was not securely set in either the economics department or the business school. I enjoyed teaching, especially in the downtown branch of the university, where many of the students were pursuing supervisory and management careers as well as attending classes, but there were strains developing within the Division of Social Sciences and the School of Business. Neither organization was comfortable with its hard-to-control, enterprising, and independent Industrial Relations Center.

By the fall of 1954, we were fatigued by new demands from my job and the growing family. With two children and another one on the way, we felt pressured to spend our weekends visiting one or both sets of parents, and Wilmette and South Shore were long drives with little children in the car. We were a happy family, but the strain was beginning to show. I began to think of alternatives. Then, out of the blue, came a call from Eli Shapiro. Eli, who had lived in our apartment building on Dorchester Avenue near the university, and who had been a professor of finance in the School of Business, had left Chicago in 1952 to go to the Massachusetts Institute of Technology. I had not heard from him since he left, and now he was calling to tell me that MIT had established, and was developing, a new management school, built on the existing foundation of a department of business and engineering administration. I knew that MIT had one of the four strongest industrial relations centers in the country associated with its Department of Economics.

In those days the field was small enough so that we all knew the distant university centers and the names, and sometimes the faces, of those who staffed them. MIT, I knew, had D. V. Brown, Charles Myers, Paul Pigors, Alex Bavelas, and younger men like George Shultz. It was there that my friend Jack Coleman had gone in 1951 after completing his Ph.D. at Chicago. Now, Eli wanted to know if I would accept the invitation were I asked to visit the School of Industrial Management. I said of course, and when I told her that evening, Betty was even more enthusiastic. Her feeling was that it would be good for us to leave Chicago. But what chance did I really have?

In a few days I had another phone call from MIT, this time from a man who introduced himself as Penn Brooks, dean of the School of Industrial Management, of whom I had never heard. Could we meet that Saturday in Hinsdale, outside Chicago, at 10 A.M. at his daughter Carol's house? I could, and did. Penn Brooks was a hearty man with a strong voice, and he was embarrassed to be seeing me in the midst of his daughter's lively household. We nevertheless had a good interview, largely spent in his telling me about the School of Industrial Management and his hopes for it.

Penn and I hit it off well from the start. A graduate of MIT in 1917, he had come from Sacarrapa, Maine. He entered the First Engineers of the First Division even before graduation, and served as a lieutenant of engineers overseas from the summer of 1917 to the end of World War I. He won a DSC and spoke atrocious French that he thought was good; he was full of great laughter and noises of various kinds, and was a shrewd judge of people for all of that.

Penn had had an excellent career at Sears Roebuck and Company, lastly as vice president of manufacturing, before returning to his alma mater as the first dean of its new School of Industrial Management. In addition to needing a younger faculty member in industrial relations who would be fully acceptable to the Industrial Relations section of the Department of Economics, the school was looking for a new director of the Sloan Fellowship Program. I had never heard of it, but Brooks filled me in on the details.

A week passed after the interview, and there was no word. I was ready to forget the whole thing when Eli Shapiro called again. Eli, it turned out, was, in addition to being professor of finance, the associate dean of the school. He asked whether I could visit MIT to be looked over by their key people. I said I could. Eli was noncommittal on the telephone about my chances, but I knew that, in him, I had a strong ally.

I spent three full days in Cambridge and MIT, my first visit there, in October 1954. I was quizzed by Elting Morison, Douglass Brown, Alex Bavelas, and some other faculty members. I also walked around MIT and marveled at the place. It had a handsome setting on the Charles River, and its School of Industrial Management was in a fine building, the former corporate headquarters for Lever Brothers before that company moved to New York. I was asked to conduct a seminar in management organization with a small group of graduate students. I was under close scrutiny, but enjoyed the tone of the place. Not as preciously academic as

Chicago, it seemed to have an atmosphere of engagement with the real world.

I sensed a wary Doug Brown and knew that my session with him was critical. I remember his first question. "How is Bob Burns and what is he doing?" He watched me like a hawk. I looked him in the eye and said, "Bob is fine, and if you know him, you know exactly what he is doing; and if you don't know him, I can't begin to explain it." Doug liked the answer, and later recounted it to me. I had refused to be critical of Burns, but I could not be an apologist for him. I stayed with Jack and Mary Coleman in their home in Acton. They described how they loved living in the area and hoped we would come.

I learned that there were at least two other candidates, one of whom had a strong reputation and a good deal of experience. The other, like me, was a relative unknown in the field. I realized that I had not been allowed a closer look at the Sloan Fellowship Program, and it struck me that Brooks and Shapiro did not want to rock the boat for Gerry Tallman, its director, while a session of the program was in full swing. I did talk to some of the Sloan Fellows—older, mature, confident young men—having coffee in the Faculty Club. When I returned to Chicago I had no clue as to the decision.

A week or more went by, and then a phone call came from Eli Shapiro. Would I accept appointment as associate professor of management and director of the Sloan Fellowship Program at $10,000 per year and moving expenses, starting the summer of 1955, with a four-year contract and absolutely no promises beyond 1959? Betty and I had talked enough about it, and I accepted on the telephone. Shapiro said I would get a letter from James Killian, the president at MIT, if there were no tie-ups at the president's office. In due time I received the appointment letter from Dr. Killian, who was only a name to me then, but whom I would come to know very well indeed.

Leaving Chicago turned out to be complicated. Our families were uneasy about our going into the unknown. John Jeuck, newly returned from Harvard, was the new dean of the Business School at Chicago. He offered me a promotion to associate professor for the next academic year at a salary matching MIT's. With mixed emotions, I turned down the counteroffer. I decided I had to go to MIT.

Aerial view of the Massachusetts Institute of Technology, circa 1956. The skyline of Boston's Beacon Hill across the Charles River changed dramatically in the next forty years

4

Becoming a Part of the Massachusetts Institute of Technology

We put our house in Chicago on the market after the first of the year. Naively, we assumed we could sell it ourselves, and we learned a painful lesson. In the spring, I went back to MIT and found a place in Concord, the home of Professor Cary Brown. He was going to Berkeley for the summer and offered it to us rent-free.

The big event of the spring, however, was Bruce's arrival on April 26, 1955. We now had three little children, the oldest two and a half years old, with no help at home, and my schedule absolutely jammed with the demands of both a responsible exit from the institution that had been my home since April 1946 and preparations for a new job. The staff at the Industrial Relations Center was marvelous at our several departure parties. Finally, in the last week of June I drove our new station wagon, loaded with cribs and other household paraphernalia, east to Boston. Betty, with the absolutely vital help of my mother, came a few days after I had arrived. She flew in with the three children, two of them still babes-in-arms and the third, Stephen, manfully helping as much as he could.

On July 1, the first day of my appointment, I drove to MIT and reported to Penn Brooks at 8:30 A.M. He was one of the few people on the fourth floor at that early hour, and he was astonished to see me. He told me that most new faculty appointees showed up at their convenience and, besides, the July 4th holiday weekend was about to begin.

I was promptly faced with a major problem. Professor Tallman had not been told I would replace him immediately; he thought there would be at least a year overlap. He had to protect his status as director of the Fellowship Program. I could see his point. The new Sloan Fellows had arrived about three weeks before. Tallman had been meeting with them constantly. The classes for the pressured summer term had begun. Miss

Gladys Murley, prima donna of the Sloan Fellows office, was in command and did not need the complication of breaking in a new director. I told Penn and Eli, nonetheless, that this thing had to be done right away—cleanly and completely—or I would never get a grip on the program. They agreed, and Tallman left the office that day.

I met with the new Sloan Fellows. They were a dynamic group of successful-looking young executives, outgoing, bright, but wary of this very young man who was introduced as the new director. I had just turned thirty-three and looked younger. They averaged thirty-five and looked older. Years later, more than one of that group delighted in telling me the story. After the meeting, it turned out that they talked among themselves and agreed that I would last no more than six weeks. "Were we surprised," Bill Mercer liked to say.

From the beginning I liked MIT. In 1955 it was still bathed in the aura of Word War II and its aftermath. The large rush of veteran students had come and gone, and, with them, their temporary barracks on the west campus. The golden era of expansion of research grants was still barely underway. Any professor with a great idea could get research support, or so it seemed. Some of the vestiges of the war mobilization were still there in temporary buildings, notably the famous Building 20, left over from the Radiation Laboratory, but the landscape was still largely unchanged from before World War II. The School of Humanities and Social Science and the School of Management were still in their early days. There was unspoken agreement in the administration and most of the faculty that the new schools would get their full chance. Fair enough, we all thought. It was a wonderful atmosphere for a young professor fresh from the Middle West. One thing was clear: MIT had a great sense of pride in what it had accomplished and of confidence in what it was going to accomplish. It expected its faculty and its students to hold that point of view. It was a place that, as Vannevar Bush said, had a habit of success.

I had free rein with the executive development program. "Make it the best" was the word from Brooks and Shapiro. I liked the freedom they gave me to manage the program but I soon learned that the program was in some trouble. The application pool was small in number and weak in the qualifications of some applicants. The faculty who taught in the program were interested in the students, but there was little cohesion about it. Erwin Schell, the founder of the program in the 1930s, was retired, but he came in every day and hovered wraith-like in the background. Relationships with the Sloan Foundation, which funded the program, were distant. There were whispers that the foundation was considering dropping its support. Miss Murley ran the schedule and was not happy to see me.

I called on Mr. Sloan in New York. Mistaking his deafness for disinterest, I found him austere and distant. Things had to change, I thought, and by the fall, they did.

I needed help I could trust. I called Ted Alfred back in Chicago and offered him the assistant director's job. He accepted immediately and soon came with Cathy, his wife. Later, I brought Tom O'Farrell from Chicago. I tried to hire Dick Thornbury, but he now had my old job and, understandably, declined. (A year later, he called to say he would come if the job were still open. Of course, it was not.) I found I needed people I could count on to ensure that I had a grip on what was happening. By late fall, many of the faculty seemed to have new interest in the program, but marketing the program was difficult in that first year. We produced new materials describing the program and made many calls. I enjoyed an almost daily chat with Schell. Williams Krebs, the previous assistant director who would rather teach in any case, became a close friend. I also developed close relationships with Elting Morison, Doug Brown, and Charlie Myers.

Elting and I became particularly close. He became a magnificent teacher for several generations of Sloan Fellows and in later years many of them felt that he was the major influence on their thinking during the program. He wrote with a lucid, engaging style about the interrelationships of technology, politics, and management, but it was in conversation that he especially shone. I would wander often into his tiny office where, feet on his desk as always, he would ask the questions that defined any problem. His impact on people and organizations would be profound.

Along the way, it seemed clear to me that MIT needed more strings to its bow of executive development than the Sloan Fellowship Program. That program was truly the Cadillac of the few executive programs in the country, but we needed, I thought, a shorter but equally appealing alternative. Why not a short program for more experienced executives to compete with Harvard's short course, the Advanced Management Program, which dominated the field? Eli was delighted with the idea, but where would such students be housed even if we did have an attractive curriculum? Our answer was Endicott House in Dedham. MIT had just

With Sloan Fellows, 1960

been given that impressive estate, but with no endowment to cover its myriad expenses. The administration wondered if MIT could keep it going. I had visited Endicott House and thought it was a stretch for students to commute to MIT every day from Dedham, but the facilities were imposing—just the thing for aspiring executives. Trudy Winquist, the newly appointed manager of Endicott House, was desperate for income sources. I could offer her two ten–week sessions of perhaps twenty four students every year, each paying premium rates through the program. Of course, we would have to do some remodeling. For one thing, we had to get rid of those big-antlered moose, deer, and elk heads in the hallways. And what about other furnishings?

But the place had been found, and Trudy was ecstatic. She became the "house mother" for successive sessions of the senior executives, and they loved her. In the years that followed, the Senior Executive Program typically carried the base budget expenses of Endicott House, and that made it possible for MIT to keep it as a viable conference center.

The final question was curriculum. Ted and I put it together and fortunately got agreement from people who would teach that first session, no

School of Industrial Management, 1955. Professors Douglass V. Brown, Eli Shapiro (associate dean), HWJ, Douglas M. McGregor, Ross M. Cunningham, Leo B. Moore, E. P. Brooks (dean), W. Van Alan Clark (assistant dean), and William A. W. Krebs, Jr.

small issue since it would be an overload in the first sessions of the program. I recall well the Industrial Management faculty meeting in which I described the program. The faculty members were skeptical. I particularly remember Tom Hill standing up and asking if this idea was actually going forward. Were we prepared to risk our reputation on this kind of program? I argued strongly for it, but I was still brand-new and Eli carried the day by saying, firmly, "We will go ahead with this and give it a fair trial."

It did go ahead and very successfully. After a first session with only eleven participants in the spring of 1956, it took off. Ted Alfred became the lead person in the program. In the years that followed, the Program for Senior Executives came to be regarded as one of the very best in the country and turned out hundreds of graduates in fifty-person classes. Long after my time in the school, Abe Siegel, then dean of the school, added a separate building to the Endicott House to accommodate larger groups of Senior Executives. It was named, at my suggestion, the Edward Pennell Brooks Center.

And so the first year passed, both hectically and productively as far as the job was concerned. At home, we succeeded in scraping by financially, and things were going wonderfully well for the family. It was not all easy. In that first summer, Boston was hit by two major hurricanes, Connie and Diane, in quick succession, and as the wind and water swirled through Concord, we wondered what kind of climate we had entered. We bought a new eight-room house in Weston at the end of the first summer, even though our house in Palos Heights still had not sold. We were allowed to put $1000 down on a $33,000 house, with a promise to come up with an acceptable down payment "soon." Luckily, the house in Illinois sold shortly afterward. We collected our $9000 equity and survived the first year on a very tight budget. We even budgeted my lunch money. I drove our lone car in every day, and Betty ran the rollicking young family home, pretty much alone and housebound all week long. I remember our biggest threat was the summer menace of polio, which was terrible for any family and especially for us with three little children. (A year later, the Salk vaccine wiped out the scourge, with every parent breathing a sigh of relief.)

At the end of the first year, I received an MIT Sloan teaching award of $1000, established that year by MIT to recognize and encourage outstanding teaching, and, fortunately, I was awarded the prize again the following year. I also began to do some consulting to supplement my income and build my experience in the field of organization. In time, I concluded an agreement with the Campbell Soup Company. The $6000 a year for one day of consulting per month with the company lifted the gloom from our financial life. I had worked with J. Paul Sticht in the Chicago plant and later in the Camden plant, and he and I touched careers again and again in the years that followed.

I was able to take on further consulting, although I restricted myself more severely than most of my colleagues. I simply could not take the time away from the job. Within three years, I was asked to join two small boards: Draper Manufacturing Company in Hopedale, Massachusetts, and Lumberman's Mutual Fire Insurance Company. I learned much from these places and used cases from them in the courses I taught. Years later, Doc Blanchard, who was in one of my first graduate classes and went on to become vice chairman of Du Pont, liked to say publicly that all my cases during his term came from the Campbell Soup Company. That may have been an exaggeration, but not by much.

And so 1956 and 1957 rolled by. Our home life was a busy one. Betty became a leader of the "Sloan wives group," and we developed many longtime friendships among those students. The Sloan Fellows Program was attracting attention within MIT. The group grew to thirty six and in time to fifty, with an ample range of applicants from which to choose. I called on Alfred Sloan and Arnold Zurcher, the director of the Sloan Foundation, every month. After a while, it seemed that Mr. Sloan was beginning to enjoy those meetings. Our field trips to New York included lively sessions with Mr. Sloan, and he welcomed their questions and sometimes astonished the Fellows with his answers. Once, one Fellow asked Mr. Sloan what analysis he used when he decided to sell a stock. Mr. Sloan looked at him intently and said, "I don't believe I have ever sold a stock."

We were constantly in need of more funds for new activities, but I usually found a way to get them. I felt, for example, that the Sloans tended to be as insular as most Americans, and I was tantalized by the idea of taking the whole group outside the country during their spring vacation; I was convinced that the Fellows would understand their own country better from that perspective. This followed an already effective visit to Washington during the spring break to see firsthand a vital part of their future lives—the Federal government.

In my first year we actually chartered a flight and went to Ottawa, where I had asked C. D. Howe, the legendary wartime genius of Canada, and originally an American from MIT, to be our host. Howe seemed to enjoy it and so, certainly, did the Sloan Fellows. Three days of meetings and sessions with ministers, bureaucrats, and businessmen with the Sloan Fellows directly responsible for developing the questions and introducing the speakers proved very rewarding to the Fellows. The trip to Canada became a regular part of the program. In later years, extensions of this idea—developed by John Wynne, who came to MIT in 1958 to direct the program—brought the Sloans to Europe and, in time, to the U.S.S.R., Japan, China, and elsewhere around the world in what became high spots of the Sloan year.

By 1957 the executive development programs encompassed the Sloan Fellows Program, the program for senior executives, and a program for Boston executives, and had become a mainstream activity of the School of Industrial Management. As the spring of 1957 approached, I proposed

School of Management Council, 1957. Front row: Jay Forrester, Douglass V. Brown, E. P. Brooks, Billy Goetz, Sidney Alexander, Eli Shapiro. Back row: Elting E. Morison, David Durand, HWJ

to Penn that we have a five-year celebration of the founding of the school. It was a big event. For the first time, many departments at the institute came to see the School of Industrial Management. It was here that Douglas McGregor read his seminal paper on two management approaches, contrasting authoritarian and participative management styles, and Vannevar Bush chaired a session on duties of board members. Shades of things to come! The field of management was never the same after that.

Another event in 1957 changed the world on a much broader front. We were electrified by the news that the Soviet Union had successfully launched Sputnik, a satellite that orbited the earth. The technical and emotional reactions were profound across the world. I remember Betty and me standing in our backyard at midnight, and, sure enough, at the appointed time, we saw the tiny bright light pass over our home and neighborhood in Weston. President Eisenhower went on the radio to reassure the country. Vannevar Bush, who was still only a name to me, was quoted as saying in an interview something to the effect that the achievement was only a "stunt." Later, when I knew him and asked him about it, he admitted he had been wrong. I wished I knew a great deal more about the physics of satellites.

One immediate impact on MIT was that Eisenhower asked James R. Killian, its president, to come to Washington to serve as his special assistant for science and technology and to consider how America could "catch up" to the Soviets. This meant that the chancellor, Jay Stratton, became the acting president of MIT. Both of these administrative moves, of course, were far from my own circle of activity.

As 1958 went on, I was about to enter the last year of my contract. I was worried, as every young professor at MIT is always worried, about chances of survival in an intensely competitive atmosphere. In those days, fewer than one in three had their contracts extended past the age of thirty six or thirty seven. In the Sloan School, the faculty had grown with each new year. Douglas McGregor had returned to MIT and Don Marquis had come, and both added real weight in human organization studies. More than twenty new assistant and associate professors, all with reputations for effective work, were working within the school in the several fields. In my field, industrial relations, three principal professorships were already filled—Brown, Myers, and Pigors—and untenured professors included George Shultz, Abe Siegel, and Jack Coleman, all close friends, with many others nearby including Stanley Jacks and Ed Schein. Elsewhere, bright lights like Bowman, Kuh, Fetter, Letwin, Bennis, Little, Kaufman, and Whitin were at work in the fields of accounting, marketing, organization, and production. The wonder of it was that we were all working well, or reasonably well, together. Under the tent of cooperation, however, ran a stream of competitiveness and an awareness that there would be only a few tenured appointments made in the coming few years.

Douglass Brown had replaced Eli Shapiro as associate dean in 1957, stipulating that it be a one-year term. In the fall of 1958 Penn asked me if I would succeed Doug Brown in the associate dean's job. Penn announced the change, and the faculty seemed to like the idea even though I was hardly a D. V. Brown. In the fall of 1958, another momentous process was under way. Although I was screened from it for obvious reasons, the school's Personnel Committee was considering whether to propose me for tenure. In the midst of that, I had a long letter from

W. Allen Wallis, the new dean of business at the University of Chicago. Would I consider returning to Chicago with a hefty salary and lofty title? He said that there would be no full professorship just yet, but that was assuaged by the offer of a multiyear and evergreen contract.

I decided not to make the visit that Allen proposed, however, choosing instead to cast my lot with MIT, and told Doug Brown of my decision. Later on, I heard that people like Eugene Burgess, formerly of General Mills and now professor at the University of California, Beverly Murphy of the Campbell Soup Company, Frederick Harbison, now at Princeton, and many others had written support for my tenure, but the key support came from within MIT from people like Ralph Freeman and other insiders like McGregor, Brown, Shapiro, and Myers. In February 1959, I was told by D. V. Brown that I was being strongly recommended for promotion to full professor and that unless things went "off track" higher up, I would be promoted to professor, with tenure, effective July 1, 1959.

I was absolutely lifted by this news. I felt as though I had made it in the toughest arena of American academics. Much later, I concluded that only a university with enormous self-confidence and a large organizational ego could afford to promote someone like me. I barely knew Stratton, who was now president while Killian was away on leave in Washington, and I was a relative unknown to the trustees. What I did have was a strong base of power with the executive programs, which were becoming nationally well known, a strong teaching record, strong support from the school leadership and the key professors, and no enemies. I probably also had important support from Alfred Sloan, MIT's number one trustee. I was now a professor, and I walked with new assurance.

In March of 1959, another event had taken place. The school had been approached by the Ford Foundation with an invitation to establish one of two American-sponsored business schools in India. Douglas Ensminger, the Ford Foundation representative in India, also wondered about an advanced management program for India. The proposal was sketchy, the financing obscure, the long-run Indian sponsorship unclear. Penn was doubtful, since we had our hands full in the United States and MIT had tended to decline foreign institution building. Nonetheless, he asked me if I would visit India and make an assessment.

It would mean a mission of three weeks or more, and I was overwhelmed as it was. But we had succeeded in appointing John Wynne as director of the Sloan programs. John, a former Sloan Fellow from my first class of '56, with his quiet and competent assumption of the job, made it possible for me to concentrate on associate dean problems. I agreed to go to India. Just before my departure, I was appointed the school's representative on a committee to assess the social sciences at MIT, to be chaired by Max Millikan, the head of the Center for International Studies. I attended its first meeting and then left for India, to return just in time for the second meeting of the committee.

I flew from New York to Rome on a 707 in the first months of commercial transatlantic jet service, and then on to India in a Lockheed constellation. My stop in Rome was my first return to Europe since 1946, and my landing in New Delhi was my first visit to Asia. India was a revelation. I spent the first three weeks traveling to Bombay, Bangalore, Madras, Calcutta, and back to Delhi. I visited factories and mills, interviewed nearly thirty top executives of business and government, spent time with Ensminger and Everett Woodman, his deputy, and came to know Charat Ram, a leading businessman and leader of the All-India Management Association. He and his wife, Sumitra, became life-long friends. When I left Calcutta late one night to return to Boston, I was exhausted but exhilarated. I was convinced that the school should enter the international arena. I thought something could be done in India, but I was not sure how.

As I flew home, stopping in Hong Kong and Tokyo for the first time, I wrote my report. I met with the faculty leaders back in Cambridge and proposed that we go ahead with an advanced management program, sponsored by the All-India Management Association funded by the Ford Foundation and using MIT faculty. We would, in the meantime, study further the proposal to establish a school of management in Calcutta, with the expectation that we would go ahead. Much depended on the Indian board of trustees to be appointed, the land site for the school, and the level of support in India.

Only a short time remained before the first of the executive programs would be held in the summer of 1960, and there was much to be done. Yet I believed the project worthwhile and so, in time, did the rest of the people who would deliver the results.

HWJ, dean of the School of Industrial Management, with his predecessor, Dean Emeritus E. P. Brooks, 1959

5

The School of Industrial Management Becomes the Sloan School

My direct role in the executive development program at MIT came to a close later that spring of 1959. It was hard to leave the program. I will always have a great admiration for the executive students and especially the Sloan Fellows. I remember now the close friends that I had in that group. The breadth and quality that we built into the program produced, as many Sloan Fellows would later say, "the best year of our lives."

Penn was thinking of retirement. He had worked hard since 1952 as the founding dean of the school, and now, a year from his required retirement, he was tired. He announced that he would retire a year earlier if he could ensure a good transition to the new dean. Naturally, all eyes in the school began to focus on that unnamed successor. President Stratton appointed Ralph Freeman, head of economics, as chairman of a search committee, and Ralph told me later that he had visited Carnegie Tech, Chicago, and elsewhere for ideas and candidates. Stratton also talked to all senior professors in the school. I paid no attention to the speculation. I only hoped that I could still work as associate dean with the individual who would be chosen.

As spring progressed, Houlder Hudgins, a management professor, exploded a bombshell when he told me, at the graduation exercise for senior executives, that he expected me to be appointed to the dean's post. Although I told him he was out of his mind, he turned out to be right. Within a week Penn informed me that I would succeed him, and since graduation was fast upon us, asked if I would mind taking office, informally, in May with official duties to begin in the fall. He also asked me to write his annual report for 1958–59 and to represent the school at graduation. He had agreed to go to Turkey to spend a year in Ankara as visiting dean of the new management school there, and he and Carol, his wife, wanted to leave on the first of June. I agreed to take over. When the appointment was announced to the assembled faculty, there was a long pause and then loud applause. Ed Kuh, with whom I had had only frosty relations, put his arm around me and led the cheer. At thirty-six, I was still so sure of myself that I did not have the sense to worry.

What a change! I must admit that although I was completely surprised, I was delighted. I met with Jay Stratton, who formally appointed me with approval of the corporation and notified me of my new salary. I spent the summer thinking how best to attack the problems. The school was full of good people and new ideas, but it needed focus, a better position within MIT, and visibility from the outside. We needed academic respectability within MIT as a field of intellectual effort. Too many of the old-line professors at MIT thought of undergraduate course XV, the numeral that designated the management course in the MIT catalog, as a refuge for those who could not deal with physics.

I thought a good deal about the state of management education that summer. The curriculum for preparing people for business careers was still stuck in the prewar business pattern. Course XV was not atypical. Rules of conduct, exhortation with an almost spiritual force, were common. The mainstays were the rationality of accounting to measure results, the engineering of plant layouts and job organization, and the marketing of products. On top of this was a layer of price theory and economics, to a large extent devoid of a sense of the realism of the marketplace. The case study method had been superimposed on this plan at Harvard as a dramatic way of injecting realism and, presumably, analysis. In my view, it was not wholly effective. The new tools of mathematical analysis and control had made possible advances, and two schools, notably MIT and Carnegie Tech, had started in the 1950s to apply analysis to a variety of management problems from capital decision-making to inventory control. Operations research had been developed in a big way and, as in economics, mathematics and statistics were becoming the principal modes of analysis. We had also begun to make headway in the study and teaching of organizational behavior. But the whole theory was still lacking. I felt that we should encourage our faculty to develop a course that could be presented in a unified theory of management. Our problem was how to achieve this and, if we did, how to market it. I spent the next several years working on these problems and my successors have continued to do so.

As dean of the school, I joined the weekly meetings of the academic council of the institute—the group of school deans and other major officers together with the president—of which I was to be a part for many years. The other school deans greeted me with all the enthusiasm of a pack of wolves meeting a new lamb. Gordon Brown in engineering, John Burchard in humanities and social science (his first words to me, "So here's our new Republican to replace Penn Brooks"), George Harrison in science, Pietro Belluschi in architecture and planning. They were all experienced and solid people, barons of their own territories, quick to protect and defend MIT but very aware of their own priorities and needs. There was also Jim McCormack, vice president for special laboratories, who had a distinguished career as an Air Force general, Joseph Snyder, treasurer, Harold Hazen, dean of the graduate school, Carl Floe, vice president for research, John Rule, dean of students, Malcolm Kispert, the council's secretary, and a few others. I soon learned that each had a style, a strategy, and a record of achievement. I felt overpowered, but I resolved that I would represent my school with a positive and straightforward presence. How I enjoyed those Tuesday luncheon meetings! Jay Stratton was an imperturbable chairman. Although he was rather remote, he had a way of presenting things as a first among equals in a most elegant way.

I began to understand the school in a new way. MIT's School of Industrial Management had begun operations in 1952, but it had deeper roots in the institute's culture than that date implies. It had begun as a department in 1917 with some minor efforts before that. MIT's administration and trustees had long realized that many MIT engineering graduates had ended up in management posts and that it made sense to provide them with some early education in the field. The course now had a distinguished alumni body, but many alumni were still getting used to the notion that their dear old department was now a school. I was sure that, in time, they would all be proud of the still-new school. But the School of Industrial Management, MIT's fifth school, still had to establish its position as a peer of engineering, science, architecture, and humanities. That was a major challenge for a new dean.

The dean's job in the school was far different from that of the associate dean. I knew all our professors, and they all, it seemed, wanted to be heard. I listened a great deal. I concluded that we were strong in several fields but could use a few key senior people to establish new ones and to create a sense of excitement. I talked to the economists in the school and in the Department of Economics. We needed strength in that key discipline. From its beginnings, the school and the department had worked closely together, rare at that time on the American academic scene for schools of business and departments of economics. The department had high standards and a strong coterie of colleagues who established a premier place for the department in the field: Paul Samuelson, Robert Solow, Robert Bishop, Cary Brown, Charles Kindleberger, Morris Adelman, Paul Rosenstein-Rodan, among others. Douglass Brown, Charles Myers, and Abraham Siegel ranked high in their own fields and took a lively interest in collaborating with the teaching program in the School of Management. It was a most happy connection.

I now proposed to Ralph Freeman, close to retirement as head of the Department of Economics, and Robert Bishop, who would replace him, that we would seek their concurrence for every economics appointment made by the school. They agreed with cautious enthusiasm. There would no longer be any hint of a different level of economics in the management school. Solow casually suggested I might try for Franco Modigliani, who was at Northwestern and rumored to be unhappy. I knew Modigliani from his earlier visit to MIT, and I thought he would make an excellent professor in the Sloan School. I called Franco during the Christmas holidays in 1959; he accepted our proposal and joined us in June 1960, adding strength to both the department and the school. Later on we tended to collaborate with the department in joint appointments, or to appoint from the outside of MIT, individuals who had a more applied bent than their theory colleagues appreciated. In this way, the School of Management and the Department of Economics appointed people like Lester Thurow, Paul MacAvoy, Myron Scholes, Fischer Black, and, in time, Robert Merton.

I wanted some additional outsiders, nonacademics, but notable in their field of practice. In this way Carroll Wilson, former Boston mayor John Collins, David Austin, Richard Morse, and Bernard Muller-

Thym came to join us. Edward Bowles, the great electrical engineer from the School of Engineering, became a professor of management. Jay Forrester, another engineer and the inventor of the magnetic core memory for computers, had joined the school earlier, but for some time he was often viewed as somewhat of an outsider by the economics and management faculties, and I decided to give him a great deal of backing and encouragement. In my view he was one of our greatest original thinkers. Some of his students, like Ed Roberts, began to excel. At younger levels, I tried to attract the pick of the new crop, and we often did. For example, Bill Pounds, just out of U.S. Navy air service, was completing a Ph.D. at Carnegie Tech. He joined us, and so did several other young stars. We had begun to build the concept of a new management school.

To support our modest growth, we needed effective administration. Fortunately, we had three stalwart administrative officers, members of the staff of MIT: Miriam Sherburne for the graduate school, Esther Merrill for the undergraduate program, and Gertrude Burns, the budget and finance officer. All were superb and for a new dean, indispensable. I later came to know that they were typical of the relatively small cadre of outstanding women who gave critical underpinning to the academic structure of MIT.

I wanted to press for the development of a Ph.D. program in management and found good support in the school's faculty but some reluctance to press for it. I decided to push hard for the program and we got it approved by the MIT faculty and the corporation in 1961. I remember the MIT faculty meeting where the proposal came up for a vote. Someone asked me, as I presented the motion, if there was really the academic substance for such a degree at MIT. I made the case and the motion passed with no audible "nays"; it was subsequently approved by the corporation. Our first Ph.D. degree was awarded later to a young man, Martin Anderson, whose thesis, published as *The Federal Bulldozer*, was dynamite in the urban planning field.

As part of the academic effort, we established a new journal, the *Industrial Management Review*, in order to have an outlet for faculty and student publications. It survives grandly to this day as the *Sloan Management Review*.

With undergraduate students, MIT, late 1950s

I realized I needed stronger and more visible help in making the case for the school within MIT to the central administration and to the deans of other schools. We had in place an advisory committee, but it functioned remotely and with too little energy. I persuaded Mr. Sloan to take an active role as chairman of the Industrial Management Advisory Council, and recruited new members, including members of the MIT Corporation who were active and former CEOs, like Bradley Dewey, Beverly Murphy, and Robert Sprague. I recruited several active leaders from outside MIT as well. They clearly enjoyed coming together for a full day every year and hearing of the school's progress and its needs. It also afforded them the opportunity to see and hear some of the great men of their world, such as Vannevar Bush and Alfred Sloan, who always attended. In time, the council became a powerful voice in many places.

One who declined to join the council because it "was not his style" was Edwin Land, the founder and active head of Polaroid Corporation.

His declination, however, included a warm invitation to breakfast with him at his offices—the first of many. After that, I went to see him often. His modest offices on Osborne Street in Cambridge were within a few blocks of MIT, and our meetings, usually over breakfast, were often attended by one of his several assistants. Land, a full-bore genius and a rare personality, sparkled on these occasions. On one, he proposed a novel plan: He would turn over to the school a Polaroid factory with a small work force, full equipment, and a new product idea to develop and produce. The plant would be operated by a group of our best students. He proposed that he and I and a few faculty members would serve as advisers or "directors," but not as managers. His concept: "Let the students learn by doing." He predicted a complete and effective education in management, as well as a profitable plant.

I considered his proposal for many days and talked it over with my closest colleagues. In the end, I concluded that we were not quite ready for it, much as I was tempted, largely because of the time it involved, and I didn't like the creation of a special anointed group. He was disappointed and in the years that followed, would often start a sentence with, " Now if we had our model teaching factory going . . ." Land was indeed a genius; he would have been a great member of the council, but he helped from the sides and we did fairly well without him in an official capacity.

In the meantime, the India project moved forward. I had hoped to go in the first summer group in 1960 as part of the faculty for the session in Kashmir, where the meetings were to be held. It was clear that my plate was full, however, and I asked Penn, who had returned from Turkey, if he would lead such a group with John Wynne as his deputy. He agreed, and the first group took off. Their reports on returning were most positive, and we planned the second group for 1961. This time I committed to go with the hope of setting forward the plan for the business school at the same time.

At home, we were going through changes, too. Betty finally had a car of her own. Although our house in Weston had served us well and Betty had enjoyed the neighborhood, we had come to like the sound and look of Lexington, and we decided to move there when the opportunity presented itself. Herold Hunt, the former superintendent of schools in Chicago, was now at Harvard, and he and his wife Isabel, Lexington residents, were especially helpful to us as we established ourselves in the area. We often saw them at their home in Lexington and through these visits we came to see more of that town. Suddenly, a month before we were to go to India in 1961, a house was advertised in Lexington, and I saw it late one afternoon. Later, Betty and I toured it together. It was a 1795 house, formerly the Raymond Tavern, with three acres of land, and only a short walk to the town center. It had bedrooms for everyone and a barn, but it needed a lot of renovation and a new kitchen. We bought it and spent spare moments in Kashmir that summer wondering what we had bought.

We loved the house, and it remains the place we all think of as our best "home," even though we were there only five years. It had been built across the street from clockmaker Nathaniel Mulliken's home and workshop, which had been burned down by the British in their 1775 retreat. We had the 1860s quarter oak floors taken up and the great wide pine floor boards underneath brought back to life. We rebuilt the kitchen wing, including its fireplace, renovated the six other fireplaces, and cleaned out the barn. The children took well to the Lexington schools, and several of our neighbors became lifelong friends. We enjoyed the old town whose history pervaded everything. April 19, Patriots Day—a Massachusetts state holiday—was an almost religious event. The parade, with enactors of Paul Revere, William Dawes, and finally the Minutemen all moving by our front door, made one's heart beat faster. Steve and Bruce became convinced that there was a benign ghost in their wing of the house and, perhaps wrongly, we did not discourage them; we enjoyed it, too. The great horse weather vane from the barn has remained with us, hung in every house we have lived in since that time.

In the School of Industrial Management, another set of events was taking place that affected our lives for years. I had been looking for someone with a business background whose teaching could help us unify the several disciplines of analysis into a whole method of thinking about entrepreneurship and management decision-making. Elting Morison told me one day about Carroll Wilson, who had been assistant to MIT president Karl Compton in the early thirties and then Van Bush's assistant at MIT and in Washington. After the war he had been the first general manager of the Atomic Energy Commission and then head of two companies. The sale of the last one left him with enough money to pursue ideas that were of most interest to him. I telephoned Wilson at his home in Seekonk, Massachusetts, and convinced him to come to MIT. He put together a program on management for less developed countries of Africa that eventually sent dozens of young people—typically young men with master's degrees in management from MIT, and their spouses—to new African countries to take up posts as assistants to their political leaders. Later, we recruited law graduates from Harvard and Yale who went to help administer legal systems in Africa.

The purpose was twofold: first, to give these young people a great learning experience that would affect their whole lives and, perhaps, tilt them toward international activities; and, second, to add an international dimension to our program—something I could see as important for the future. Obviously, too, we were trying to help solve some of the problems associated with the transition of colonial states to effective self-determined republics. Individuals from the MIT Fellows in Africa Program later became college presidents, judges, district attorneys, and world bank officials. If I cannot say we added much in the long run to Africa, at least the short-term results were positive. Nation-building is a difficult process, and grafting from the outside without long-term follow-through is not effective. Our efforts at long-run institution-building, such as those we began at the Calcutta Management School, were far more effective.

There was one additional bonus from our work on the Fellows in Africa Program. Carroll needed assistance in administering the program. In response to this need, I recruited and hired Constantine Simonides, who was at the beginning of his long and effective career at MIT. Later, Kathryn Willmore, a graduate of Mt. Holyoke, came as an administrative assistant to the program, and has remained to do many fine things at MIT. She became secretary of the MIT Corporation, having succeeded Constantine in that position. Constantine and I became close personal friends and remained so until his untimely death in 1994. I can see him now: bright and optimistic, with a wonderful quizzical look, conscious and sensitive to the nuance of human behavior and warmly open to every human association. The sudden loss of Simonides would leave a serious hole in MIT's administration.

And so the school, day by day and term by term, went ahead. Some influences on us were separate from the MIT experience around which most of Betty's and my life revolved. I was asked to join the Putnam Funds as trustee by Charles Werley, its chairman. Charlie impressed me by his steady wisdom. "Remember, we have a responsibility to the widows and orphans in Maine," he would say. It turned out that the funds were governed by four outside trustees in those days, and it was Horace Ford, the legendary financial officer from MIT, whom I replaced. For a number of years the other trustees were Vannevar Bush, whom I came to know very well; Louis Hunter, long-time treasurer of the Massachusetts General Hospital, and Donald Hurley, a distinguished Boston lawyer. I learned some things about long-term investment judgments and large-scale analysis that served me well through the years.

The fee that I received for this service put our household on a sound financial basis for the first time. I never again had a major worry about financial pressure on the family. I also joined the board of Hitchiner Manufacturing Company, and this experience with a small, struggling casting and foundry shop in New Hampshire, which achieved a major success, was a vital part of my education.

Although the school was doing well, I sensed the beginnings of administrative problems centered largely around the man to whom I reported. Jay Stratton had recruited Charles Townes of Columbia University to become provost—the principal academic officer of MIT—a post last held by Jay Stratton, himself, and not filled since he became chancellor in 1956. Charlie Townes delayed his coming until the fall of 1961, but it was clear to the deans, based on an early meeting, that his presence would be formidable. He was a star in the science firmament, widely mentioned as a prospective Nobel Laureate, which he did indeed achieve in 1964; a super-bright physicist and a soft-spoken, hard-working academic with great ambitions.

Although there were seldom any negative words between us, it cannot be said that there was any warmth in our relationship. That apparently was also characteristic of Townes's dealings with the other deans. The Academic Council meetings became more pro forma. Robert Bishop had become dean of humanities and social science, and soon after, Lawrence Anderson became dean of architecture. As the terms continued to pass, the council morale was often low.

In 1961 MIT was celebrating its 100th anniversary, and a campaign was inaugurated to raise $66 million. Associated with this campaign was a plan for creating a number of new centers for interdisciplinary research. The Schools of Management and of Architecture and Planning, I felt, were already interdisciplinary, but were largely left out of the original plan of fund-raising. I, naturally, had to raise enough dust to get my school on the list. Most of the money was going to come from companies and management graduates, and I argued that we ought to be part of the stated purpose of the campaign. I think the two schools were finally listed as needing $1 million each, but, as it turned out, I raised much more than that.

The School of Management had two major needs. First, we had to get a sustained source of income from the Sloan Foundation for the Sloan Fellows program and for the school. I was finally able to get Mr. Sloan to understand this. I also worked out a concomitant agreement with the MIT administration for the school to receive a "credit" for tuition funds earned from students majoring in other fields who took some courses in management. By increasing the number of master's students, and receiving a credit for income earned from the Sloan program and the Senior Executives program, we balanced our operating budget. "A miracle," said Stratton, and so it was.

The second need was, predictably enough, more space. The Sloan Building had filled up. Because of a growing social science component in the curriculum and the expansion of the school's programs, there was a need for more office space, classroom space, and space for the over-burdened Dewey Library. With great help from Vice President Phil Stoddard and Planning Director Bob Simha, we hatched a plan: a new building behind the Sloan Building to provide office space, a new library, additional classrooms, and a remodeled Sloan building to reclaim the basement and other marginal spaces. Professor Eduardo Catalano of the School of Architecture, who had the commission to design the Stratton Student Center, agreed to develop the architectural plan. I made two additional suggestions as I sensed growing enthusiasm among the faculty members. Why not two high-rise residences for our graduate students and a small auditorium, seating 300 or so, for larger meetings? Underneath these buildings, Catalano proposed a large parking garage to re-place the entire Sloan parking lot.

There were some major problems. The administration, mostly Stratton and Townes, were not convinced that the additions were a priority. Be-sides, MIT did not own a piece of property crucial to the plan: more than an acre on the corner of Wadsworth and Main Street, then leased as a gas station and owned by the Bright brothers. MIT treasurer Joseph Sny-der came to the rescue. The institute, he said, already had its eye on the Bright site. After negotiations with the owners, MIT bought it and one other parcel from the Brights for what seemed at the time to be a terribly high price, using funds from the institute's real estate budget. My problem now was where to raise the money for the new structures. It was clear I would get no help from the MIT campaign people; they had many other fish to fry.

I developed a reasonably clear explanation of the new building and went to New York to talk to Mr. Sloan. By this time he and I were able to communicate pretty well. I had managed to outgrow my feeling of awe in his presence, and he began to see me as an individual and not just one of the many minions around him. Many years later when I became chairman of the Sloan Foundation, his secretary, then retiring at age sev-enty, told me that Mr. Sloan looked forward to my visits and seemed to enjoy our conversations more than any other. Mr. Sloan quickly agreed to send a check for $1 million to me at MIT, earmarked for our expansion. It was the biggest check I had ever seen. But we still needed an additional $2 million for our building and $1 million each for the institute's share of the debt financing for two high-rise buildings, and, of course, unspecified additional money for the raised plaza, as Catalano loved to call the park-ing space.

Suddenly a new possibility emerged in the midst of otherwise dreary prospects. George Bunker and William Bergen of Martin-Marietta, cor-poration members and members of our advisory council, came to me with a thought. Grover Hermann, the retiring chairman of Martin-Marietta, had a lot of money and no college affiliation. They arranged for Mr. Hermann to come to Cambridge, and I spent a morning describing the plan to him. He was a gentle and generous man, and he was most im-pressed by the thought of being a partner to Alfred Sloan, a point that I

Alfred P. Sloan, Jr., at MIT, May 1962, School of Industrial Management convocation. James R. Killian, Jr., is at the left; HWJ, Mrs. Killian, and John M. Wynne

tried to emphasize. We then walked over to Jim Killian's office. I told Jim, privately, that Mr. Hermann was ready to hear the question, and $1 million seemed possible. Jim taught me something that day. Without blinking, and with that marvelous country-boy-turned-university-president personality, he looked Hermann in the eye and said: "MIT needs $2 million to finish the Hermann Building and $1 million for the high-rise building for our graduate students." Hermann did not blink, either, and after further discussion, agreed in principle, with confirmation to come later. At that point, I would not have had the nerve to ask for the whole amount, but Jim Killian did. As he said later, that was the chairman's job. Many times, later on, I found it increasingly easy to do the same thing.

The plan was a solid one, and the work began in 1963. The academic programs proceeded on schedule and the building was completed in record time. The architecture of the Hermann Building and the single high-rise were in the same style as the Stratton Student Center: fortresslike, it foretold situations that became grim realities before the end of that decade. I accepted the plan (although in later years would not have done so). Catalano was a great engineer as well as a solid architect, and he stayed precisely on the budget. We also raised a little more money for the Millikan Bridge, as I called it—Max's practical idea of linking the third floors of the Sloan and Hermann Buildings. It demonstrated a proposition that was later followed in many buildings on the campus: Communication and intermingling of faculty members is more likely when direct passage is readily available. Professors do not like to go outside, especially in rain and snow.

Funding for the second high-rise and the parking plaza became terribly difficult and, finally, impossible. Jim Killian and Jay Stratton were not sure they liked the idea, even when I agreed that married students other than management students could occupy it. Many times in the following years I wished we had both buildings. It would have been a great bargain. A delightful plan was developed for a small auditorium but this was also a nonstarter. Now, thirty years later, the latest Sloan addition, the Tang building, includes this much-needed facility for the East Campus.

The years rolled on. I do not think I could have been happier with a job up to that time. The School of Industrial Management was developing a stronger presence on the campus. Our faculty members were seen increasingly as the equivalents of their colleagues elsewhere in the institute in every sense. On the international front, Betty and I had gone (with Douglas McGregor, Houlder Hudgins, Mike Gordon, and Sydney Alexander) to Kashmir for the All India Advanced Management Program in 1961. We were reinforced by Jack Coleman, who had become Ford Foundation representative in India.

When the Indian sessions were concluded, we boarded a flight in Bombay and flew to Entebbe, Uganda, to join Carroll and Mary Wilson and Max Millikan in the first session of the African Fellows Conference in that beautiful country in the days before Amin. We roared in from Bombay in the evening of the first day of the session. The party went on until the early morning hours. Clearly, that able group of young people, half finishing their first year, half heading out for their two-year assignments, were having a productive and happy time.

On the way home we stopped in London for a luncheon date with Peter and Anita Gil that had been arranged weeks before as we had passed through the Centre d'Etudes Industrielles in Lausanne, Switzerland. We badly needed a new head of the Sloan programs. John Wynne had become my associate dean, and Ted Alfred, while still available for some help, was also trying to finish his doctorate. A multilingual firecracker, Peter had completed his work at the University of Geneva and spent some years as an expatriate in Europe. He and Anita were both ready to come home. After a long lunch at Rules in London, I hired him, and he agreed to come in the fall of that year. John Wynne was very glad to see him, and Peter served ably in that post for many years.

We went back to India in 1963 for a full six weeks plus two weeks of travel. Houlder Hudgins, who had had a near-fatal fall from a river bank in 1961 in the Kashmir, visited me with a gloomy prediction of dire events if we were to go to India once again. I can remember him saying, "Don't go, for God's sake, Howard," but I felt it was important to show the MIT flag. The faculty was committed to the Calcutta program, it was up and running, and we had to show support for the members of the faculty there. This time, the MIT team was composed of Doug Brown, Ned Bowman, Tom Hill (who had remained on in India as the head of the Calcutta Management School), Peter King, and me.

The sessions had become popular and were held this time in the Bombay area at a first-rate hotel, Sun and Sand, thirty miles from the city. Indian government ministers and well-known managers like Charat Ram came to speak and observe. The sessions were serious and the participants were enthusiastic in their reactions.

A horrendous problem developed, however, the memory of which would cause Betty and me to break out in a cold sweat for years after. I had come to India two weeks earlier than Betty and the children to travel around the country as part of a series of faculty appearances before beginning the program in Bombay. Betty arrived, having traveled Boston-Paris-Cairo-Bombay, with Steve, Laura, and Bruce. Within a few days after arrival, Stephen came down with a dreadful stomach and bowel upset, accompanied by vomiting and fever. Getting medical help was difficult, but a participant in the program from Indian Airlines got the chief medical officer of IAL to come to the hotel. The verdict: acute gastroenteritis. The recommendation: do not put him in the hospital—that might be fatal—but keep him here in a cool room. The only treatment was to try to get liquid into the sick little boy. So we took turns, sitting up around the clock with him. Betty would stay with him through the day while I participated in the program, and then take turns in the night shift. The fever finally went down, and after four or five days, he was on the mend; we felt very grateful that he had survived. He lost fifteen pounds on his little frame during the illness.

After the program was completed successfully, we went to Greece for the sessions of the African Fellows Program and then on to Italy, Germany, and Austria, having a wonderful time all along the way. By the time we arrived home, Steve had completely recovered and was declared fully fit by his doctor.

The contribution of our Fellows in Africa program made me wonder whether a similar program might be possible in Latin America. We had developed close relationships with the large group of alumni in Colombia, and at their invitation, Bill Pounds, Ed Kuh, and I visited Bogota, Cali, and Medellin. We had productive discussions with a number of the Colombians: Virgilio Barco, then the mayor of Bogota, Rodrigo Botero, and others. We tried to establish a program there, but it did not produce the same kind of enthusiasm that we had experienced in Africa. There were obvious reasons for this shortfall and outcome: First, we lacked a strong and committed leader on the MIT side, like Carroll Wilson; second, there was the grim threat of *la violencia*, the irrational combat that went on between the shadowy peasant guerrillas and the government forces.

I had two exposures to that problem in Colombia on earlier trips. I had been the guest, for a few days, of Harold H. Eder, class of 1923 at MIT and our oldest alumnus in the country. His home outside Cali was protected at night, as other suburban homes were, by guards, barbed wire, and dogs. He was obviously deeply worried about the violence. Within days after my departure, Eder and his ranch foreman were kidnapped by the outlaws while they were riding on his ranch a few miles outside Cali. The foreman returned with a ransom note, but Eder never came home. Much later, he was found dead, murdered by the outlaws.

In a second instance, Bill Pounds, Rodrigo Botero, and I, during an early trip to Colombia, had had dinner with the president of the Universidad de Los Andes on the outskirts of Bogota. Returning later after dinner, our car was stopped in a traffic jam entering the fully darkened city. Pounds, on my left, suddenly opened his door and, despite my warning, began to leave the car. "I have no choice," he said. A uniformed soldier with a submachine gun was beckoning him. Soon Botero and I were ordered out the other side. The soldiers, when we could see them, were young—surely in their teens—and they looked nervous as they kept their fingers on the triggers of the Sten machine guns. After ransacking the seats and trunk of the car, they allowed us to go on. The next day we learned that they were looking for explosives rumored to be arriving in the city for the work of the rebels.

This undercurrent of danger made it difficult to design a useful collaborative effort. I will always regret that we could not get an effective program moving in that beautiful country. The experiences dramatized the clear lesson that countries, like organizations, need a sense of order and civility for progress to be made. The thin line between order and repression is, of course, an issue for constant study and concern. In any case, we did achieve close relationships with many admirable citizens of Colombia, including Virgilio Barco, class of 1943, who became in time the president of the Republic of Colombia and who also served ably as a member of the MIT Corporation.

Back in Lexington, Laura and Bruce were both in advanced classes, and Steve was doing well in his local school. One disappointment, however, was that there was not a good Boy Scout troop either in Lexington or in Weston. The activity that had meant so much to me was absent in our boys' lives.

We bought an old house on Lucas Pond in Northwood, New Hampshire. We used it year-round for weekends and additionally in the summer. It encouraged our habit of collecting antiques, which had begun in Weston. As we needed furniture, we began to buy old pieces at auctions and at a few inexpensive dealers. It was our therapy, and Betty and I became interested in antiques of all kinds. Over the years, we have found fascinating items and have learned a great deal. I had an interest in the Civil War and began to collect all kinds of material from that era. This was back in the days when Civil War documents, artifacts, and books could still be had for a few hundred dollars. We bought as many as our confidence and wallets allowed.

Our parents came out to New England at least once a year. My mother was an especially welcome guest. The children loved her, and she and Betty got along very well. I remember those many holidays with gratitude when she and my father were able to spend time with us.

The autumn of 1963 brought a calamity on the national scene—the assassination of President John F. Kennedy. Like everyone who was present on that day, I can recall the precise moment that I heard the news. I was returning to MIT from a meeting outside Cambridge on November 22 and turned on the car radio. The news from Dallas was terse and terrible: President Kennedy had been shot while riding in a motorcade in that city. He was, clearly, severely wounded, as was Governor Connolly riding in the same car. Soon came the word that Kennedy had died at Parkland Hospital. At about that time I arrived back at the School of Industrial Management, parked my car on Memorial Drive in front of the school, which was never allowed, and walked into the lobby, which was filled with milling students and faculty members. At their invitation, I spoke briefly to them about what we had all heard, and urged a steady and reflective mood rather than any sense of panic. After a few days of national confusion, then mourning, and then the tearful ceremony of the funeral procession in Washington, the nation steadied and under Lyndon Johnson began to breathe again. The questions surrounding that gloomy day remain, but the most complex to me revolves around whether Kennedy would have pulled the country out of Vietnam early had he lived. Lyndon Johnson apparently could not, and thus began the greatest disaster the nation was to face in mid century. But the country moved on and a period of uneasy regularity ensued.

For us, sad events were occurring. Even before Betty had arrived in India the previous year, we received word that Houlder Hudgins had died, and in 1964 we suddenly lost Douglas McGregor, a great professor and a dear friend, and also Erwin Schell and Ross Cunningham. We were beginning to experience personal losses of friends and colleagues, a process that continues to the present day. It remains for me one of the most depressing passages of our human existence, the loss of those close and dear.

The school, despite all, continued to move ahead. The new buildings were coming along, the faculty was growing stronger, and our finances were improving. The school was now seen in the public record as one of the best business schools in the country. We were still behind Harvard and Stanford in the polls, but surely in the top group.

On the broader front of international affairs, there were increasing tensions. The Berlin Wall had gone up in 1961, and the tensions between the United States and the Soviet Union continued. I was serving a six-year term as a member of the Board of Visitors of the Air Force Electronics Systems Command, and as part of that assignment, I was a member of the subcommittee that looked at some serious problems of the Air Force Systems Command organizational system. The report was useful, but I remember it best because of one dramatic incident. During our study, we flew into Homestead Air Force Base in our Air Force plane on the tensest night of the Cuban missile crisis. It was a grim experience flying into an air base on full war alert. The crisis had brought the world closer to a nuclear war than anything before or after, and our committee spent two days in the south of Florida during its most severe phase. Later, I co-chaired a panel with General Jack O'Neill to propose the future of the not-for-profit special laboratories of the Air Force. It was good preparation for the events surrounding the special laboratories of MIT at the end of the sixties.

A singular local event in the fall of 1964 also reminded us of the ongoing tensions between the United States and the Soviets that we had all learned to live with, however uneasily. We had a full and active social schedule within the school, of course, and from time to time participated in both professional and political events in the wider world. In early November of 1964, we invited Charles and Frances Townes, along with General O'Neill and his wife Mary and one other couple, to join us for dinner at our home in Lexington. The day, November 9, was Betty's birthday, and we chose that date only after many other efforts to fit people's schedules. It turned out to be a memorable choice.

At 4:30 P.M. I left my office a bit early in order to drive home to Lexington to help with the preparations. My car radio news told me that there were some power outages occurring around the Boston area, and a Boston Edison spokesman said that there were no explanations, at present, for the shutdowns. As I drove west along Memorial Drive in the gathering evening of that November day, I became aware that the lights in the office buildings across the river were going out. So, abruptly, were the street lights. Soon, the headlights of cars were the only source of illumination. The commentators on WBZ suddenly sounded uneasy. They had switched to emergency power. The power grid up the coast to Canada and down through Connecticut, and finally to New York, began to shut down. Only one cause seemed possible: a United States/Soviet confrontation.

I arrived home at 5:45 to find Betty, at that time unaware of the extent of the problem, wondering how to finish preparing dinner with no electricity. We were not surprised then to get telephone calls (the telephone was the only utility not affected) from the offices of our guests, saying that they would be unable to come. By this time, all offices in greater Boston had shut down in the pitch dark, and the streets of Lexington were completely black. It was an eerie scene.

At home we had earlier made an effort, on the widespread advice of Civil Defense authorities, to stock up some emergency things in a section of our cellar, but I had little confidence in the general survivability of home shelters. This evening we gathered the children in our kitchen and had a rather uneasy cold meal by candlelight while trying to remain cheerful. The same thing was going on in many homes in New England. By mid-evening came the authoritative explanation, received with much relief: the New England power grid from Montreal and Quebec to New York had shut down in a domino effect. When, after several hours, the lights began to come on again, a grand sigh of relief seemed to go up all over the East Coast. But the experience drove home again the feeling of vulnerability that the nuclear overhang generated among all of us. The event reminds me to this day of the constant threat of a nuclear exchange that loomed at that time. Now, with that threat lifted, it is hard for the present generation to imagine what it was like.

As 1965 dawned, all of the deans were aware that big changes were in the offing, and not all were eagerly awaited. Jay Stratton's retirement date was June 30, 1966, and it was expected that his successor would be named by the corporation at the June 1965 commencement meeting. As provost, Charles Townes was the obvious front-runner. I thought I could continue to work as a dean under Townes but, after one serious run-in, had no enthusiasm for the prospect.

That spring the Ford Foundation awarded funds to MIT for nine professorships, with emphasis on areas affecting the international arenas. I had made, I thought, a strong case for one of those chairs to be assigned to the school in international management—a still new field that I was eager to initiate. I was surprised and troubled to learn—by telephone when I was on a trip to the West Coast—that the president and the provost had chosen to place all the chairs in engineering or in the social sciences, but none in management. I called Charlie Townes immediately. It was clear to me then, as now, that the case for international management studies was strong. I argued with him against his decision, but he would only say that they might reconsider sometime in the future. I saw this as a sign of miscommunication, and I took his decision as a poor portent for the future. Nevertheless, I had no thought of looking elsewhere. Occasionally, I had feelers from other organizations, but I had no interest in another university. I knew most of the deans in the leading schools of business, which now included several old friends such as George Shultz, who had gone on to Chicago, and George Baker at Harvard, but I was completely at home at MIT.

Jerry Wiesner had become dean of science at the institute in 1964, replacing George Harrison, and we developed a special connection on many issues. Having just returned from Washington, where he had served as science advisor to Presidents Kennedy and Johnson, Wiesner was deeply aware of management issues. We spent a lot of time talking about management of big systems. I thought he would make an excellent MIT president, as would Gordon Brown, but there was little support for either one in the faculty or in the corporation, and what support existed was badly split between the scientists and the engineers. The Corporation Committee on Succession, chaired by James Fisk, the president of Bell Telephone Laboratories, met with me briefly with questions about the three possible contenders: Townes, Wiesner, and Brown.

In the late spring something occurred that put into play events that changed my life. We had appointed Robert Greenleaf, the well-known

AT&T senior personnel executive, as a visiting professor at the Sloan School for a year. Greenleaf had a good year at MIT and then went on to Harvard. He was so impressed by his academic exposure that he never went back full-time to AT&T, and turned instead to consulting with that company and others.

It was as a consultant that Greenleaf came to see me at the Sloan School for "serious conversation." It turned out to be very serious. Would I, was Greenleaf's question, consider taking a job as executive vice president of Federated Department Stores? The more I heard, the more serious it became. Federated was the largest department store group in the country, with major store divisions in many cities. I did not know much about it beyond that. Its major problem, it turned out, was reconciling decentralized management with maintaining central control of key financial and personnel decisions in its Cincinnati headquarters. Top management had decided to move the process of selection of management and compensation, and control of management development, to the portfolio of a new officer who, along with an executive vice president of merchandising operations, would report to the chairman and CEO, Ralph Lazarus, and to the president, Paul Sticht. Sticht, again! He had moved to Federated a few years before from the Campbell Soup Company, and he and Greenleaf, Federated's consultant, had hatched this unusual plan.

There were many reasons to consider the job and many not to consider it. I had been the dean of management for six years and a professor in the field for longer than that. On some kind of theoretical level, I faced the pointed challenge: Could I *do* as well as *teach*? At the practical level, MIT was about to change presidents, and I was not sure I would be as happy with the obvious front-runner. After several serious discussions with Federated's chairman Ralph Lazarus, his brother Maurice, the financial vice president, his father Fred, who was honorary chairman, and Paul Sticht and other top people at Federated, I decided the proposal was very promising. They showed how much they wanted me by offering a six-figure salary package, deferred compensation, a five-year contract, and, most important of all, a surprisingly free hand in designing a new kind of management system. In addition, Ralph hinted strongly that he was looking for a successor; Sticht was not it, and he thought I might be the candidate. At home, Betty was open-minded. Administration politics at MIT, as they were developing, were not attractive to either of us. I mulled it over and put the decision aside until the term ended.

We were riding a wave of progress within the school. I had proposed to Jay Stratton and to Jim Killian that we rename the school in honor of Alfred Sloan, and have its new designation be the Alfred P. Sloan School of Management. This change would recognize both Sloan's support and the fact that the preparation of our students was broader and more encompassing than only industrial management. The corporation agreed unanimously, and I know that Mr. Sloan, when he got the proposal, was very pleased. The change certainly stabilized our connection with the foundation. We had a grand corporation and school event with Sloan and Hermann and all of the key individuals from our advisory council and the corporation present. I had a growing sense of accomplishment and, perhaps, closure at the school.

I talked to Stratton right after the MIT commencement to tell him I had decided to leave. Jim Killian soon visited me in my office and urged me to stay at MIT. More surprising, Vannevar Bush, whom I had come to know well at the Putnam Fund, came to me to propose a plan of his own. Would I consider becoming executive vice president at MIT when the new president (presumably Townes) was named? I told Bush such an appointment was unlikely since the new president would have to make it, and I doubted that he would. I never heard any more of that plan.

MIT agreed to a mid-August announcement of my leaving MIT and going to Federated, and Federated also accepted that schedule. Jay Stratton sent a very gracious letter to the corporation and to the faculty to the effect that I was leaving on December 31, 1965, and that the institute would miss me. The Sloan faculty was surprised and appeared to be genuinely saddened, and they showed this in many supportive ways. I felt a terrible sadness at the realization that I would be leaving MIT. At the same time I was heartened by the increasingly positive reception at Federated headquarters and around the company. When the announcement was made, the *New York Times* gave much notice to the appointment, and deans around the country expressed delight at the news and offered their consulting services. It was rare in those days for a business school

With Alfred P. Sloan, Jr., New York, December 1964

dean to be appointed to a top management post. I had become one of the better-known management deans in the country, but the proposed appointment was still an uncommon one. Later, it would become more common, as indeed would the reverse: top management becoming deans of business schools.

As fall began we were still awaiting our announcement on the new MIT president. The October meeting, when everyone finally expected the word to become official, came and went as did the December meeting, to general surprise. Three days after the December corporation meeting, I was interrupted at a Sloan School committee session in the dean's office and was told that a group of corporation members were on their way over to my office to see me. No, I need not appear at a place convenient to them; they were coming to my office. I assumed it involved the position of executive vice president.

I met with the somber assembled committee in John Wynne's vacant office. Jim Fisk, the chairman, Vannevar Bush, Crawford Greenewalt, Ed Hanley, and Robert Gunness were all grim faced. Their first question was direct and abrupt: "Your name has been proposed as president of MIT. Is that a good idea?" I was surprised, but I began to realize I was suddenly a front runner. I told them I thought MIT's new president ought to come from one of its central fields of science or engineering, and the discussion went on from that point. When the committee members filed out forty minutes later, I didn't know what to think. As Betty and I discussed the future that evening, the whole process seemed to be suddenly pointing toward me, yet neither of us could believe that I would be named president of MIT. The journal *Science* would later note that, as Townes and Wiesner faded in the committee's review, "Johnson, not even a dark horse in the speculation, then came to be seriously considered." It was all beginning to put a strain upon us.

At the end of that week, the Sloan School faculty had a farewell party scheduled for us at the Faculty Club. Two days before that event, I had a call from Jim Killian. He wasted no time on preliminaries. Would I accept the presidency of MIT if I were elected? I said I would, and I telephoned Betty. I also called Ralph Lazarus in Cincinnati, and said it was important that we have a meeting immediately. He said that he and his father were going to be in New York that evening and asked if I could meet them there. In their suite at the Pierre I explained that I was about to be offered the post of president of MIT, fully mindful that I had a contract commitment to Federated. Fred immediately offered to release me from my contract if I were to be elected MIT president. He added that the MIT job was clearly more beneficial for the country. Both said they hoped I would work with Federated until the end of June in order to find a successor, but that I could then go with their blessing. I could not have asked for a better reaction from the Lazari.

We went to the farewell party at the school on Friday night with, of course, instructions not to say a word to anyone about the election. We were presented with a silver tea service (which, later, the Yankees among the faculty thought we should return). Much later, Penn Brooks, who had come back for the party, said my "farewell speech" was the worst speech I had ever given. I agreed with him. I did not enjoy the deception of saying good-bye when I knew I was going to remain at MIT.

By now it was time to move to Cincinnati—MIT presidency or not. We had already sold our Lexington house and our retreat in New Hampshire, and we had bought a fine new home in Indian Hill, a suburb of Cincinnati, on the basis of one quick viewing.

The children had been remarkably understanding about the whole process of leaving school. We had planned to move our household things on a Friday and Saturday of the week before Christmas. Betty, the children, and I would stay at the Lexington Battle Green Motel after the vans had loaded on a Friday night, and Betty would then drive with the children to our new home, staying in a suburban hotel until our furniture arrived. As a final touch and at the last moment, we decided that our favorite tall clock, made by Nathaniel Mullikan in 1767, would not be going to go to Cincinnati. I asked our neighbor, Charlie Barrett, if he would take care of it until I was ready for it and he readily agreed, adding it to his own clock collection. He must have wondered why.

On Friday evening, Jerry and Laya Wiesner unexpectedly came to our home. As we sat around the kitchen in the almost empty house, we chatted over coffee. They could not have known what was transpiring, but I will never forget their solicitude and concern and their genuine friendliness in a very unusual situation. The week before, there had been an Academic Council farewell party, given at Gordon and Jean Brown's house in Concord. That had been a somewhat strained affair with everyone being cheerful toward us. Charles and Frances Townes were especially pleasant.

We closed the door on our Lexington house with a deep sadness. Leaving the scene of so many happy times for our family, we felt that we were really moving into a new and unknown chapter of our lives.

Doug and Mary Brown had invited me to stay at their home in Brookline for the few remaining days of my scheduled duties before Christmas vacation and my departure for Cincinnati. On Saturday evening, as I joined them for dinner, they were their usual warm and cheery selves. The situation now moved very quickly. Telegrams were sent to members of the entire faculty on Sunday afternoon, with a call to a special faculty meeting for Monday afternoon. Doug Brown's telegram was delivered to his home, and as he showed it to me, he said, "I wonder who is going to be named president."

I couldn't bear to keep the news from him in his own home, and I knew I could trust him, so I told him, in his quiet living room, that I believed I was going to be elected president. Doug looked at me, unbelieving, wide-eyed. He began to dance around the room, shouting and singing and behaving in a way I had never seen him behave before or since. Mary, hearing the shouts, came into the living room to find her husband doing a vigorous Indian war dance, and asked, "Has he gone crazy?" I told her the news and she began to cry with delight. I was very moved by their reaction.

A special corporation meeting had been called for early Monday morning. Vincent Fulmer, the able corporation secretary at that time, ushered me into his office, where I was to wait alone and uneasily for the next hour. I was finally escorted into Killian's office, where the meeting was being held, packed shoulder to shoulder with the members of the corporation. Looking at that sea of faces, I recognized only a few. I was introduced as twelfth president of the institute, the vote having been taken and unanimously passed just before my entry. I spoke briefly, and I am afraid quite inadequately. No one had briefed me on the steps that would take place. Now they did. I met with the executive committee, most of whom I knew.

Bush, Killian, Stratton, and I then walked from the office of the chairman of the corporation and entered Huntington Hall, which was packed to the rafters with the members of the faculty. Somehow, in the throng, I could see Douglass Brown. Poker-faced, as always, he managed a big wink. Following a brief opening by Stratton, Killian and Bush spoke. After Killian described the process and named the new president, there was an incredulous pause. The faculty stood and burst into applause. I thought Bush was especially eloquent that day. He said MIT was now entering a new period in which it would be severely tested. We were now recognized as the leading technical institute in the country; we would become a leading university of the country.

My own words were brief; I had little time to prepare for this unlikely event. I said I would do the best I could, and with God's help and theirs, we would meet the challenge of the future. The audience responded again with enthusiastic applause. Gallantly, I thought, Charles Townes came up to me first as the meeting ended and congratulated me warmly.

The general uproar continued. After greetings from all sides, some pictures and press conferences, I was able to call Betty. She was still at the inn in Cincinnati and had heard the news on a radio newscast. I said I hoped to get home by Thursday. I went back to the Sloan School for general back-pounding, and dictated a letter to the Sloan faculty starting with the line, "A funny thing happened to me on the way to Cincinnati . . ."

Jim Killian offered to resign the chairmanship of the corporation if I would feel more comfortable with someone else. I assured him that his staying on was critical. Jay and I talked at some length. He said he would spend some time each week that spring at the Ford Foundation in New York where he had been elected chairman. He invited me to all the executive committee meetings and, of course, I already was a member of the academic council. I suggested that in a few months we appoint a new dean of the Sloan School, and said I would have a recommendation to make.

The *New York Times* carried a front-page story with a continuation: "Man in the News." A few days later, the *Times* had its lead editorial on the "wise" choice of a "social scientist" for president of MIT. Jeff Wylie, the head of the MIT News Office, had always seemed rather dubious about the Sloan School, but now he was ecstatic about the public relations effect of the story.

Back in Cambridge I met briefly with John Wynne, and asked him to take on the increasing burden of administration at the Sloan School. Under our new plan I would continue to function as an absent dean, he as the present associate dean. I also talked to Constantine Simonides, now the assistant dean, and told him I would want him to come with me to the president's office as my assistant there. He was enthusiastic and helpful, as always. I also asked him to put some notes together for me on staff needs in the office. I knew I would not take Peggy Adams, the able dean's office secretary, with me to the president's office. She was first-rate, but as a single mother, was sharply restricted in time available for work.

I headed for Cincinnati and Christmas. Our new house was now ready, and we moved in. The children, after several days on the road and at the inn, were ready to stretch, and Betty was more than ready. So was Napoleon, the big poodle, and Tigger, the orange tomcat. The house on Waring Drive was a great new experience. New, large, well laid out with all the amenities, it was our first house on that scale. But the situation had changed completely from when we had bought it just two months earlier. Now it was going to be only a short-term house, to be vacated and sold again by June 30th, when we would return to Cambridge. Not surprisingly, the children had some doubts about the future, but they were in good form. Stephen had the biggest chore. After the holidays, he would return to the Fenn School as a boarding student, and he was stiff-upper-lipped about that. It was a wholly new situation for him and at thirteen, he was not at all confident about it. Laura and Bruce went to the Indian Hill School and, understandably, never quite felt part of that student body because of their short term. My own schedule was going to be especially awkward. I spent weekends in Cincinnati and usually three days at Federated, often traveling to divisions. I tried to return to MIT for at least three days every two weeks, but it was difficult. Just before Christmas I received a rare phone call from Mr. Sloan. He could not hear on the telephone at all, and it was embarrassing for him to use it. Nonetheless, he came on and said in a croaking voice, "Howard [the first time he had ever used a first name for anyone at MIT as nearly as I could tell], I want to tell you how happy I am that you are the new president. I will help you in every way I can. Good-bye." I was deeply moved that he had tracked me down to Cincinnati and even used the hated telephone.

I saw him again early in January in New York, and he made clear that he would support MIT with new enthusiasm. He then raised a surprising question: how much would it cost to move MIT out of Cambridge to a place where more land was available for facilities and housing? He said if a place could be found and the cost were not prohibitive, he would fully support such a move. He also reiterated his support for the MIT Sloan Research Fund—a proposed $25 million fund—whose income was dedicated to supporting MIT faculty research. The first payments had been made, and he now intended to fund the remainder. Finally, something that would be useful to me years later, he said to make sure that the fund was diversified in its investments. It would come to MIT in General Motors stock, but "no company in the world is immune to problems." What a giant! It was the last time I saw Alfred Sloan. He died in March and I attended his funeral at the Riverside Church in New York.

Over the years it had been my good fortune to have seen and known several exceptional men and women whose lives and works had made large imprints on the world around them. Alfred Sloan was surely one of the best. His focused intelligence on an industry and a company made history in management and in organization. While I knew him only in his last decade, I saw frequent flashes of his giant intelligence and his insight into industrial society and the world at large. I have no doubt that he stands in the top tier of individuals who represent the best in American management in the twentieth century.

The spring of 1966 moved at a snail's pace even though we were terribly busy. I was eager to get into harness at MIT, but there were important tasks to be finished before I left Cincinnati. I visited every one of the sixteen divisions of Federated and set up a plan and program in management organization. The concept of a two-person top team was extended to all divisions, and it continues to serve Federated despite the battering by corporate raiders. I did find a replacement: John Paul Jones of Union Carbide, whom I had known through Douglas McGregor. He was appointed a senior vice president and had a good start, but he never really developed the full confidence of the Lazari and his effect was diminished because of that factor. Sadly, he died of a heart attack a few years later.

Ralph Lazarus asked me to join the board of Federated in March of 1966, and I agreed, with some reluctance, because I wanted to devote my full time to MIT. We came to know only a few people in the city, and found ourselves frequently joining either Fred and his wife Cele, or Ralph and Gladys, and their closely associated families. They were a generous and gracious lot. When it came time to leave and return to Cambridge, we were sad that it meant the loss of our frequent associations with that group.

Of course, the board associations were just beginning. It was still early enough in Federated's history so that some legendary retail leaders like Sydney Solomon, Milton Berman, and David Rike, and great financiers like Paul Mazur were with the company. Newer members like Dillon Anderson and Alfred Gruenther had invaluable insights even though their experience was in fields far different from retailing. Later, with new appointees, the board became a more standard business board. To me the old board was stronger. Those board members were close enough to the business in one way or another to enjoy the feel and sound of merchandising, and they were astute enough in their other business exposures to understand the heart of the management process. It was an excellent experience to be with Federated, even though its closing weeks, years later, as the company was taken over by a mindless corporate raider, were painful and sad.

HWJ's inauguration, October 1966, with James R. Killian and Vannevar Bush in the foreground; on the left are members of the corporation

6

Early Years as President of MIT

My MIT life was coming into focus even as my Federated life was fading. I had time, mostly on Federated airplanes, to think about both the long-term questions and the insistent, immediate, demanding problems facing MIT. On the long-range issues, I had the opportunity to ponder MIT's five schools: Science, Engineering, Architecture, Humanities and Social Science, and Management. Together, they formed the structure on which the whole teaching and research program of the institute rested. Each deserved support. After nearly seven years as dean of one of the five schools, I had come to know the other four fairly well, but there was much I still needed to learn. All were composed of departments that ranked at or near the top of their fields in the country, and I was certain that the continuing reputation of MIT depended on the quality, competence, and ideals of its faculty. At the outset, I resolved not to show any favoritism or special interest toward my old school, the Sloan School. I apparently did that so successfully that, later, some of my old friends in the Sloan School intimated that I had forgotten about it completely. I hope I did not go that far. I resolved to concentrate on the other four. I would focus on the School of Science because I knew it least well. I was determined to pay special attention to the needs of each of the science departments. The School of Engineering made up nearly 50 percent of the resources and staff of the institute, and its largest departments, Electrical Engineering and Mechanical Engineering, were massive engines of accomplishment. Gordon Brown, the dean, and his department heads had a plan and a momentum that promised strong results. Humanities and Social Science deserved new support and encouragement. On the social science side, I knew economics, political science, and the Center for

Betty with Stephen, Bruce, and Laura at inauguration, 1966

International Studies very well. The humanities side carried a heavy and exhilarating responsibility for the liberal education of the undergraduates, and, at the same time, it was moving to the same high graduate and professional standards as the other four schools in several areas, notably history, linguistics, and philosophy. We had a common purpose: to make sure that these advances would take place. The School of Architecture and Planning was somewhat special: a professional school of long standing—its architecture school was the first in the country—with a distinguished roster of faculty and alumni, and seeking to deal with the dramatic changes in the field. The school needed space, like almost every activity did, and it needed the strongest kind of encouragement.

The activities of the schools and the departments included major commitments to both undergraduate and graduate programs, and the inevitable tension between those two parts was an issue of long-term importance for the institute. With all this, I had much in mind that MIT was an

With Julius A. Stratton, president, and James R. Killian, chairman of the MIT Corporation, December 1965

institution that based itself on merit. We were inherently an American institution, but I had to remember that one-third of all faculty had been born outside the country, and the richness of this diversity gave great strength to the confederation of talents. We intended to yield no ground to our best sister institutions on the scale of merit or accomplishment. There would be no right-angle turns in MIT's program. It was time to resolutely speed ahead. I could not know that the years to come would force their own agenda upon us.

In the short term, I had to consider the immediate appointments that had to be made. The provost job was the most important of these. Charles Townes still held the post, but he had indicated to me that he would shortly leave MIT. He was to become a university professor at California and continue his remarkable career as a scientist. I worked with Townes and Stratton on the matter of replacing the dean of the Sloan School. I proposed Bill Pounds, and he was appointed to take office in the spring. He led our old school for the next fourteen years.

I discussed the matter of selecting a new provost with Stratton and Killian. They had no names to propose. It would be my choice alone. Jerome Wiesner was first on my list. There were a few others, but Jay Stratton warmed to the idea of Wiesner. The question was whether Jerry would accept. Stratton rather doubted it. When I asked Wiesner to join me, he was pensive—somewhat doubtful—about the idea; after thinking about it for a day, however, he accepted the position. Thus began the most remarkable and professional partnership I would ever know. I was sure we could work well with the faculty. We trusted and supported each other without qualification. I never knew any man to whom I felt closer. For the next twenty-eight years we worked together—president and provost, chairman and president—on many projects and many fronts. Jerry remained provost throughout my term, and at the end of it succeeded me as president. In 1968, we appointed Walter Rosenblith as associate provost; he became provost during Wiesner's term. Paul Gray was appointed assistant provost, also in 1968, when the brewing campus turmoil required still more strength in that office. He, in turn, succeeded Wiesner as president in 1980. Thus did we form an unbroken chain in the leadership of MIT for the next twenty-five years, and the institute benefited greatly from that continuity.

The corporation and the faculty were, of course, the principal structures for running MIT. They were the major policy, communicating, and problem-solving groups of the institute. The president plays a critical role in both of these bodies, and, over time, has a large influence on the leadership, style, and tone of the organization. If everything goes well, that is. As president, I worked closely with the chairman of the corporation. I chaired the executive committee and presided over the monthly faculty meetings. During some periods, these roles may not be critical. During the decade of the twenties, for example, the equivalent roles were apparently almost inconsequential. But, as I was to learn later, the decades of the sixties and seventies would surely be different.

Having Wiesner as provost meant that the science dean's post was now open. We discussed prospects within MIT, and I spent a lot of time visiting key professors in the sciences, especially physics, where I had few contacts, mathematics, and chemistry. I called on physicist Victor Weisskopf. He was just back from CERN in Switzerland, and Stratton won-

With Jerome B. Wiesner, 1966

dered whether he would stay at MIT. Weisskopf wanted to meet the new president. We hit it off well, and Stratton later told me that he thought that Weisskopf had fallen in love with me. I doubted that. Elsewhere in physics, Jerrold Zacharias was reserved, as was John Slater. In chemistry, there were problems; in mathematics I was delighted to have very good sessions with Norman Levinson and Ted Martin.

In investigating outside candidates for the dean's post, Jerry and I made two false starts, but a suggestion from the head of chemistry led us to a distinguished biochemist at Wisconsin, Robert Alberty. We were interested in giving biology a greater push, and the chemistry department was suffering from a serious slump following the death of a long-time head. Alberty seemed to be an excellent candidate, knowledgeable in both fields. After some conversation, he agreed to come as dean of science at year-end.

I knew we had an excellent dean of engineering in Gordon Brown, and I knew many of the engineering faculty from earlier times. Other able deans were happily in place: in management, Bill Pounds; in architecture and city and regional planning, Lawrence Anderson; and in humanities and social sciences, Bob Bishop. At the department-head level we made several new appointments. Alfred Keil was already on his way to MIT when I took office, and I concurred in his appointment as head of Naval Architecture and Marine Engineering. In those early years we appointed such remarkable scholars as Ray Bisplinghoff, head of aeronautics and astronautics; Milton Clauser, director of Lincoln Laboratory; Victor Weisskopf, head of physics; John Ross, head of chemistry; Louis Smullin, head of electrical engineering; Boris Magasanik, head of biology; Donlyn Lyndon, head of architecture; Ithiel de Sola Pool, head of political science; Norman Levinson, head of mathematics; and the biologist Irwin Sizer, dean of the graduate school.

Several difficult long-range issues lay before us. As the dean of the Sloan School, I had had little direct experience in government funding processes for research and, of course, MIT relied on federal funding in the most fundamental ways. Looking at the two major labs—Lincoln and Instrumentation—we were fully dependent on the Department of Defense. Even for on-campus research, the DOD was our major source. Jerry was well experienced in this arena, although he was, it turned out, not in the best graces of some people in the DOD.

One earlier experience became very useful. In the early sixties, Elting Morison and I, ruminating about MIT's future, had come up with the idea of an in-house study of the Lincoln Lab and the Instrumentation Lab to be conducted by a small group comprised of Elting Morison, Carroll Wilson, Will Hawthorne, and me as chairman. Jim McCormack, the vice president to whom the two laboratories reported, supported the idea, and Jay Stratton also agreed to give us some official standing, which was critical in getting into the largely classified labs. We asked Arthur Singer, John Burchard's assistant, to join us for additional support, and he cheerfully did.

We spent several days a month over an entire term discussing the situation with the leadership of each lab, the financial people at MIT, and the MIT central leadership. Clearly, there was no easy solution to an ever-growing problem for MIT: laboratory growth beyond limits of internal control and uneasy and unsure long-term financial support by the federal agencies. We raised the idea of spinning off one or both of the laboratories to private companies or establishing an arms-length relationship with an entirely new entity. That idea was so unpopular with Stratton and McCormack that we quickly abandoned it. No one was enthusiastic about dealing with a problem that appeared to be many years in the future. The experience had given me more depth of understanding of the two great institutions, and I came to know well Stark Draper, the legendary founder-leader of the instrumentation laboratory. Little did we know that in a few years this laboratory would be the center of the social and political storms that engulfed us all in the late sixties.

Now, as president, I was introduced to another big issue involving the instrumentation laboratory. It, and hence MIT, was a prime contractor for the guidance and navigation system of NASA's Apollo Program—the moon landing project now well under way. I was introduced to the project in depth and learned that, as the chief executive officer of MIT, I would soon be part of the periodic meetings of the dozen or more prime contractors for the program who formed a council headed by the vice president of the United States but, in practice, led by James Webb, the remarkable leader of NASA.

I maintained close contact with this project and traveled frequently to Cape Kennedy to witness the Apollo shots until the successful conclusion of the moon landing. Watching the lift-off of the successful lunar orbit shot and watching the first moon walk live on television were heart-grabbing events. As a dean, on several occasions I met with the astronauts who trained with the lunar navigation equipment mockups set up by Stark Draper and his staff at the instrumentation laboratory.

The seven original astronauts who formed the first contingent of that remarkable group all had the wiry, muscular, and surprisingly slight build of the fighter pilot, and they also had the piercing eyes of those who had seen something denied to ordinary mortals. It seemed to me that Shepard, Glenn, and Grissom, the first three, were especially impressive. At the faculty reception to which the astronauts were invited, I was amused to see notables of the MIT faculty lining up, obviously impressed and eager to meet the astronauts—this from men and women who seldom were impressed by anyone.

Now, in my new role, I was to see the project at much closer range. The moon landing before the end of the decade, as Kennedy had proposed, was a magnificent achievement, producing a sense of pride that the whole nation shared.

In 1966 I had an urgent call to meet with James Shannon, the director

Former first ladies Margaret H. Compton, Elizabeth P. Killian, Catherine N. Stratton, with the new first lady, Elizabeth W. Johnson, MIT, 1966

of the National Institutes of Health. Killian, Wiesner, and I were stunned by his proposal: Would the new administration of MIT accept a grant in the range of $50 to $70 million dollars and further commitments of annual funding to cover operating costs in the range of $10 million for several years to start a medical school at MIT? It was an exciting idea that had been mentioned over time as one that MIT might consider. It was fairly heady stuff for a brand-new president interested in getting off to a running start. Moreover, at first blush it seemed to be a good idea. We had many professors in the sciences and in engineering who were conducting joint research with counterparts in the medical schools and hospitals around Boston; a significant percentage of our undergraduates went on to medical schools.

Fortunately, there was a faculty group already in place that was well qualified to consider this idea. Gordon Brown had earlier appointed a Committee on Engineering and Living Systems with an ad hoc committee

to deal with medical research at MIT. Both were chaired by Walter Rosenblith, a professor of electrical engineering, and he was planning a 1966
summer study on the medical research questions. It was most timely. I
asked Rosenblith, with whom I had developed close working contacts
during my Sloan School years, if he and the group would take this additional question under advisement for the provost. The answer was an
enthusiastic yes. It gave the ad hoc committee a strong focus and a firm
deadline. We needed to know how MIT faculty in related fields felt about
the idea, and we needed to know quickly.

In the early fall the Rosenblith committee concluded that it would be
unwise for MIT to inaugurate a medical school, a conclusion with which
I concurred as I came to understand the financial implications. Such a
school would be prohibitively expensive even in the unlikely case that all
promises of the NIH were kept. Sources of funding of other important
units at MIT would be affected. We concluded that MIT had an important contribution to make in medical research, but not if we became enmeshed in the machinery of medical school and hospital administration.

We informed the NIH of our decision and asked Rosenblith to consider
another avenue for MIT contributions to medical research.

An even more intriguing proposal came from Robert Ebert, dean of
the Harvard Medical School. Ebert suggested a close collaboration between the medical school and the departments of science at MIT, with a
closer working relationship and better teaching and research access to
science fields, especially in physics, biology, and chemistry, than existed
at Harvard. Ebert also felt there were important new aspects of engineering that could be made accessible to the medical school that were
not available at Harvard. At MIT, Rosenblith reported on the needs of
our faculty and students that emerged during the work of the ad hoc
committee on medical research. Many of those could be provided by regular access to the resources of a medical school.

There began a series of discussions that culminated in a proposal to
form a joint Harvard-MIT Program in Health Sciences and Technology.
I found the concept both exciting and practical. Apart from the academic
hurdles and opportunities involved, there were financial implications of
the first order. We worked through the debates and final approvals by
the full faculty of MIT and by the faculties of the Harvard Medical School
and the School of Public Health. We also sought the full approval of the

boards of both MIT and of Harvard, no mean feat. We had earlier been fortunate in finding Dr. Irving M. London to head the program, and he was appointed to the rank of professor at both Harvard and MIT, an uncommon event in itself. London gave the program leadership, inspiration, and character. Over the years that followed, twenty-five additional slots for students seeking the MD degree at Harvard were created, and the candidates who were admitted through a fierce competitive process had, in addition to the requirements for the MD at the Medical School, an intense exposure to science and bioscience and bioengineering at MIT. As many as 30 percent of the students also qualified for the doctoral degree at MIT. By 1977, a new medical science and medical engineering degree program leading to doctorates in medical engineering and medical physics was created at MIT. Many of these students would additionally take their preclinical work at the medical school. The graduates of all these programs began to make medical research history. Twenty-five years later, more than three hundred physician scientists and one hundred biomedical engineering graduates of these programs have entered the healthcare professions.

The program was taken up by Daniel Tosteson, the medical school dean who succeeded Ebert at Harvard, and he used one aspect of the joint program as part of the design for the medical school itself; that is, organizing the medical students into cohorts of roughly twenty-five who went through training together. It turned out that building a strong identity within small groups raised morale and improved productivity.

In time, MIT needed new facilities and organizational structures to accommodate this broad effort. Rosenblith and Wiesner were an excellent team in all of this, and on the Harvard side Ebert and Tosteson were equally effective.

MIT's deeper involvement in the world of medicine, biology, and health care have made it a broader institution. In this we have been guided by outstanding medical practitioners who are also philosophers. People like Albert Seeler, Michael Kane, and Arnold Weinberg of our medical services must be rare, and I and my predecessors and successors have learned much by their approach to human health as well as their approach to life and, in the end, death.

But rubbing shoulders with the people of several great medical institutes in the Boston area—from the medical schools to the hospitals—

was also instructive. For example, soon after becoming president, I was appointed to the three-person scientific advisory committee for the Massachusetts General Hospital. My cohorts in this endeavor were Lewis Thomas, then dean of the Yale School, and Francis Schmitt. I knew Frank as a distinguished biologist and colleague on the MIT faculty and came to know him better when he began the Neurosciences Research Program. Thomas was new to me; he was a magnificent individual in his knowledge and wonder about science and medicine, and he wrote like a poet. What a pair of instructors I had as we sat for long evenings of discussion over dinner. Other eminent medical doctors I came to know well over the next many years included George Thorn, Gerald Austen, both members of the MIT Corporation, and Francis Moore. Their way of thinking helped me to understand the impact of medicine on our own institution. Around 10 percent of our graduating senior class entered medical school, and the percentage of our faculty broadly involved in biology and engineering-related medical research was surely in that same range.

This was only the first of several collaborative efforts with other institutions in the Cambridge area that were begun in those years. The Harvard-MIT Joint Center for Urban Studies was given new financial support after extensive earlier planning. The major grants from the Ford Foundation to the two sponsoring institutions were announced in November 1967 at a press conference involving President Nathan Pusey and me, and Daniel P. Moynihan, the director of the Joint Center. The most memorable question, after the professionals all seemed satisfied, came from the rear of the room: Why doesn't the foundation give those millions directly to the people of Cambridge rather than to you rich institutions? Nate and I explained carefully—and academically I am sure—the broad long-term benefits of research in this field not only for Cambridge but for the whole country. Unsatisfied, the man persisted. Pat Moynihan, a bit ruffled, said something like, "Look, the foundation gave it to the universities, not the city, because it apparently feels it could get a much higher return for society in general," which instigated a lively discussion. Pat Moynihan, whom I came to know well and much admire, went on to Washington two years later to work for Richard Nixon and to begin his long and productive political career.

The second collaboration with other institutions had more specific results. In May 1968, Paul Fye, president of the Woods Hole

With Paul M. Fye, director, Woods Hole Oceanographic Institution, September 29, 1968

Oceanographic Institution, and I formally began a new collaboration between the two institutions in a program of joint doctoral studies in several
fields of ocean science. The laboratories and classrooms of MIT and the
research vessels of WHOI formed a perfect base for collaboration, and
they became open to students from both institutions. Hundreds of joint
degrees have been awarded over the years, and the ocean fields have been
advanced because of this constructive collaboration.

I have reported on the medical and health sciences and these other
collaborations as though these efforts were a fully formed entity within
the president's domain. In reality, I found that the president's job, in com-

parison with the dean's, had more dimensions, constituencies, and channels of communication. Multitudinous layers of concern, aspects of problem-solving, levels of complexity—all working interdependently—define the president's job. As dean of the Sloan School, almost everything I did, all of my responsibility, was related to the domains of management. Despite its considerable complexity, its central themes and the central emphasis can be described clearly and more or less concisely. This is true for the most part in corporate management responsibilities as well, as I have observed them from the vantage point of my Federated position and other corporate directorships.

Not so the task of a university president. A different order of complexity marks the president's job. The range of fields of study, the many constituencies, and the varying time dimensions make the job notably more complicated. Fortunately, I took to it and enjoyed it for a long while. I believe that the frequent cases of burnout seen in the many presidents who left their jobs in dismay and in exhaustion in the late sixties were the result of multiple layers of complexity simultaneously heaped on them.

I remember Elting and Anne Morison visiting us in Lexington one evening in the early sixties. As we talked after dinner in our sitting room in that old house, Elting suddenly said, "How do you keep everything straight in your mind? How do you keep things sorted out?" I had not thought of the matter at the time, but as I reflect on it now I conclude that the ability to focus on specifics while keeping the whole in sight is the central requirement of the university presidency. Warren Bennis, among others, has classified various approaches and styles in meeting this requirement. In his book *An Invented Life,* he has classified me as "the problem-solver," that is, one who focuses large resources on defined issues. I can appreciate his definition, but I resist it a bit. It understates—and perhaps ignores—the need to keep the entire effort in some kind of balance as the work on the problems goes forward. The principal task is to build an organization in which all members become problem-solvers toward a set of common goals, and, at the same time, carry active responsibility for a specific area. To sum up my view of a complex administrative operation: the leader must be able to hold several often opposing and conflicting ideas in mind simultaneously and over a long period of time, while maintaining a consistent forward effort on track for the entire organization.

I mention these points to put my account of the activities in perspective. As we finished the first months of my administration, the focus on what could be done became clearer to me and to the team that we had assembled. Little could any of us, or anyone in university administration at that time, have imagined how overwhelmed the universities would soon become with Vietnam and the social upheaval that followed before the decade was over.

My days and nights were occupied with learning as much as I could about MIT. I asked for reports and summaries, talked and listened to all kinds of people, and began to learn more about this remarkable place, where I had worked for many years but which I never expected to lead. I especially enjoyed my exposure to the executive committee of the corporation. They were a gracious and sympathetic group, and I came to know them and their successors extremely well. As the committee re-formed for 1966 onward, I came to know the key people—James Fisk, David Shepard, George Gardner, William Brewster, Ed Hanley, William Coolidge, Beverly Murphy, Jeptha Wade, and, later, Carl Mueller and George Thorn—both of whom would soon become mainstays of my administration. Fisk, Murphy, and Coolidge were also among the advisors and leaders for the corporation.

Jim Killian was, of course, the chairman of the corporation and a member of the executive committee, which I chaired as president, and I came to know his style well. Despite his many outside interests, MIT was always paramount. Vannevar Bush was a much closer contact for me in those early days of my presidency. He would frequently walk unannounced into my office at 8 o'clock in the morning and greet me cheerfully. We became close friends; I often regret that I did not learn more about his experiences during World War II. He was the director of scientific research for the Free World during the war, with access to Roosevelt, Stimson, and Marshall. There was so much I could have learned from him. Instead, we usually talked about MIT and the contemporary university and science scene. He often talked of prewar MIT and his experiences as a faculty member in the twenties and thirties. He would become my hero in a lot of ways, and when he died in 1974, I lost a prime influence in my life. Along with Sloan and Greenewalt, he occupies the top tier of the pantheon in my experience.

The spring of 1966 had been tough on my family. The corporation had been willing to rent a temporary home or apartment for us, but Betty's program was a full one in Cincinnati, and I commuted to Cambridge, usually staying at the Eliot Hotel on the corner of Commonwealth and Massachusetts Avenues, occupying a small sitting room and bedroom. Living there as a commuter, I was often able to duplicate that experience dear—but only in retrospect—to the hearts of MIT students through generations: walking across the Massachusetts Avenue bridge to the institute on a windy and wintry day.

This time of transition was not easy for our children. Laura and Bruce needed to enroll in new schools, and so did Stephen, for whom the Fenn School was no great joy. After much visiting, reviewing, and discussion, Steve was enrolled at Belmont Hill, Laura at Winsor, and Bruce at Shady Hill. I have often regretted that public schools in Cambridge were not possible for any of them, but all advice at that time strongly emphasized the benefits of the schools we finally selected. For the month of June we moved into the Continental Hotel in Cambridge and continued preparing for a new life, and a new home in the MIT President's House, which was still occupied by Jay and Kay Stratton, who could not depart before July 1.

One incidental, happy note considerably lightened that month of June for us. With the Strattons' good advice, we had decided that a retreat away from Cambridge was absolutely necessary, and Betty Simonides, who had experience in real estate matters, volunteered to take on the task of finding some possibilities for us. On an early spring weekend, she lined up three houses for us to look at, each one meeting our requirements: a private place, a home that did not need major remodeling, with room for everyone and potential for expansion, and within two hours of MIT. The one we liked best was in Strafford, New Hampshire, six miles from Rochester. It was an eighteenth century house and barn on sixty acres with great views and lots of peace and quiet. Our offer was accepted, and the house proved a wonderful place in all seasons for us, especially in those early hectic years; we kept it until 1980, when we sold it, retaining some acreage nearby.

Another special event for me was MIT commencement in June of 1966. I had sat on many commencement platforms during the previous seven years as a dean, of course, with the usual assignment of reading the names of Sloan School candidates for degrees. This time, I was there as president-designate to hear Jay Stratton's farewell and observe the exercises in a new light. The exercises were subdued and traditional and a far cry from what they would become in the next five years all across the country and the world.

As I sat on that platform, I remember cautioning myself not to get so wrapped up in the day-to-day operations as to exclude thinking about what MIT could become in the remaining thirty-five years of the century. MIT was a world-class institution and deserved to be. My first requirement, then, was to be sure that neither I nor anyone else would hurt the institute during my years, and, further, that we would continue to build on its considerable strengths.

I knew that the vision of MIT's students should be broadened to meet the requirements of a new era. Watching the commencement procession fill Rockwell Cage, I was keenly aware that the graduates were essentially all white and all male. Happily, the new first wing of McCormick Hall, a residence for women, was now complete, and the freshman class for the coming year had room for more women, but specific goals were still a long way off.

The nature of the campus itself was also a large concern. It was a Spartan, functional place. Only the Great Court itself was green, and it was an underused space. More landscaping of other sections of the campus and some color in the corridors would make our surroundings more attractive without sacrificing our traditional puritan austerity. MIT could never collect, much less conserve and exhibit, the great art collections the older universities had. But we could build an outdoor collection of sculpture, and, in time, we would establish the campus of the institute as one of the leading outdoor art collections in New England.

It all began with the installation of Alexander Calder's *Big Sail* in 1966. The sculpture was commissioned during Jay Stratton's time, with the advice and urging of the committee for the arts, but it was completed and installed as I took office. The campus was not unanimous in its regard for the Calder when it arrived. I remember Jerrold Zacharias telling me that it ought to be removed. He said that, like the emperor's clothes, most

The Calder stabile under construction, spring 1966

people were seeing something that was not really there. He was not alone in thinking so.

The committee for the arts, which had been appointed during the Stratton administration, continued to flourish throughout my term under the leadership of Paul Tischman, Ida Rubin, and Kay Stratton. It would become the base for the council for the arts after 1971.

In another assessment of the physical campus, I had come to understand that the land we now held was inadequate for our future. As one who had walked almost daily from the main buildings of the campus to our eastern outpost in the Sloan School, I knew further that there were square blocks separating the two parts of the institute, nondescript areas of commerce and light industry unrelated to MIT. Beyond was Kendall Square, a desolate place with little human presence after 5 P.M. A plan and program to expand our holdings could be developed. Over the years that followed, our planners and our operations and finance groups developed a program, and we executed a systematic process for acquiring land within our existing borders from Memorial Drive to Main Street. There were only one or two small and difficult pieces that we missed in the process. Kendall Square itself was developed over a longer period, and its atmosphere and character improved. In 1969, we completed the purchase of more than fifteen acres of the former Simplex property on our south boundary for longer-term ancillary purposes. I felt that we had assembled the land needed for our campus to accommodate MIT's needs until 2050, our set goal.

Of course, program and curriculum improvements would be necessary. The humanities program inspired a fair amount of muttering. The corporation's visiting committee reports that I had studied indicated significant weaknesses in both chemistry and chemical engineering. Civil engineering, as well as naval architecture and marine engineering, struggled to stay alive in the modern era. Both needed reformulation. In a dynamic place like MIT, almost every department needs renewal. I felt that biology, especially, needed major expansion, and that would become a first priority.

There was also the general inadequacy of our student resources on campus. Already aware of the shortages in space that had made student housing a priority at the Sloan School, I became even more conscious of MIT's broader needs in student housing in my visits around the campus that spring.

As I assumed the office, I came back to the central idea of keeping the faculty strong and adding to the institute's financial strength. I thought I was ready to take on the task.

Before July arrived, Harvard and Florida's University of Miami asked me to participate in their commencements to receive honorary degrees, and I was honored to do so. George Morison, an old Harvard alumnus, told me he thought his university could have waited a while, but I could see he was pleased nonetheless. And for my part, I realized again how visible MIT was in the field of education.

Staff issues began to press in those days before July 1st. Constantine Simonides had come up with a suggestion for the secretary's post in my office. He had known Elizabeth Whittaker in her job as assistant to James Austin, director of the summer sessions. I met Betty, recognized her competence and professionalism, and asked her to join me. Of all the people I asked to join me in those early days, she took the longest to say yes. But she held the job as my administrative assistant—first to the president, then to the chairman—and stayed on until 1983 to become associate secretary of the corporation, finally to retire in 1993.

I asked John Wynne to come over from the Sloan School to be vice president for administration, and he served well in that increasingly complex job, assuming more and more responsibility until his retirement. Kenneth Wadleigh, having joined the academic council in 1964, was an old friend, and he was willing to stay on as dean for student affairs. I welcomed his decision. Philip Stoddard agreed to continue his responsibility for the physical plant and the operation of the campus. Phil was a superb head of our complex physical operations, with strong support from William R. Dickson, who went on to succeed him. Paul Cusick, soon to be joined by Stuart Cowen, added strength to the management of our financial operation. These bright, good-hearted men were the iron of our team.

As I dealt with these staff appointments, it also became clear to me that one of the problems with the planning of the academic structure was the lack of information at the top about the direction and speed of many of the programs. The deans were unevenly informed about the departments in their schools, and the new deans, especially, required time to develop information about the forward motion of their departments. MIT had had a history of strong decentralization in the schools and departments after World War II. There were many merits to this approach, particularly during a period of growth, for we essentially controlled department budgets by controlling appointments and salary increases. Early in the administration, with the full agreement of the provost, I asked each dean and each department head to prepare a summary of his five-year plan in terms of programs and the number of faculty and undergraduate and graduate students expected.

This was a touchy subject, and the approach had to be carefully prepared. The history of faculty entrepreneurship in developing new fields and new programs deserved to be defended. As we all often said, a professor at MIT with a first-rate idea could go forward if he could also find the funding to support it. I had often used that approach in the Sloan

School, and much can be said for this kind of support for new directions. As a result, the heads of the departments, to varying degrees, ran their programs without interference as long as the programs remained solvent. The main central control lay in the appointment, staffing, and promotion functions. We were coming into new times, however, and most deans and many department heads gladly accepted the idea of the need for better planning. Over a period of time, we made progress in creating a total plan for the teaching and research effort of the institute. By 1968, most deans had a much clearer understanding of the planning tool, but these efforts, interrupted by the upheavals of the times, were surely preliminary. I felt, however, that good progress had been made, and it was a great learning process for me and for all of us. In later years, the pressures of slower growth in research budgets and finally a slowdown in federal funding made new efforts of control and coordination absolutely vital. These early steps were useful in developing a process and a way of thinking.

Another area in which we were trying to get some forward movement was in the hiring of women and minorities, especially African Americans, at the institute. Efforts in the departments at MIT and elsewhere were only spasmodically effective. I asked the help of the executive committee in seeking black candidates, and Bev Murphy told me of a promising young black man, Frank Jones, at the Scott Paper Company, where Murphy was a director. Jones had impressive credentials and I was immediately impressed by him. On invitation, he would join up with Charles Miller in civil engineering as assistant director of the Urban Systems Laboratory. Miller at that time was on the way to revolutionizing that long-established field with computers.

The focus on what could be done became clearer as we finished the first months of my administration. Our new team was strong, but needed more cohesion. I had enlarged the academic council by adding the comptroller and the head of financial operations to it. With Jerry Wiesner as provost, the academic operation began to cohere. Anderson and Pounds were relative newcomers. Gordon Brown, a fellow dean and long-time friend, had to make the biggest adjustment. After all, I had been somewhat junior to him as a dean and now I was president. In addition, he was now reporting to Jerry, who had been a fellow dean and, in a sense, a long-time competitor. Gordon managed this new relationship with grace. Later, I invited the chairman of the faculty and his successors to join the council; their inclusion served MIT well in the years that followed.

A second council, which assumed greater importance as time went on, was the faculty council—a group of about forty-five individuals, including deans, department heads, and laboratory directors. This had been largely a pro forma assembly, but the press of events in the following years made it a vital vehicle for communication. Less influential, but still important, was the administrative council, which brought together all of the units, including the alumni organization, that formed the institute's administrative understructure. MIT was, and is, enormously strengthened by a strong staff, from administrative personnel through the academic and service departments to research and support personnel in the laboratories. These people make the academic and research function effective. I found these two groups extremely helpful and can remember, even thirty years later, detailed agenda and exchanges with them.

The faculty and its monthly meetings were the principal structure for communicating and monitoring the goals of the institute. To find myself suddenly in the role of its presiding officer was like being dropped by parachute into a new country, even though I knew the faculty well and had long attended its meetings. Not that faculty meetings were lively events; the meetings had a reputation for being soporific affairs for which it was sometimes difficult to raise a quorum. A typical meeting numbered sixty to seventy members; committee reports were heard, along with a few comments from the floor and an occasional speech by someone with a problem, but most remarks were reinforcements of comments already made. When I became president, the elected chairman of the faculty, Charles Kindleberger, distinguished economist and an old friend, was about to begin the second year of his two-year term as chair of the faculty. Charlie had been through the routines once before and was an old hand. He was also an ideal initiator for me. He did not take himself seriously, nor did he take me seriously, and we got along very well. Kindleberger loved to tell the story of how he was consulted during the last days of the presidential search. He loved to say, also, that all was peace and quiet during his and Stratton's days, but when they turned things over to Howard Johnson, Jerry Wiesner, and Walter Rosenblith, all hell broke loose.

I will always be grateful to Charlie for his tutelage. He was to be succeeded in 1967 by Walter Rosenblith, with whom I was to work in harness for the following two years. Later, as associate provost, he was indispensable.

The faculty meetings became major events on the campus in the late 1960s. I found presiding over and running these meetings both challenging and rewarding. I particularly liked the interplay of the people and the chair, and I tried to make sure that there was a chance for members to speak out. I made it a point of getting to know almost all the professors by name. We rarely had uncivil outbursts, even at the worst moments, although I can remember a few. As things got hotter, we soon had to set up an observer section for these meetings, and we had increasing demands for what came to be called "speaking rights" by nonfaculty members. We worked through a laborious system of designating outsiders with "speaking privileges" from among undergraduate and graduate student groups and from staff groups as well. These additions added time requirements and put restraints on the faculty discussions.

The meetings grew, and at the height of the antiwar activities in the late sixties, it was not uncommon for the faculty meeting to be held in Kresge Auditorium and come close to filling that large hall. The first time it happened, it was a continuation of a meeting begun as usual in Huntington Hall, and which I transferred in mid-meeting to reconvene in Kresge. The entire attending faculty—perhaps 600 strong—walked, marched or meandered to the new venue. One can now only imagine the drama of these events. In any case, we had put together a structure of communication that served the institute well. At minimum, it reduced the level of distrust, provided opportunity for discussion, and gave the appearance, at least, of covenants openly arrived at. It also made the process unpredictable at times and sometimes unbearably long. But it worked. The openness of the process helped diffuse a lot of tensions.

To return to the early fall of 1966, as I was entering into my term as president, we moved into the President's House at 111 Memorial Drive in the first ten days of July. There was some fairly extensive redecorating and a complete refurnishing. Betty secured the assistance of the Bloomingdale's decorating staff to help her, and using our Federated connections, bought the furniture and floor coverings for the house. Betty also

With Betty at the President's House, 1966

had a good deal of support from our longtime friend Vallie Hudgins, whose good Boston eye was very helpful in every aspect. Coats of paint were removed from original brass fixtures and fittings, and from walls, and the necessary major refurnishing had to be planned and carried out. We found a splendid Georgian dining room table at Shreve's, along with a massive Dutch chandelier, for the dining room. Both pieces remain in the President's House today.

The need for larger paintings and works of art was also a major requirement. Boston's Museum of Fine Arts, which we came to know so intimately in later years, was quite a mystery to us at the beginning, but we did arrange the loan of several paintings that were not on active exhibition there. We borrowed Sorolla's *Biarritz Beach Walk* for the dining room mantel. It remained there throughout our years and beyond until the museum recognized its dramatically escalating value and reclaimed it for an important gallery wall. William Lane, through the MIT Committee on the Arts, placed three paintings on loan for the house, including a splendid Feininger, which opened my eyes to the greatness of modern painting. Later at the MFA, I came to know Bill and Saundra Lane, and they became much closer to the museum during my term as president of the Museum of Fine Arts. Eventually, Bill Lane left much of his great collection of mid-twentieth century art to the MFA.

By summer's end there was perceptible interest in seeing what was going on at "111" on the part of the MIT community. We fixed the date for the October corporation reception and the traditional reception for entering freshmen as the dates to show the house, and narrowly made that self-imposed deadline. Above the first floor, the furnishings were not a major problem since we had our own things to fill in. I was never quite sure whether the children thought of the house as their home. Generations of presidents' children had the same problem.

A new experience for us was the fairly large staff: butler, upstairs and downstairs maids, cook and helper, and some yard help formed an ingrown family group. We soon found that the cook and kitchen helper spent most of their time preparing food for their fellow staff people, all three meals each day. In a short time we reduced the numbers by half, and relied on Ed Fields as manager and Frances Driscoll as housekeeper

The Johnson family, 1966

for our day-to-day support. Ed took on the chore of driving the children to school every day, and he also supervised the operation of the house.

The President's House was an architectural wonder. Given to MIT by the engineering firm of Stone & Webster, builders of MIT's main building structures in Cambridge that opened in 1916, it was designed by Welles Bosworth with a gracious set of rooms for many visitors while providing a certain privacy behind its stern Florentine facade and its interior garden. It was flanked on two sides by Senior House, student dormitories since the 1920s. Despite a fringe of trees, some of our backyard activities took place under the scrutiny of Senior House occupants, as it had for generations before. Students occasionally critiqued our actions; I remember playing catch with the two boys early one fall evening and having a voice from Senior House float over the yard: "Nice catch, Ho Jo."

Another student communication from Senior House had humorously grim overtones. When we moved into 111 Memorial Drive, the children had kept their pets including Tigger, our large yellow tomcat. Tigger frequently visited the students at Senior House, and they seemed to enjoy

Student/faculty baseball game, 1967

him. He was often absent without leave overnight, making friends with the students there. One morning, just after I had announced the first raise in tuition in several years, Tigger returned home with a carefully printed tag attached to his collar. It said, "Ho Jo, the next time you raise tuition Tigger will not come back."

We formally inaugurated the house at the October meeting of the corporation, the meeting chosen as the time for my inauguration. It was one of the last of the large inaugurals in the Boston area for quite a while. Delegates were invited from universities across the country and around the world, and the usual representatives of federal, state, and city governments were present along with a jostling crowd of well wishers of all kinds. Carroll Wilson, our old friend, was appointed chairman of the inaugural committee, and the whole exercise was done with great MIT style. Governor John Volpe and other Massachusetts political stalwarts attended. The speeches were many, and mine was well received. When I reread it recently, it seemed unreal in some places. I sought to reassure the faculty segments concerned about deviations from our technology heritage, and to encourage those who hoped for even more breadth in the MIT curriculum. The receptions that followed were fatiguing, yet heartening. MIT loves a spectacle, and this certainly was one. Betty's parents and mine attended, making it a grand reunion with our families.

Many attended the reception in addition to the university delegates: delegations of students, faculty members, and Boston and New England friends and associates. Fred and Ralph Lazarus came. I remember Fred walking to where I was chatting with Penn Brooks and Herold Hunt in one corner of the crowded reception room. "What do you think of my boy?" boomed Penn, who knew Lazarus by reputation and admired him a great deal. Fred, in his quiet way, said, "You mean, don't you, 'What do you think of *our* boy?'" Herold roared approval.

The freshman reception that took place a few weeks earlier had really inaugurated the institutional uses of the house for us. This time-honored event brings the parents of the freshmen to the President's House for a walk-through and punch and cookies. The president and his wife shake hands with each and all. In 1966 it happened on a warm September Sunday, and all seemed to go well until suddenly, an hour into it, a student bolted from the garden throng, raced through the big Bosworth doors that opened onto the garden, and headed for the front door. He never made it; on the exact center of our new light V'Soske carpet in the main reception hall, he threw up his cranberry punch. Although we spent hours trying to remove the stain, I used to think I could see it, mocking us, repeating the old adage about the best laid plans. I was not sorry, many years later, when, worn out, the carpet had to be replaced.

As the sixties wore on, the dress of the freshmen changed remarkably, but the students remained respectful to Betty and me. At commencement, I often received tokens of the graduates' esteem as I passed out diplomas: coins, kisses, and hearty handshakes.

Since MIT did not have a hotel or guest house nearby, the President's House had long served as a place for distinguished overnight guests of the institute. Many were visitors to the United States. One who stayed longer than overnight was Dzherman Gvishiani, head of the Committee for Science and Technology of the Soviet Union. Gvishiani was an affable official well known to several MIT people, including Jerry Wiesner and Carroll Wilson, and he was the son-in-law of Premier Aleksei Kosygin. On his brief visits to Washington and New York, he was occasionally given permission to visit the Boston area. Our children found him fascinating, and he was eager to talk about his home and family. He was also very much interested in the gadgets with which the American home was filled. He found the description of the snowmobiles, which we used in New Hampshire, to be especially intriguing; while the Soviets had large snow machines, they did not have smaller vehicles available to individuals.

We and others at MIT found him enormously helpful in clearing the bureaucratic underbrush when we visited the Soviet Union. In those days of the cold war, science and management were the two chief avenues of conversation available to the governments of our two countries. They were the channels by which the government kept the doors and discussions open. Both Wiesner and I found these helpful and so, I am sure, did Gvishiani.

Local and national politics were new points of focus for me as I became president. Jerry was an old hand at the art. At the federal level, I made it a point to communicate with the major cabinet officers: Defense, Labor, HEW, and Commerce. I also sought out a few committee heads and our own delegation in Congress. Tip O'Neill, our district congressman and later Speaker of the House, was consistently helpful. The first time I called on him, he pretended amazement that I had no specific request in mind, but later we did need his help. Our senators were Ed Brooke and Ted Kennedy. Kennedy was especially helpful over the next seventeen years of my terms as president and chairman. Interested, effectively staffed, straightforward, he was an excellent senator.

I had an early, light-hearted exposure to some opinions of Cambridge citizens. A small band of well-mannered protesters demonstrated at my inauguration waving signs saying, "President Johnson save our house,"

"Save our houses from the inner belt highway," "President Johnson we love you." While the inner-belt problem was an old issue soon to be completely resolved, I decided right then to make known my views on improving the working partnership between the educational institutions and the city. After I gave a speech to that effect at the Annual Meeting of the Cambridge Chamber of Commerce, Nate Pusey, who had done so much to make us feel welcome, cautioned: "Be careful, Howard. They are difficult." I later came to know exactly what he meant. MIT did not have the layered scar tissue of hostility from the city that Harvard did, but the rueful joke at City Hall was "MIT and Harvard are having a race to see which one will reach Central Square first." Nonetheless, we tried, as MIT presidents before and since have tried, to foster good relations. Fortunately, Walter Milne continued as my assistant, as he had been to Jay Stratton and Jim Killian, and he was an excellent ambassador to the city. Over the years we sought to cooperate on every front. We encouraged our students to engage in all kinds of teaching efforts, and we extended a hand to generations of city councilors. We made a strong effort to help mitigate the housing shortage for older residents in Cambridge. Because we could move with greater speed in financing, design, and building, we actually bought land and built large apartment buildings for elderly residents on several sites of the city on a "no loss, no gain" basis under a federal program that on completion transferred ownership to the city. It turned out to be a very constructive thing to do, and Walter Milne saw it through to the end. Still, any canny politician in Cambridge could always find a way to jab at us or Harvard to gain popular support. The wonder of it was that we had as good a relationship as we did, for the town-gown relationship is always a complex one. Fraught with difficulty as it is, it demands constant attention.

Lobby of Building 7: a demonstration against the Vietnam War, 1969

7

Grim Years for the Nation and the Universities

So the events of the fall passed, one tumbling on top the other. In thinking about the years from 1966 on, one must recall all of the social and economic and political streams of change that were engulfing the nation. It is against the background of those upheavals that the events on the campuses must be examined.

First, there was the war in Vietnam—the largest upheaval to embroil the country in the last half of the century. U.S. involvement there had grown from the small contingent of U.S. advisors after the fall of the French in the old French Indochina during the late Eisenhower years, to increasingly larger groups of U.S. Army advisors under Kennedy, to whole divisions under Lyndon Johnson. By mid–1967 there were 450,000 Americans joined with the South Vietnamese Army fighting against the North Vietnamese and the Viet Cong, and American involvement was growing. Inevitably, the fighting expanded in intensity and range. First one and then another regime of South Vietnam was propped up and in time fell. The Johnson administration, with its "best and brightest" advisors, made the fundamental miscalculation of assuming that our country could support large increases for the cold war and war-making expenditures in Vietnam, and at the same time support large budget increases for the "Great Society," all without increasing taxes. It was a fundamental mistake, and the country is paying for it still. As the war expanded, inflationary pressures built, and the country was in for more than a decade of inflation pressures and their attendant problems. Meanwhile, to keep the armed forces at appropriate levels of manpower in spite of the fall-off of enlistment rates, draft calls became progressively larger. Deferments were obtainable for college enrollees, however, and it is now widely accepted that the war was fought largely by individuals from the lower economic levels of the country. Those who could afford college found it easier to avoid service, and those not able to go to college ended up as the riflemen of the Vietnam War. Many young men avoided the draft by evasion or emigration. College students with shaky deferments joined the National Guard.

The war ground on. Campuses felt the strain in many ways: professors felt compelled to inflate grades and students extended their college stays to keep their deferment status. How can I give the grade of D or F, one well-known professor asked me, when that could be tantamount to sending a student to his death? Not surprisingly, college campuses across the country began to bristle with guilt, dismay, and discontent.

By late 1967, with a presidential election looming, the U.S. administration was facing large-scale citizen dissatisfaction with the war and its conduct. President Johnson was under great personal pressure, and his sagging hound-dog eyes and jowls began to show the strain. I was frequently in the White House Executive Offices in those days as a public member of the President's Advisory Committee on Labor-Management Policy, which included people from management, labor, and the public sector. I remember working with this committee late one evening when the president, with his characteristic need for an audience, walked in brandishing photographs showing the results of the latest Hanoi bombing campaign. However promising things might look at a given moment, though, hopes for victory were always dashed by new reports of Viet Cong resistance.

The turning point for many Americans came in January 1968, when the North Vietnamese Army, believed to be beaten in the field, mounted the Tet offensive campaign across South Vietnam, including Saigon itself. Large and small fire fights were waged at many points including the boundaries of the U.S. Embassy in Saigon. The administration called it the last gasp of the Viet Cong, but it soon gave the lie to its own pronouncement when word began to circulate that a large increase in U.S. manpower in South Vietnam would be needed to further strengthen U.S.-South Vietnamese positions. Rumors of the need to increase troops by 200,000 to 250,000 surfaced. With campuses already uneasy and the stability of academic programs threatened, it seemed to me and others in the Association of American Universities that Lyndon Johnson's administration should know how such large-scale escalations would affect the universities. Several of the university presidents—Brewster of Yale, Goheen of Princeton, Perkins of Cornell, Knight of Duke, and I—met in New York at the Princeton Club on an early March evening to discuss what we might do. Pusey of Harvard was unable to attend, but Brewster, on his own, had invited McGeorge Bundy, the former national security advisor, out of the administration and now president of the Ford Foundation. We decided to have a discussion with the secretaries of state and defense, since the president, typically, was unable or unwilling to see a group of academicians. Douglas Knight and I were the only two presidents who were available when the secretaries agreed to see us the very next weekend. Speaking for the others from a set of notes agreed upon by all of us, we went to Washington that Saturday, March 9, to meet with the secretaries of state and, we hoped, defense.

We first met in the State Department in mid-morning with Secretary Rusk, accompanied by William Bundy and two others. We stated our view: a call for massive additions to the U.S. armed forces in Southeast Asia would not be acceptable to an increasingly large number of Americans. Both student and faculty bodies on most campuses would greatly escalate their antiwar activities. Rusk, who surprised me by offering drinks to us at 10:30 in the morning, seemed unfazed by our review. The colleges and universities and especially their leadership should understand, he said, fixing us with his hooded eyes, that we had a vital national interest in South Vietnam, and that we must win decisively or that whole part of the world would become Communist. The administration felt that the United States had no choice but to persist in the war and win. Not to do so, having expended so many resources and lost so many lives, would be deadly national policy. Equally coldly, we stated our disagreement with his conclusions. He was polite but unmoved. Bundy listened and took careful notes; I felt that he must have had conversations with his brother earlier. I do not think that Rusk gave any credence to all our counterargument. He seemed to be living in a sheltered world.

We hurried over to the defense department by noon to see the secretary but had doubts about whether we would succeed. Robert McNamara had resigned in the previous days to escape his own devils, and the president had appointed Clark Clifford in his place. The new secretary was literally in the process of moving into his office. That large room in which I had seen McNamara from time to time was full of boxes and framed pictures and other memorabilia. Where I had last seen the well-organized McNamara, surrounded by graphs, charts, and maps, we saw Clifford surrounded by unhung pictures and stacks of paper, books, and documents. He said that he had time and would meet as long as necessary.

As the conversation went on, Clifford seemed to be trying to make up his own mind. We recounted the situation as we saw it, and emphasized the almost complete unanimity of our group. He put his fingertips together and looked at the ceiling. He told us that the president had given him a few days to come up with his best assessment and that our views would be considered. After an hour we left, feeling that he had listened and would give our arguments careful consideration. At that time Clifford struck me as a thoughtful and able political personality who was carefully assessing a complex situation. I came away, however, with no great feeling of achievement. The future for the campuses and the country looked darker to me than ever.

Much later we learned that soon after our meeting Clifford had switched to the antiwar side of the argument, along with George Ball, and the president had begun some very serious rethinking. I never knew if our visit played any part in Clifford's conversion, but it might have done so. Perhaps, in the supercharged atmosphere of the time, that was the best we could have hoped for.

The overall conduct of the war, the never-ending stream of TV reports of the escalating disasters in Vietnam, were producing a general repugnance about the U.S. position. In mid-spring, Lyndon Johnson, shocked by Eugene McCarthy's strong showing in the New Hampshire presidential primary, and no doubt haunted by the overwhelming morass that the Vietnam War had become, announced that he would not be a candidate in the 1968 presidential election.

Concurrently, opposition to the war was rising to a new pitch in the Cambridge–Boston area. Demonstrations involving tens of thousands became frequent events. In 1969 about seventy-five university and college presidents signed a letter to the president urging an end to the war, but I think it was lost in the noise of the time.

Clamorous as it was, however, the war was not the only source of dissent, dissatisfaction, and even rebellion roiling the surface of the nation. There were in addition the tensions generated by the civil rights situation in the United States. From the late fifties and early sixties, dissatisfaction was growing among black Americans and a large part of the rest of the society with the lack of progress in securing full civil rights for minorities. Martin Luther King, Jr., who preached nonviolence, was the principal leader of the civil rights movement. But there were many other leaders including Malcolm X and Stokely Carmichael, with a large base of support in black churches and the NAACP. There were also many white people, frequently based on the campuses of the country, who felt that progress had to be made and soon.

The pressure of integration efforts in the day-to-day social life of America was dramatic; so was the backlash, especially in the South, where bombings of institutions and the homes of those favoring integration were not uncommon. Marches for voter registration were regular events in all parts of the country. On the college campuses the relatively few blacks in the student body often took on radical programs to enforce their demands for more black student enrollment. Occupations of campus offices and buildings were frequent events. In the spring of 1968, when Martin Luther King, Jr., was assassinated, civil uprisings took place in the black communities of many American cities. Whole neighborhoods of cities like Detroit and Los Angeles were devastated. Boston, with a relatively small black population, had major fires, and I remember several nights when the skies glowed red in the distance across the river from Cambridge.

At MIT, where I thought we had succeeded in adding significantly to our black student percentages, the progress was not considered sufficient by our black students' organization. The dean for student affairs did his best to deal with the group's carefully phrased request, but the group wanted to see the president, and I agreed to see them along with Jerry Wiesner, Paul Gray, John Wynne, and Constantine Simonides. They were led by a young woman with the Afro haircut that was de rigeur in those days for both males and females. She was Shirley Jackson who, steely eyed, without emotion, and in a flat voice, laid out the program they insisted be executed—a largely reasonable one featuring greater efforts for recruiting and access to tutoring. Much later, Shirley became a close friend. She went on to finish her doctorate in physics at MIT, and become a well-known figure in the scientific community and a life member of the MIT Corporation. In 1995, the president appointed her chair of the U.S. Nuclear Regulatory Commission. But in 1968 there began a long period of tension, with occasional intimations of possible building occupations. In the end, however, accommodation was achieved. Many were involved in these efforts, notably Paul Gray, but real progress came more slowly than we wished.

On other campuses the landings were not so soft. Black students, as we soon came to call the whole group, demonstrated, paraded, held teach-ins, and, in many cases, occupied offices and buildings. The most publicized situation was probably that at Cornell University where, after a series of ugly confrontations with administration and faculty members, the Black Student Union, armed with shotguns, seized the student union building and held it under all kinds of threats. A famous newspaper photograph of the leaders holding firearms aloft in revolutionary style at the entrance steps of the building remains one of the classic documents of the period. As the result of this and other large-scale student problems, and growing faculty and trustee unhappiness, James Perkins, the president of Cornell, resigned. He was regarded as one of the most able of the university presidents of the period, but events combined to overwhelm him. One of the student leaders in the news photo, holding a shotgun aloft and wearing a menacing scowl, was Tom Jones; twenty years later he became treasurer of the John Hancock Mutual Life Insurance Company where, as a director, I came to know him quite well. He later left Hancock to become president of the TIAA-CREF organization, and he was elected a trustee of Cornell.

Black student upheavals were common in many places. At Yale, another stalwart president, Kingman Brewster, made some controversial statements during the ominous, tinder-dry situation there, where a group of militant black extremists was arrested and brought to trial. The situation eventually calmed without major damage in the community, but there was damage to Brewster's standing in the collegiate community from which he never recovered. Brandeis was also the scene of an occupation by black students and white supporters that eventually brought down a brand-new president, Morris Abram, who left the university on a few days' notice. Harvard and Boston University had serious problems as well, as did many of the universities in the West.

These events by the dozens were only incidental acts before the ominous race upheavals in the cities in general. As always, extremism begat extremism. There were also symbolic acts that I remember. One in particular occurred at the Olympics in Mexico City in 1968, when two black American medalists in a major track event refused to salute during the American anthem at their medal award ceremony, and, instead, eyes on the ground, held up the fist of the black power salute—this in a city where hundreds of rioting students had been killed the same year by soldiers intent on keeping order. The full story of that grim episode is still not clear, nor is the number of dead.

A more peaceful revolution of those years was another civil rights issue: equality for women, especially in the workplace. This movement would have been enough to shake and rattle the American campus, along with all other American institutions, even without the Vietnam War and the racial upheaval. Coming concurrently, it was an unsettling event of significance on many campuses. The institute had enrolled female students since the 1870s, but the numbers were a small percentage of the total. In the early sixties, in a freshman class averaging 850 students, the number of women averaged about thirty. In my early teaching days at MIT, I recall only one woman in all of the classes I taught. The same low proportions were true as well in the faculty. These low numbers reflected that individuals who succeeded in coming to MIT typically were self-selected; they wanted to come to MIT to study in disciplines that historically had been male-dominated. But I had become increasingly aware that this was both an unjust and an unwise situation. I remember using "Women in the Workplace" as a topic in my weekly seminar with a group of senior executives in 1960, taking the position that women were the underutilized resource in the American work force. Few in that group agreed.

By the time I became president, there were the beginnings of real progress, and the springboard was in place for more. The first half of McCormick Hall had just been built. That residence hall, the first for women on the MIT campus, was the gift of Katharine Dexter McCormick, class of 1904, who cited her MIT education as the most important factor of

With James R. Killian and Vannevar Bush at commencement in the late sixties

her life. She was elderly by the mid-sixties, when I spoke to her at the dedication of the first tower of McCormick Hall. Through her I came to know her Cleveland attorney, William Bemis, who handled the details of her benefactions. Jim Killian had worked through all of the process of the first wing of McCormick Hall, and I took office just in time to participate in the dedication of that building. We then began planning for the second wing, which was dedicated in 1968. The increasing numbers of women began in 1966, my first year, but our admissions office took a year to understand fully the complexities of recruiting women in the nation's high schools. And it took time to fill McCormick Hall. At one point, the admissions office predicted that the percentage of females in the entering class would never be more than 25 percent because of the relatively low numbers interested in our core fields of science and engineering. By the academic year 1995–1996, the institute had reached the 40 percent mark in the undergraduate classes.

Increasing the numbers of women and blacks in the faculty was a longer and more difficult process. Progress for women was evident as the pipeline of qualified candidates filled, but for African-Americans, the process of adding top-level faculty was difficult and vexing. It was here that Professor Albert Hill of the physics department played such a large and effective role in encouraging black students to go on to graduate work. Of course, there were stops and starts in this whole program for MIT.

For many years the situation in South Africa had strong resonance with the American black students. In later years, when I served as chairman of the institute, the issue of investing endowment funds in companies that had operations in South Africa became a point of contention. When the almost miraculous progress made by Mandela and de Klerk changed the issue virtually overnight, students and others who had demanded a pullout of American companies in South Africa were urging new reinvestments to help rebuild the country. That ironic development was far in the future.

Another project consumed a great deal of my time and energy after 1966. I had become aware that the new additions of women—undergraduate and graduate—made possible by McCormick Hall would not significantly change the look of the campus. The idea of developing a cross-registration program with Wellesley College came to me, and as Constantine and I talked about it, it assumed major proportions. Wellesley College, less than twenty miles away, had large numbers of talented and able young women with high academic standards. It also had a beautiful suburban campus. Its president, Ruth Adams, had imagination, I was told. Could the two of us, new presidents both, envision a joint program where Wellesley and MIT students could easily and without red tape take courses on each other's campus? We created a plan—which she later told me she kept in a locked file labeled "Ice Cream."

We each had our own interests. Wellesley was feeling the pressure to consider coed enrollment as it noted the increasing push for enrollment of both sexes in traditionally single-sex schools. It was in this era, for example, that Vassar went coed. Among all-male schools, so did Princeton, Yale, Annapolis, and West Point. MIT had women students, of course—albeit only a few—and was under less pressure. But an association that permitted an MIT student to take classes in fields in which Wellesley had strength and that permitted a Wellesley student to take classes at MIT in, say, science, management, and engineering, had many practical advantages. Significant issues needed to be resolved, such as establishing a system of transportation between the two campuses, but, first, we needed agreement among the faculty and trustees. It was not easy given the air of caution at MIT.

When approval came, we even found some money to fund a bus system. A position was created on each side to provide encouragement for the program, and a joint committee was appointed that surveyed, studied, and reported. New experiences at MIT helped Wellesley women shape careers, and the college could remain a single-sex college while still having wider opportunities available for interested students. At MIT, the effects were not as significant, although I have heard many MIT students talk positively about the program. More than 25 years later the program is still in effect.

I became a trustee of Wellesley in 1968 and remained one for eighteen years. I saw that college go through all the stresses and strains of the period, and I saw the growth of the MIT-Wellesley program and how much it meant to both sides. My experience at Wellesley increased my awareness of what it meant to be a professional woman in a male-dominated society. I had a similar experience at Radcliffe, where I was a trustee for six years. Often, I found myself the only male in a committee or discussion group, and I learned much by listening. It is an instructive experience for any man. I remember, too, at the Wellesley commencement exercises in 1969, hearing the student speaker make a brief statement following the commencement address by Senator Edward Brooke. Her comments were extemporaneous and delivered with deep passion. They were very well received by the students, if not by the faculty and the parents. The name of the student speaker was Hillary Rodham, and I predicted to the trustee sitting next to me, that she was bound to amount to something. She certainly did.

Ruth Adams, for reasons unrelated to the joint program with MIT, left Wellesley in 1972, and, happily, successive Wellesley presidents and MIT presidents have supported the program with equal enthusiasm. Although MIT's size and the relatively rapid growth in the number of women on campus lessened the impact of the Wellesley students, it was still an effort worth the time and money that was spent on it and, at minimum, it emphasized that women at MIT were now more important than ever.

Movements of deep and underlying social significance during that revolutionary time need to be recalled in recounting what happened during the sixties. The rise of the counterculture loosely describes the rapid changes in the use and abuse of substances to stimulate the body and mind. Marijuana was easily obtainable and eagerly sought. Other, more worrisome drugs were soon available throughout society and, inevitably, on the college campus, often the experimental edge of society: heroin, LSD, cocaine. It would be a rare college student who did not have first-hand experience with some drug, and, increasingly, the problem was present in high schools and in society at large. Widespread experimentation took place at MIT, typically with marijuana, with some disastrous consequences. No one was immune, including our own children. I remember the unreal night when Timothy Leary, the Harvard professor, debated MIT Professor Jerry Lettvin—hardly a model of convention—on the use of drugs. Before a packed house, Leary urged the students to "turn on, tune in, and drop out." Lettvin was violently against Leary's idea of experimentation with drugs and the philosophy of dropping out. In a booming voice he summed up his reaction: "Bullshit." Such was the intellectual style of the day.

The language is a pallid sample of what happened in those years to the style of communicating in the societies of the world. Written and oral communications, books, movies, the stage, and common interchange were laced with obscenities. I can recall the language of the wartime army where obscenities as verbs, adjectives, and nouns were part of the structure of language. All that and much more became the order of the day in the sixties. Women students, still with the ingenuous faces of girlhood, used language that would make an old infantry sergeant blush. With it, came the change in the way people acted toward one another. Civility was no longer a mutually agreed upon process, nor was it valued.

Somewhere, along with all this, came large changes in the sexual mores of the time. The coming of effective birth control pills reduced a major barrier to active sex among younger and younger people. On every campus this became an issue. The principle of *in loco parentis*—the college acting as parent to students enrolled in its programs—lost most of its meanings. For many parents this became a point of bitterness. While MIT was by its nature more detached from the extremes of this kind of activity, let no one assume it was not a big problem. Although most of the students returned to what might be called a less heated way of life and love as they entered the real world, some did not. No single incident better illustrated the new modes and mores, of course, than Woodstock in 1969, that delirium of music and weird individual and group behavior involving tens of thousands of young people—the flower children—in a New York country setting.

Along the way new music, new tastes, new ways of thinking about the world took hold in the styles and patterns of the young. Some of the music and some of the performance artists were outstanding, but the gulf between generations, always present to a degree from ancient times onward, was probably wider in the sixties and seventies than at any time in this century.

This was true not only in the United States, but in France, Japan, Mexico, Germany, and many other places around the world. Clashes with police, often resulting in killings on both sides, and ineffectual programs to deal with differences were the stuff of headlines every day.

One rare area that had intergenerational agreement was the environment, as seen in the rise of awareness of the damage being done to our fragile world. Again, the college campus served as a focal point for the issues. The task of protecting and improving the environment was multidisciplinary, and we formed an environmental laboratory that included on its policy-controlling committee people from several engineering, social science, and management departments. The venture never got off the ground. Developing interdisciplinary approaches in a strongly disciplined institute had proved to be difficult. It was one thing to bring the several fields of science and technology together, as in the Materials Science Center, but quite another to bring in economic and political and management policy as effective ingredients in the technical broth. Yet it was a beginning. MIT now has several successful efforts in interdisciplinary research and education to show that, with time, it can be done. Progress has been made in teaching programs involving management and engineering disciplines, now a major effort at MIT.

In 1970, we took the lead in an event supporting better environmental awareness that became known as Earth Day. The all-day teaching and discussion effort worked well. The then-governor of Massachusetts,

Frank Sargent, MIT class of 1939, came at my invitation to open the general session in Kresge, and he did a superb job. Some of the hangover from other campus problems, however, intruded on Earth Day, and Sargent's speech was loudly interrupted by some group. He listened to their views as I sat with him on the stage, then he began again. Again interruptions. This time Frank, with his wonderful raw-boned frame and craggy New England face, got angry. "I've listened to you. Now it's my turn. Hear me out." After a smattering of applause from a not wholly friendly crowd he completed his speech. Years later, the biologist Salvadore Luria, one of MIT's first Nobel Prize winners, wrote in his autobiography, that he admired the governor's position that day and felt he presented the classic American stance of listening and then insisting on being heard. In any case, the first Earth Day was a success at MIT, and we took a lead position on the university campus scene.

Although large-scale consensus on the environment had been achieved on our campus, the Vietnam war remained a powder keg of disagreement, large-scale agitation, and violent reverberations from many other campuses as the mid-sixties progressed. What had begun in Berkeley had spread to the east like a wildfire of protest, fueled by the tinder of the civil rights and women's rights movements and changes in lifestyle. In the New England area there was a sporadic press of student and other protests verging on violence as the spring of 1968 went on.

Columbia, for example, had occupations of the president's office and large-scale teach-ins and walk-outs. Grayson Kirk, its long-serving president, was forced from office, replaced by an acting president, Andrew Cordier. Outbreaks of violence occurred with regularity around the country. At Stanford, a fire in the president's office destroyed President Sterling's library. But those problems still seemed far away to many people in Cambridge. Then our neighbor, Harvard, had its own incident.

An increasing level of student-faculty-administration distrust and dissatisfaction had been occurring at Harvard, culminating in the occupation of University Hall on April 9, 1969. Harvard administrators, pushed back and forth, and committees of well-intentioned but bumbling faculty members sought to deal with the crisis. After a deadline to evacuate the hall predictably passed, President Pusey and his colleagues made the definitive error of sending in the Cambridge police, backed up by additional forces from the Metropolitan District Commission and Harvard. All hell broke loose. In the resulting furor, which spread over the next several months, Nathan Pusey, that gentle and decent man, was effectively sidetracked on day-to-day decisions by the Harvard governing board; and Archibald Cox, John Dunlop, a faculty committee, and others became mediators and tactical heads of the administration, with serious long-range consequences for the university. I remember that the Harvard "bust," as it came to be known, occurred shortly before a faculty meeting at MIT, the tone of which was apprehensive. I told the faculty that we would be consultative and encourage discussion with all factions. The Harvard bust and its aftermath destabilized the tensions within the universities of the Northeast. In a sense, the center had not held, and for many on all sides MIT became the new focus of interest.

An earlier test at MIT gave me and my colleagues a certain experience with the tactics of the radical student movement. That test, which could have ended with a similar hurtful polarization on our campus, involved the sudden arrival in the Stratton Student Center of an AWOL soldier. A large group of our and other radical students had heard of this soldier deserter through their network in Boston, and brought him to the MIT campus to one of the main rooms of the Student Center. They proposed to keep him there "in sanctuary," and to keep him safe from the military and the university. Within an hour, hundreds of students were surrounding and guarding their AWOL private, a draftee who was out of his element, confused, afraid, and in the end, pitiful. His benefactors were not wholly motivated by his welfare, however, and it was clear that they hoped we would "bust" the sanctuary and return the soldier to the MPs. I was not willing to do that, and most of my administration agreed. Accordingly, we informed the MPs that the AWOL soldier was at MIT and monitored the situation very carefully. There was an old dictum that had become accepted in dealing with this kind of upheaval: early bust or no bust. It was expected, I was told, that I would do an early bust. I rejected that as counterproductive.

We confounded the radicals by essentially ignoring their uncomfortable captive. After a few days, he stopped being news, and the TV cameras, hitherto at the beck and call of the radicals, no longer kept monitoring the situation. The MPs, on advice from above, wanted no part of him as long as he was on our premises. In fact, we asked the MPs to stay off our campus unless they meant to recapture the fugitive, for I had made it a point in principle to keep an outside police force off our campus on the justification that under ordinary conditions we were responsible for our own conduct. As the days went on, a large part of the student body and faculty lost interest in the idea of sanctuary, although I received a few phone calls urging me to "get that deserter," and the story became a non-news item. The radicals also lost interest, and their nighttime vigils became sparsely attended. The deserter was not a very engaging conversationalist, it seemed. Noam Chomsky, the distinguished professor of linguistics, proposed the bizarre idea of awarding an MIT scholarship to the deserter, to be taken up at some future date. Even the most extreme of the protesters found that proposal hard to support.

Finally, after a week or so, I called the head of the New England military district, at this time an admiral, who came over to the President's House on a late evening to talk over the situation. He was prepared to pick up the deserter, who by that time was very tired of the whole matter. The next evening the admiral called me and said that the pick-up would be that night after midnight. Sure enough, at midnight a small squad of naval shore patrol entered the back door of the center, and with the dean of students' representative, walked into the large common room and escorted the unresisting soldier out. I had been fairly sure that would be the result, for I had seen deserters during the war; they were usually lonely, dispirited, and scared. So it was with this soldier, and I felt sorry for him. The case was closed.

Another kindling point for the faculty and the student body that raised pressures throughout the 1968–1970 period was ROTC. As the war in Vietnam ground on, the ROTC program of the Armed Services came under increasing attack. One by one, we saw the ROTC programs across the entire Ivy League, and most of the other private colleges and universities in the nation, ruled off their own campuses. Once it would have been impossible to imagine that in New England the great private institutions—Harvard, Dartmouth, and Tufts—as well as the great metropolitan universities like Boston University and Boston College, would kick the ROTC off their campuses. But it happened. MIT and Northeastern continued their programs, but not without debate. In our case, I expanded our faculty committee on the ROTC to study the matter. After an initial report, this expanded group came back with some proposals for improvement, including changing the appointments of all of the military officers of each service to reflect visiting, rather than regular, appointments and reducing the MIT credits awarded for completing ROTC subjects. In heated sessions that endured over several meetings, the vote was, finally, overwhelmingly to keep the ROTC. I had made it clear that for me it was a stand-or-fall issue, and perhaps that helped. A strong civilian officer component in our military was vital to our democracy, and ROTC was the major way to ensure such a component. I was glad the faculty came out with such a large majority, and most of the MIT community applauded this resolution.

I occasionally run into alumni, however, who still assume that MIT, like many other universities, dropped ROTC. The program at this writing, more than twenty-five years after those votes, still goes on and actually provides ROTC training for students from Harvard, Tufts, and now Wellesley.

At the edge of all these happenings was a series of potentially violent incidents, more common on other campuses than on ours. The tenseness it generated in our institutional life required close attention.

MIT's biggest flash point developed around the issue of "war research." It was an understandably vexing issue. The instrumentation laboratory was covering itself with glory on the inertial guidance systems for the Apollo moon shot, but the same technology was central to the guidance systems of several navy long-range ballistic missiles. These systems developments were generated by contracts with the DOD and the U.S. Navy, and MIT was responsible for them. As new generations of the systems were required, employment at the laboratory had expanded dramatically, with the staff housed and working in several old industrial buildings bordering the institute. And as new developments such as the guidance systems for the multiple warhead missiles (MIRVs) became part of the laboratory's program, there was growing criticism of the institute's role in running a large laboratory employing 1800. The criticism came not only from antiwar protesters, although that was by far the dominant factor, but it came from companies such as General Electric that were unhappy with the institute's role as a hardware supplier (and competitor) to the government.

At that time we were engaged in the hottest phases of the cold war, and the country was caught in the step-by-step dance of defensive-cum-offensive weapons. To stay with that race increasingly meant danger of the most drastic kind; to lag in it might well mean disaster. Opinion was all over the lot. Some felt that we had a moral responsibility to end, or at least reduce, the laboratory's work. Many others felt we had a responsibility to the nation to continue. Doc Draper was the charismatic leader of the Instrumentation Laboratory, his laboratory, and a polarizing force to many on the faculty. I remember asking him on one occasion to describe the current activities of the laboratory to the faculty council. He came on initially as a modest little man from Missouri, and ended up as the fire-eating rocket scientist. He alarmed several of the department heads. One of my colleagues called him Dr. Strangelove.

Draper and I began to meet regularly, usually over lunch at Locke-Ober's, the venerable restaurant on Winter Place in Boston. Stark would invariably have a straight-up dry martini to begin his lunch, usually oysters in some form. I was always glad that we had the MIT driver, and not Draper driving his Morgan open car, to take us back to the institute. He was an authentic engineering genius, as Jim Killian liked to call him; he was tenacious and fearless, and he was very tough. He once told me he was not an aggressive boxer while engaged in the sport at college, but he was "a hell of a counter-puncher." And so he was.

My agreement with Draper when I became president had been that he would stay past the normal retirement age of sixty-five, until the conclusion of the Apollo project. I felt it was important that he remain in command until then. In the meantime, he would prepare a successor; as is common with such strong leaders, he never did. With all the tumult, he decided he would not step down. He turned sixty-eight in the fall of 1969, by which time the Apollo Project had achieved its mammoth goal of placing men on the moon and returning them safely. I thought that we would do better in dealing with the laboratory situation without Doc as the active head. He would remain in some kind of honorary administrative post and would continue as an emeritus professor. We could have some respected administrator take his place.

With Cambridge mayor Walter J. Sullivan and astronaut James Lovell, February 1969

How wrong I was! My choice for his replacement was Charles Miller, the respected head of civil engineering, who was nationally known as a leader in the application of computer capability to large-scale technical problems. I thought he could expand the range of the Instrumentation Laboratory and take some of the heat from it. It turned out I had put him in a very difficult position. Charlie never uttered a word of complaint, but the new situation did not work. He moved on, in time, to new and important assignments, but I will never forget his resilience and decency in the process.

Doc Draper, among his many gifts, loved to talk to the press, and I remember, ruefully, the headline in the *New York Times* that featured an interview with Draper: "I didn't resign; I was fired." Of course, many people sympathized. It was one of two large press counterpunches that I experienced. But for the most part, our personal relationship with the media was good. In the meantime, as the saga of the laboratory evolved, I was determined that we would honor our contracts with the DOD. MIT's good name was on the line, and we would not go back on our word. Meantime, we kept the operation going on schedule. I frequently visited the DOD people, as well as the NASA people and the congressional delegations. They needed us as much as we needed them.

Lincoln Laboratory, our other large special laboratory, was more like an academic facility than was the Instrumentation Lab, although it, too, had important production functions. It was situated at a distance, in Lexington, Massachusetts, and not on the edge of the campus; it never became the lightning rod that the instrumentation laboratory soon became. I had appointed Jack Ruina to replace James McCormack in 1966 as vice president for special laboratories. Ruina had strong academic credentials as well as excellent DOD and Washington experience. Unfortunately, he never developed an effective working relationship with the Instrumentation Laboratory management, and with Stark Draper particularly. Eventually, I had to move him out of that assignment, and it was then, in 1969, that I turned to Al Hill as vice president for research. He would have responsibility for both the special laboratories and for our research on campus.

Hill had self-confidence and a kind of bull-dog tenacity. After a most effective career in weaponry project leadership during World War II, Hill had declined physically and psychologically to the extent that his career had virtually ended. Talking to me in the middle sixties, he promised that he was going to "straighten out." He did, going on to new achievements and areas, some of which are cited in these pages. It goes to demonstrate that an individual should never give up. He had become once again a physicist of note at the institute, serving at one time as deputy department head. From this point on he stayed with the laboratories through thick and thin, and is memorialized by a building named in his honor at the new Draper Laboratory, and most deservedly so.

Long after the battle was over, he sent me a letter that described the whole effort, in which we had been engaged, with approval and agreement. A great supporter all during the upheavals, he used to slip me short pep-talk notes. They usually said things like, "Atta boy." But once he wrote, "Howard, show them you've got the balls to do it." Those notes always lifted my spirits, and he knew it. I wish I had that last one, although I'm not sure how it would translate in the next century.

As pressures on all sides mounted, we formed advisory groups of faculty members and, separately, of students—both graduate and undergraduate—to help with our communication channels. The advisory groups became known with the inelegant acronyms of FAG and SAG.

The laboratory question was in the foreground of all other activity. The student opposition was led by Jonathan Kabat and a graduate transferee from Cornell named Feigenbaum. They would hold teach-ins on an almost continuous basis. They once invited Draper, Killian, and me to a large rally in room 10–250. It turned out that although I was invited, I was not allowed to speak. Draper was, blithely going on despite being berated and shouted at. I could see Feigenbaum circulating through the audience, leading the shouting, first at one place, then another. As I looked at the jeering crowd of faces, calling out names and shouting epithets, I remember having the fantasy that if I had my old squad from Camp Robinson there, I could clean out the whole group in a hurry— exactly the wrong thing to do, of course. The session bought us time because I did not want to have those several hundred people in my office, but as John Wynne said, "It was a chilling experience."

Indeed, the whole country was enduring a chilling experience, with the war going badly and support for it unraveling. I remember vividly a group of visiting college administrators at MIT the evening Lyndon Johnson announced he would not run for reelection. After our reception and dinner at the President's House, we brought a TV set into the living room at everyone's request, and the several university presidents and provosts gathered around to hear what we expected would be another of the president's gloomy accounts of the war. At the end of his speech, he looked directly at the camera and concluded his speech with the statement, "I shall not seek and I will not accept the nomination of my party." We were all startled.

Two grim and terrible events took place in the season that followed: Martin Luther King, Jr., was assassinated in April, and two months later Bobby Kennedy was assassinated in Los Angeles. The Democratic National Convention in Chicago was an unruly wreck of an event, complete with large-scale police riots and charges of brutality on all sides. All of these events were magnified on college campuses around the country. I issued a statement of my own views at that point, and it was picked up by the nation's press. In it, I said that the college campuses of the country could not return to full concentration on education until the war ended, and I urged the president to take steps to end the war. In the midst of all this on the national level, I was brought back to a very personal reality by the death of my father in October 1968. The grim lines from *Hamlet* came to me: "When sorrows come, they come not single spies, but in battalions."

Hubert Humphrey was nominated by his party to succeed Lyndon Johnson, but he did not distance himself from Johnson's Vietnam position until it was too late. Such was the turmoil associated with the war that he lost to Richard Nixon in November. After the promise of a plan to end the war, Nixon and Kissinger, now Secretary of State, seemed to be working not for peace but rather for an escalation of the war.

During this period the uproar surrounding the instrumentation laboratory increased, and by early 1969, the laboratory question was near an explosive point. To my surprise, Jim Killian asked if he could sit in on a faculty meeting where questions were to be raised about the laboratory contracts. I thought he would be helpful, since the contracts involved the corporation directly. At one point in the argument, when I felt confident I had the majority with me, one well-meaning member of the faculty asked if there was any reason all new contracts, or renewal of old contracts, could not be tabled with the understanding that existing contracts could go on. To my dismay, Jim Killian rose from his seat and said he saw no reason from the corporation's point of view that new or renewal contracts could not be held up pending further review.

This seemed to the opposition to be a welcome concession; it was quickly put to a vote and then passed as a resolution by the faculty as a recommendation to the corporation, with Killian saying again that he would accept something like that on behalf of the corporation. He meant to be helpful by diffusing a tense situation, but it had the opposite effect, and the fat was now in the fire. Draper, after the meeting, told me some vital renewals were up for consideration, and I wondered what, indeed, further study meant. Jim quickly washed his hands of the matter; he had not meant for that to be binding. I had a long talk with Vannevar Bush the next day, and he urged me to think of some plan to remedy this unfortunate turn of events. It was the last faculty meeting that Jim Killian attended as chairman of the corporation.

The student press and the leaflet press, which were very active, made much of the deed. The affair did stimulate me further, however, to arrive at some new method of operation for this large multimillion-dollar laboratory. But it had made the administration look distant from the corporation, and I resented it. To move ahead, I came up with the idea of forming a campus commission on the whole range of issues surrounding the two laboratories. We wrote the terms of reference for the panel very carefully. It was to be not a decision body but an advisory one. I asked William Pounds to chair the panel, which became known as the Pounds Panel. Its members included individuals from the laboratories and distinguished faculty members of all stripes and reflected a full range of opinion. Seeking balance, I also invited students of the left and right, including Kabat, and the president of the interfraternity council, George Katsiaficas. I thought Katsiaficas had seemed like a middle-of-the-road or a slightly conservative student the previous term. As it turned out, he became an all-out radical who later disappeared into the underground. I also asked alumni members and corporation members to serve, and my memory now is that everyone said yes. The core of the panel consisted of responsible MIT citizens representing several points of view. The pressure surrounding the situation began to subside, with an audible sigh of relief from everyone except for the real Luddites. I asked Bill and the panel to give me their view on the question of pending renewals of contracts as a first order of business.

The panel worked prodigiously, often for long stretches, with testimony heard and papers prepared on all issues and from all sides, largely at the Endicott House, MIT's off-campus conference center. Bill Pounds's skill and sincerity led to the cooperative and effective work of the panel, avoiding potential splits and walkouts.

The first recommendation was that the institute should renew the pending contracts and await the final report, and I proceeded to reinstate them. Then the commission went back to work with relatively few leaks and disruptions in the grueling sessions that followed.

That process took the steam out of the lab situation, but it did not end the turmoil in the city and on our campus. As the fall term of 1969 began—and even before—it was clear that we were in for a major blow. We heard that the SDS, with its running cavalry, the Weathermen, would call for November actions; and that term—November Actions—became a rallying cry, its leadership enlisting support from all over the campus, the area, and the country. Many of the faculty members who supported the protest against the war drew back a bit as the impending, much-heralded events grew closer. I and my colleagues went through an around-the-clock effort at communication and cooling off and, in the end, developed a clear resistance to events that had the potential to turn violent. Violent acts occurred sporadically, but so far MIT had avoided a big explosion. I consulted people from various venues to make sure we had strong support for the administration. At one point, I called Ramsey Clark, who had recently resigned as attorney general; he came to the campus and quietly consulted with us, concluded that we were doing all the appropriate things, and slipped out of town, refusing to take a fee. I also met frequently with the corporation and its subgroups.

Although we held the corporation meetings in reasonably secure places, the October meeting was stormed by the SDS and its unpredictable circle of supporters. In the midst of the meeting, the noise outside grew louder and louder. As I listened to the pounding and furor, I conferred briefly with John Wynne. I asked him if he could arrange for a small group to enter and speak their piece. The agreement, negotiated in less than five minutes, was brought to me as a proposal from John Wynne: a group of twenty students would be allowed to come in and speak their minds for a total of ten minutes. I agreed, as did the crowd outside. I don't know how they selected their twenty, but in they came, most half-crouching, looking for trouble. I grabbed the hat off the head of the student undergraduate president and handed it back to him, warning him to mind his manners. Out of the corner of my eye I saw Paul Gray jamming Katsiaficas's head against the wall and telling him to quit yelling. The group finally calmed down. Two spokesmen from the group presented their case for the corporation to digest: all military research on the campus was to end. This was done reasonably quietly, and, I thought, rather well. The corporation took it with surprising equanimity. I heard later that the SDS leaders were impressed by the attention and interest of the corporation group. But I cannot over-state the air of tension that was building up as the first week of November approached.

I decided that we needed a special counteraction to the threat of the November Actions and talked to Bob Sullivan of Herrick and Smith. It seemed like a good idea to get a restraining order against violent action as the situation heated up, with the threat of police action to enforce the order if necessary. I took the position that the university was an open place for ideas and debate, but that our very openness made us vulnerable. In this unusual situation, we had to turn to society for protection if violence or danger to people or property were imminent.

On Sunday evening before the week of November Action I went to the judge's home with our counsel. After lengthy discussion, the judge granted a wide restraining order to go into effect the following Tuesday, the opening day of the series of planned November Actions. The first thing Monday, I called a special faculty meeting. By then we had a system of rapid communication to almost every faculty member, and therefore had a large turnout in Kresge Auditorium. I requested the faculty's endorsement in asking for a restraining order. In the subsequent debate, some argued that I already had the confidence of the faculty and didn't need a special vote. I argued that I did not intend to call in the police for routine incidents but that this was an extraordinary situation and might require such an action. In the end, Victor Weisskopf introduced the motion to support the president and the restraining order plan and it carried overwhelmingly, to great applause.

The wind behind the November Actions subsided noticeably. Their planning group suddenly was thrown into some confusion. Nonetheless, there were difficult and tense days, with lots of unruly parades, meetings, and demonstrations, but even the extremists drew back from the violence that might provoke police action. The Cambridge tactical squad of police—all one hundred of them—stood ready. So did the MDC special squad I had requested from the governor. We publicized that readiness, and we came through unscathed, if tired and worn. All sides felt that the integrity of MIT had been preserved. Although there were many flash points to come, I felt that we now had the method: communication with all, flexibility, active resistance when necessary, and always a visible administration. Our team was outstanding, from Jerry Wiesner, Walter Rosenblith, and Paul Gray to Constantine Simonides and John Wynne, and to all of the deans. One night, after midnight, walking the corridors as

Protest march to the administration offices crossing Massachusetts Avenue, November 1969

I often did, I came across Lawrence Anderson, the dean of architecture, who was the dean-on-call that night. With his usual gentle countenance, he was walking through the silent long corridors with a cup of coffee. "I never knew being a dean would be like this," he said, ruefully.

And, as the faculty member said as he stood up in the faculty meeting, "I didn't accept appointment at MIT to be doing all this kind of thing." I responded, "I so sympathize with you, sir. I didn't become president of MIT to do this kind of thing either." The faculty roared with laughter, and that took some of the pressure out of the situation. Some years later Professor Ben Snyder, dean for institute relations, wrote a book on the use of humor to defuse tense situations and cited my meetings as examples.

The major explosion during the November Actions was the clash at the Draper Laboratory. Frustrated by their inability to close the corridors of MIT, the leaders proposed to shut down Draper Lab by preventing employees from entering the workplace. Early on that Friday morning of

Demonstration on the steps of the Rogers Building, November 1969

the last day of November Actions, several hundred demonstrators gathered at the entrance of the lab. I had tried to make our position with the
city very clear. We believed that MIT laboratories and offices off the campus should be fully accessible to those who worked in them, and we
would support police efforts to ensure this access. As usual, we believed
we could handle the activities on the campus ourselves.

The Cambridge tactical squad quickly mobilized at one end of the street
and moved steadily forward in their measured and practiced way. At first,
the demonstrators didn't move, but they were blockading city streets and
were warned by bullhorns to leave the site. They were soon routed and,
after some rocks were thrown and a few arrests made, the demonstrators
panicked and broke ranks. Included in the group, it turned out, were
several of the instigators of the recent Harvard bust.

The entire week was photographed by Richard Leacock, the filmmaker
from MIT, with the cooperation of all parties. Years later I saw an
abridged version of that film when Ricky gave me a copy, and it remains
a compelling chronicle of the period. I remember one vignette of a well-

Demonstration, lobby of Building 10; on the wall behind, part of the list of MIT alumni killed in World War II

known faculty member, a future Nobel laureate, saying innocently to the TV reporter that he didn't see why the police had to break up the peaceful demonstration. Since the film had just shown people in full riot, his comment seemed disingenuous.

The interminable meetings of the faculty and student advisory committees and the air of impending disaster permeate the Leacock film. My own statement, "It came out just about the way we hoped it would," can be heard toward the end of the film. Hoped, indeed. *Time* magazine, television, the daily newspapers, and other media gave MIT full coverage, and I believe that the *Globe* was disappointed that disaster hadn't occurred.

Time magazine ran yet another cover story on the student dissent movement in the country, on student uprisings at Fordham, Michigan State, Texas, Notre Dame, and other universities. It featured a long story on MIT, "The Man Who Cooled MIT." It was a strongly positive article about our situation and reached many of our alumni and friends in a way that no internal publication could. I must admit to feeling a certain lift as a result. The general situation, however, continued to be grim. It was a somber time for the nation, and for college campuses in particular. An explosion at the University of Wisconsin, set by radical students, resulted in the death of a graduate student, and several students were killed by national guardsmen at both Kent State University and Mississippi State in 1970. The country was in upheaval.

MIT had survived, but we had to endure the rest of the academic year under a constant threat of explosive events generated both within the campus and beyond it. In the spring of 1969 many colleges and universities were forced to curtail the school year, canceling classes and examinations and closing early for summer vacation. We did not. The next year, 1970, was tougher. We worked through the year in reasonable style, but many examinations were canceled. Graduation was an uneasy event, but it passed and I was glad that we survived intact.

During that grim period, classrooms were periodically invaded by over-zealous individuals who harangued students and pushed professors aside. Sometimes the professor acquiesced, but not John Wulff, the fiery metallurgist. John fought back like a tiger on one occasion, joined quickly by the majority of the class. Eventually, we expelled some of the invaders.

Another professor who felt the pressure was Max Millikan, the head of the Center for International Studies. Like several other professors and staff members who were targeted because of the activities they led, Max Millikan was singled out because of research sponsorship by the Department of State. Max, along with others, notably John Wynne and Constantine Simonides, had on one occasion stood in the way of a large rampaging group of protesters on the Sloan plaza at the entrance of the Hermann Building. It took a lot out of Millikan, I was told. He died a few months later, and many of his colleagues in the CIS and in the institute felt that his condition had been made worse by the turmoil of the time.

Most professors were prepared to endure a certain amount of jeering, pushing, catcalls, and yelling but they did fray one's nerves. I got used to it, perhaps because of my army experience, and I actually felt myself on occasion becoming a bit combative—a very bad response in these situations. Toward the close of one faculty meeting, Constantine quietly slipped up on the stage of Kresge, where I was presiding. He handed me a note that said something to the effect that, "we have information that there may be an effort at kidnapping you after the meeting. We have campus patrolmen behind the curtain of the stage!" Actually, nothing happened, but it was not the kind of communication that calms the atmosphere or the presiding officer.

The campus police always assigned a patrolman to accompany me and Jerry, and sometimes others, as we made our rounds of the campus, but, even so, we were sometimes jostled. A campus patrolman was also stationed at our door at 111 Memorial Drive, especially after a four-foot length of steel pipe was thrown through a large window on the first floor, and one of the regular protesters climbed up to another of our first floor windows. Betty was unruffled through most of this, but in time it began to tell on her and on the house staff. The final straw was a call from the campus police chief late one afternoon to tell us that we would have to evacuate the house, perhaps for some days, because the FBI had reported that some men armed with rifles or shotguns were seen driving around MIT and had asked for the location of the President's House. Betty quickly arranged to pick up the children, all on their way home from school, and left the house in a hurry. We spent the night in Brookline, courtesy of John Wynne. The suspects were spotted, but we heard they were somehow scared off and did not appear again. We returned to our home the next day, but Betty never felt quite as secure there as before.

It was about that time that the Cambridge chief of police called on me in my office and insisted I accept a permit to carry a concealed weapon. He also offered to secure a pistol for me. I assured him that although I had some training and presumably could use such a weapon, I had no intention of ever carrying one again. The city of Cambridge, incidentally, regularly renewed that license for the next fifteen years, and I still carry in my wallet the outdated version, which gives the reason for carrying the weapon as "protection of life and property." That says a lot about the position of the university president in those days.

There were, however, some lighter moments. Most of the students were extremely friendly and walking through the halls, I would occasionally hear a student call out encouragement and support. I remember appearing with some trepidation on the stage during the Tech Show in 1969 and, to my surprise, getting a burst of warm applause from the student audience. It probably helped that I entered stage right carrying a swimsuited coed in my arms and depositing her in the center of the stage. She was one of the show's producers and had suggested the idea as an entrance, including the line which I delivered with a mostly straight face, "I thought you would like to see my idea of an outstanding student body!" I overhead one student say as I left Kresge, "Well, if HoJo isn't uptight, I won't be either."

About that same time, *Fortune* magazine came out with a major article about MIT and me titled "Come Squeeze or Bust In Ho Jo We Trust." That was a quote from some of the signs that had appeared in the main corridor before the November Actions. The article was subtitled "Under fire from all sides he still comes through . . . as the best damned university president in the U.S." The story described student support for the administration. The fact was that a large number of students were distant from the uproar created by the antiwar groups and hoped that the traditional MIT atmosphere of study and work could somehow return. Of course, that was impossible at the time, but the *Fortune* article was positive and influenced alumni and student attitudes. During this period, we had large volumes of mail, mostly from alumni but also from individuals outside the MIT community. For example, there were over 800 letters at the time of the AWOL soldier incident, and that was only the beginning. Emotions ran high in those days, and communication was often distorted. Bruised feelings about alma mater were common. One thing was certain, however: I never had anyone—faculty, administrator, or alumnus—volunteer to take my place. I was determined that we would try to answer all letters addressed to me. Donald Severance, the executive director of the alumni/nae association and successive presidents of the association did a remarkable job of reviewing the letters and replying to many. Between us, we were able to respond to most of these letters, and, in general, our response effort served the institute very well.

More complicated and difficult was the process of staying in touch with our entire alumni body. It was gratifying to see the level of interest of our graduates, tens of thousands of whom were scattered around the country and the globe. In general, the alumni showed deep concern and solid support despite a national press that tends always to over-emphasize the negative. The leadership of the association and the elected presidents of the association rarely failed to back me and my associates.

Membership issues for the corporation also received some long overdue attention. I recommended for membership my old friend Jerome "Brud" Holland, not an MIT graduate but a distinguished Cornell alumnus, whom I had met when he was president of Hampton Institute. Later he was U.S. Ambassador to Sweden and a member of the Federated Board. Many African Americans were to follow him as members, including the early appointees Whitney Young and Vernon Jordan. We also appointed the first female member of the corporation, Mary Frances Wagley, soon joined by Emily V. Wade. This appointment and others like it, all long overdue, added strength to the corporation.

We also urged the corporation and its chairman to adopt a plan for permitting election to the corporation of younger alumni. We soon had a procedure that elected five recent graduates from both the undergraduate and graduate ranks. The program, unanimously adopted by the corporation, brought new voices and dimensions to the corporation. To provide further access to corporation discussions, we formed a trustee-faculty-student advisory committee to the corporation, called CJAC. That committee, chaired by a succession of hard-working corporation members, served to provide important new perspectives. I remember how effectively the corporation functioned during this period. Like the faculty, it had to make adjustments for the changes roiling around it. This it did with great aplomb under Jim Killian's leadership. In many other institutions the president had to worry about a rear-guard action that had the backing and support of the trustees. I never had to worry about that, a sign of the fundamental strength of MIT.

Cartoon by Paul Conrad, *Los Angeles Times*, 1969

8

Education in the Midst of Turmoil: The Close of a Presidency

After all these stories, one might ask whether any academic work was going on at MIT during this period. The answer, or course, is a resounding "yes."

Students have told me, and I agree with them, that they found the institute to be academically vibrant during that time despite the uproar. The class of 1969, meeting for its twenty-fifth reunion in 1994, invited Betty and me to their final dinner at Faneuil Hall and assured me with great earnestness that they did not really mean many of those statements that the radicals made in 1969. Besides, they said, they got a great education at MIT. Maybe so. I also know, however, that many, too many, took the advice of the Learys and others to "drop out," that many altered their motivations as well as their minds with drugs, and that many never fully got back on productive tracks. Unquestionably, however, the majority, certainly more than ninety percent, survived in reasonably good shape. I cannot produce the data for this but anecdotal information and the example of the class of 1969 helps to prove my point.

Much that was positive emerged from the upheaval, and, as in the aftermath of every revolution, it is important to build upon the good results and minimize the damage. That is what we tried to do at MIT, sometimes with success.

Criticism of curriculum and culture from student and faculty surfaced over the years, as at many universities. In some institutions, faculties and administrations reacted by removing specific requirements for a degree and allowing more individually determined courses of study. At MIT, we did not choose such an unwise course. We—the president, the provost, the chairman of the faculty, and several powerful faculty committees—

believed in the science core of the undergraduate curriculum. Consequently, the Educational Policy Committee and various departments reviewed the situation. The chairman of the faculty and the provost were typically the linchpins making progress here and elsewhere. In my terms as president and chairman, MIT was fortunate in its faculty chairmen: Charles Kindleberger, Walter Rosenblith, Ted Martin, Hartley Rogers, Elias Gyftopoulos, John Ross, Bob Hulsizer, Sheila Widnall, and Felix Villars.

Several experimental undergraduate programs, sponsored by committed professors and departments, were introduced and received my strong support. Professor George Valley's Experimental Studies Program and numerous additions of new course work in mathematics and physics were among those efforts, and helped many acquire a genuine sense of participation in devising their own course of study.

The principal venture of this kind was the program to encourage undergraduates to participate directly in research efforts of faculty members. An important and original preamble for this idea came, once again, from Edwin Land. In the 1957 Arthur D. Little lecture, Land proposed that undergraduate students be purposely and regularly involved in research efforts at MIT beginning in their freshman year. An obvious connection existed between this lucidly presented proposal and the one he had pressed on me about working students in factory management in the early sixties. I had not then been ready for that proposal, but now, Margaret MacVicar, a young assistant professor in physics, had a great idea. She was the chief spark behind the new effort aimed at substituting real and vivid involvement in research in place of the cookbook exercise that had so long dominated undergraduate laboratory work. With the strong support of Al Hill in physics and Paul Gray, the assistant provost, she came to Jerry and me asking for support. We enthusiastically decided to press the plan with the faculty, and soon it was a major experiment with Paul Gray as the leading proponent.

The program grew with added support from the faculty and financial support from members of the corporation, eventually encompassing a large proportion of the undergraduate class. The program, the Undergraduate Research Opportunities Program (UROP), is a notable part of the undergraduate experience in all fields. Margaret became a professor and, eventually, dean of undergraduate studies. Tragically, she died several years later, but her imprint on the academic program of the institute, and programs it inspired elsewhere, was profound. Many people consider UROP to have been the major curriculum innovation at MIT during my term, and Gray deserves special credit for his support of the program.

A few other changes had a long-term impact on MIT. For years, I was aware of dissatisfaction with the semester system, in which the fall term continued to the two-week Christmas break and concluded after the break with a three-week period of review and examinations in January; then, almost immediately, the spring semester began in the first week of February. Through the appropriate faculty committees, we supported proposals to begin the fall term right after Labor Day (with the freshmen coming a week earlier) and ending the term with all examinations completed by the Christmas break. We then proposed that January be an independent studies period, later called the Independent Activities Program, with time for special academic efforts, nonacademic subjects of all kinds, independent research, and real relaxation, including skiing. The spring term then began a little earlier, and the whole semester ended in late May in time for a typical early June commencement. The proposal was fiercely debated by the faculty, but was passed; with the help of special funds raised for the purpose, it got off to a splendid start and has improved through the years. Many students told me then and later, that they got their bearings again during January, and used the time productively in ways that later had a favorable impact on their academic and professional careers.

Another effort involved the freshman grading system. Our freshmen arrived at the institute with academic records that placed them at the top of their high school classes, often as the valedictorians. They entered MIT's very demanding first year, took their examinations, and 50 percent found that they were below average. Those initial grades were often devastating for the students. Fortunately, most recovered, and like survivors of a marine boot camp, insisted in later years that the freshmen go through the same drill they did. But the idea of pass-fail grades awarded in the freshman year seemed to have a great deal of merit. I took the lead, with Ben Snyder's support, in championing this idea with the faculty, as did Jerry and the dean for student affairs, Ken Wadleigh. The experimental plan was approved by the faculty and established; it has been reviewed and renewed numerous times since then.

Against the background of these and many other active efforts I felt that it was time for an overall look at MIT education, for the institute had undertaken no such wide review since the early postwar years and the Lewis Committee in 1948. We established a commission to be chaired by mathematics professor Kenneth Hoffman that involved a wide range of participants from the campus. The group selected to serve on the Commission on MIT Education worked long and hard, held campus-wide hearings and discussion sessions, produced papers, and deliberated at length with all comers. They also toured other institutions and explored the whole range of educational issues.

Their final report was a lengthy document. It reinforced several principles for depth and breadth. I was ever grateful to Hoffman for giving up a solid eight months of his life in this endeavor, but it has to be said that it changed his life, too. After serving as head of the Department of Mathematics, he became a leading spokesman for the importance of the study of mathematics in the nation's colleges and high schools. The report of the commission proved to be a solid piece of work for MIT and put the whole case for curriculum and cultural reform at MIT on a cooler and more considered basis, away from the heated and hysterical discussions taking place on many campuses at the time.

But such long-range studies, valuable as they were, took a back seat to the upheavals of the period. At our university and those around us, there continued to be demonstrations. One point of friction that typically generated some heat was the job recruitment activities of companies of all kinds on the campus. Formerly these annual visits by company representatives coming in the late fall and early spring to interview prospective job candidates on campus were warmly welcomed. Not so by 1968. Even noncontroversial companies were suspect and, of course, companies with connections to defense industries were pariahs to the antiwar activists. Companies like Dow Chemical and General Electric were especially singled out, as were government agencies of all kinds, particularly the CIA.

Many campuses endured shoving matches and other violent acts between protesters and campus police. At MIT it never quite reached that stage, but aggressive picketing was a concern and a real threat. On one occasion there was a much-publicized visit by representatives of General Motors, at which time the SDS demanded to know the details of the company's "war production" and the profits resulting from such production. We tried to brief the GM delegation, headed by its then-treasurer, Roger Smith, on what was in store for it when it arrived. Smith managed to get through the session, which involved over 200 participants, and a reasonable level of civility was maintained, but I think he left an impression of narrowness and insensitivity.

Speakers on campuses were also subject to a possible barrage of catcalls and heckling, and if they were at all pro-administration or in favor of the war in Vietnam, they were in for a very difficult time. It remains one of the deepest scars for me that even on our campus diverse views were no longer tolerated and were frequently stopped altogether by angry protesters. One case at the institute involved Walt Rostow, a professor on leave from MIT who was serving the administration in Washington. He was invited by the Center for International Studies to speak in Kresge Auditorium and all hell broke loose at that session. It was chaired by Robert Bishop, dean of the School of Humanities and Social Science, and the level of noise and interference forced Bob to move to better-controlled facilities in the Sloan School.

Sometime later, the Rostow affair took another twist. Walt, whom I had known in the pre-Kennedy days, had gone to Washington with the Kennedy Administration in January of 1961, eventually becoming national security advisor during the Johnson Administration. He had been given the usual year's leave, which was renewed for another year. The institute's policy was to continue such public service leaves where requested for a reasonable time. My predecessor, Jay Stratton, had agreed to Rostow's request to extend his absence from MIT for 1963 and 1964. In 1965, after discussions in the Academic Council, Stratton wrote Rostow and warned him that if he did not plan to return by the end of that year, he would have to vacate his professorship. Five years away from the institute, Stratton said, was the limit, and a precedent set by another current case. Walt's response confirmed that he felt he must stay in Washington at that difficult time. The parting was congenial but final.

Three years later, in 1968, he let it be known through Max Millikan that he would like to return after the election, and wondered whether his old post would be available. It was proposed by the Center for International Studies that he return as a professor. The Department of Economics, however, which was Rostow's former faculty home, turned down the proposal, which ended the matter as far as MIT procedure went. When the news became public, a furor arose in the faculty. My mail, however, overwhelmingly supported the department's conclusions, and Jerry concurred strongly with me that Rostow should not be renewed. Max Millikan suggested that we bring him back as a visiting professor, but I felt that was a compromise that was not useful. I informed Rostow of our conclusion.

Meanwhile, the affair was leaked to the press, and James Reston of the *New York Times*, of all people, ran a very sorrowful column in which he said that MIT, while following its regulations, certainly was not following the spirit of permitting a public servant to return to his institution after service well rendered to the republic. Jerry called Reston and complained, and although Reston agreed not to publish further on the matter once he was better informed of the details, Laya Wiesner, who knew him, said that this was Reston at his most mischievous. Perhaps that is the best way to put it.

What happened at MIT when Walt Rostow tried to speak at Kresge Auditorium was inexcusable and I regretted it, but it was even worse on other campuses. Robert McNamara, visiting Harvard, not only had been prevented from speaking, but his car was stopped on campus and stoned. He was very seriously threatened until the police got him safely away.

At Edward Levi's presidential inauguration at the University of Chicago in November 1968, demonstrations all but shut down the celebration. George Shultz, then at Chicago and awaiting a call from Richard Nixon to become secretary of labor, and I, as the representative of MIT, attended the inaugural ceremony together, which took place in Orchestra Hall in downtown Chicago. We were aghast at the malevolence of the demonstrators and the uproar that almost prevented the ceremony from taking place. Later, Levi had to deal with the longest siege of any university when students occupied the administration building for many weeks. When they finally left, several were expelled, and the incident left multiple scars on the institution.

When I returned to Chicago in June of 1969 to receive the alumni medal, an honor I treasure, the commencement celebration and the alumni activities were held behind barricades. And so it was in many places. I was invited to give the commencement address at Ohio State in 1969, but was warned by the university's president that it would be delivered against the potential background of student violence. I had to say no in any case because I assumed that we would have our hands full on our own campus that spring, but I was very sorry I was not able to accept an invitation from a great Middle Western university.

When I went to Caltech to give the address on behalf of academic institutions at the inauguration of its new president, there was a heavy police presence, as there was at ETH in Zurich when I spoke to a large convention of students and faculty there. On many campuses, and perhaps especially at the most prestigious universities, a kind of denial of free speech had developed, something that had been anathema to the concept of the university. It disturbed many an alumnus and many a parent. To me it was the most discouraging aspect of the whole period. The physical threat to discussion, to speaking publicly on unpopular subjects, meant a complete negation of the free intellectual character of college and university life.

MIT at this time had plenty of unfinished business. The Pounds Panel report had effectively channeled debate around the laboratories, but we were still left with the decision of what to do. Innumerable discussions among the administration and the faculty and the corporation ensued following the Pounds Panel report. Some wanted total disassociation; others wanted a military guard around the laboratory. It was at this time that we experienced the second counterpunch in the press soon after the Pounds Panel report was presented. I had a call from McGeorge Bundy. Mac informed me that I could expect a stinging column from Joseph Alsop, and there was nothing I could do about it. I knew Alsop only by his vitriolic archconservative tongue, and I wondered what was coming. It soon came. Alsop, in the first of two columns, said that MIT and its president had demonstrated leftist leanings by depending on the Pounds Panel report. He claimed that the panel was loaded with radicals and that the report, which he had not read, not only was unpatriotic, but it seriously threatened the defense strength of the country. He pictured Draper himself as a man of great patriotism who had served his country well and was now being driven out by his colleagues.

Through Jim Nichols, an old friend from my Federated days, I contacted Alsop and told him that he was misinformed. He agreed to come up for a breakfast with me to hear more. I have seldom met a more mean-spirited man, one who was totally sure of his point of view in advance. He recalled that MIT, under Killian, had been "lily-livered," as he put it, in the days of the McCarthy hearings and threatened to be so again. I could tell I had made no headway with him. His second column appeared, and it was as distorted as the earlier one. Noam Chomsky, a member of the panel, responded to Alsop in a letter to his Washington paper, but all that produced was another venomous piece from Alsop, more evidence of the tenor of the times in which it seemed impossible to air divergent viewpoints.

Such attacks were no help as we tried to arrive at a decision on the laboratories. I spent a weekend focused on the matter in the isolation of our New Hampshire house. I came up with a plan, which I discussed with my closest colleagues—Jerry Wiesner, Jim Killian, and some of the deans—at great length. I then tried it out on the academic council. It was basically this: MIT would spin off the instrumentation laboratory, which would become an independent, not-for-profit organization, maintaining its effectiveness as a developer and producer of guidance technology for the defense department. We would, at MIT, appoint a board of directors, chaired by Al Hill and including several MIT Corporation members and a few other public people. Al was once again in a critical spot where he would perform magnificently.

I proposed that we would achieve this separation over a period of up to three years, but we would begin immediately to take some first steps to separation. We would continue to provide certain infrastructure supports for the laboratory organization, including health and other benefit plans, and facilities like libraries, especially in the early phases. All contract negotiations would be transferred immediately to the new organization. I had concluded that this plan was the right step for MIT. I felt further that it was a fair response to the Pounds Panel, which essentially had said to preserve in the national interest the unique technological capacity of the laboratory, but gradually shift to progressively larger nondefense purposes. That second part, I concluded, was going to be impossible to achieve in anything less than a decade. We tempered the abruptness of the financial impact on the institute of the loss of overhead, which all of the financial types had been bewailing. We maintained the laboratory as a learning and teaching place for our students and for faculty and staff participants.

Despite some problems, the plan was a sound conclusion. Earlier in the year, I had proposed to the corporation that we rename the laboratory in honor of its founder and technical leader, Charles Stark Draper, and it was now known as the Draper Laboratory. With all of that, I assumed we could make the transition. We kept the Lincoln Laboratory on the basis that it was more academically oriented in its work and in its association with the academic departments, notably electrical engineering and computer science. In that sense it was a more appropriate connection, and, as a practical consideration, it was also more distant from the campus.

But the basic reason for the difference in MIT's position on Lincoln Laboratory, in contrast to Draper Laboratory, was not something that could be broadcast publicly. The fact was that MIT's corporation and administration basically controlled Lincoln's policies and operations. The president of MIT appointed the director of Lincoln and approved all major appointments and programs in the laboratory. All this was supported by a network of connections with several parts of the faculty. Draper, in contrast, was already very much an independent laboratory. Appointments, nominally MIT's, were actually controlled by the laboratory; its programs were, in a much more direct sense, the function of the government defense agencies. MIT, under Killian, Stratton, and now me, was not in full control of Draper, and we knew it. In time, after Stark Draper had retired, all this could be changed, but it would require peaceful times, which we did not then have. I decided that the situation was not a healthy one for either MIT or our defense department clients. My colleagues in the faculty and the executive committee agreed.

In discussions with the academic council and eventually the faculty council, I swore everyone to secrecy, and to my relief, there was not a single leak. I visited the senior officers of the two laboratories. The leadership at the Draper Lab, including Draper and his chief lieutenants, accepted the proposition somewhat reluctantly as the best they could achieve. Lincoln was delighted. I worked closely with the executive committee of the corporation and visited the DOD leadership. After some modest fine-tuning, it was ready to be presented to the faculty and to the corporation at special meetings in which the principal agenda item would be the administration proposal on the laboratories.

I had worked almost around the clock for ten days, and had reinjured my lower back. By that time, the medical department had fitted me with a kind of brace, but the pain was still severe, exacerbated no doubt by the psychological factors involved. This was in the days before Ibuprofen, and I did not want to take available pain killers because they were also mental-dampeners.

The big day arrived, presaged the day before by a front-page story in the *Boston Globe* by reporter Victor McElheny saying that I would announce at Monday's special faculty meeting that we would keep the instrumentation laboratory and conduct business as usual. Victor, who later joined the MIT staff, was most surprised when I reported our conclusions to a hushed faculty meeting to which the press, incidentally, was invited. When I finished, there was a muted response. The antilab elements were confused, not expecting this development and now not knowing what to do. The vociferous laboratory supporters were also mute. Stark Draper gave a short but gracious speech saying that he and his laboratory colleagues were saddened and felt they really were not understood by their MIT colleagues. A motion was made and carried by a large majority to endorse my proposal, and a few comments of support were made about my actions on this matter. The meeting adjourned, and I was glad to see it end.

In the corporation meeting two members were especially critical, including my old friend Bob Sprague who was a Naval Academy graduate, and who felt that we had made a large mistake. The corporation, however, overwhelmingly approved.

The transition took longer than I had hoped, not being completed until during my term as chairman of the corporation. Over the years since, I have often had the chance to discuss and review that decision, and I believe now as strongly as I did then that it was a wise one. The laboratory continues to be an effective operation. It became even larger and was able to improve its facilities in a way that would never have been possible for it as an appendage of MIT. Finally, I believe the institute also benefited. Not only did we lift that burden from our backs, but we were also freed from dealing with large personnel problems that had union implications on campus. In addition, we were no longer dealing with the financial pressures of an up-and-down budget, at least in relation to the Draper Laboratory.

Most of all, we dealt with the very basic question of principle: Should MIT have total responsibility for a large facility with production capabilities that we did not fully control? While the ensuing financial problems and pressures resulting from the spin-off were real, MIT learned to deal with them, since they came on gradually. In the long run, our decision saved us from the potential calamity of having two large laboratories that could suffer similar blows simultaneously. We have, in a sense, therefore, kept a close association with the wider and broader technology and, at the same time, hedged the potential financial hazards. I remain content with the outcome, and except for the views of one or two critics, the aftermath has been positive. Jerry Wiesner often told me during his presidency that he was grateful that the decision had been made or the institute could have been in deep trouble later.

In recent years, I was invited to speak at the memorial service for Dr. Albert Hill at the Draper Laboratory. Most of the surviving former leaders of the laboratory were present. They went out of their way to say that the arrangement, which they had not always supported, had produced the best outcome.

Only history, of course, can make a final judgment of what we did. On the campus, however, the laboratory question now essentially disappeared and with it the broader issue of the war research question. The subsequent demise of an aggressive Soviet Union and the ensuing step-down of the large, multiple missiles have put the MIRV missile question on the refuse heap of history. All of that, I hope, is now behind us. May it remain there.

Of course, the removal of the laboratory question from the active agenda had no effect on the national uproar. That continued at a somewhat less intense level with "peace talks" begun between the North Vietnamese and the United States going on in Paris. Bombings by B–52 formations stirred up everything once again, but, in general, even though individual families still suffered losses, the national scene became somewhat quieter, if only from exhaustion.

Just before Christmas in 1969, I received a package from Goodspeed's, the Boston bookseller. It contained a framed Civil War document: an original order from Ulysses S. Grant to George Meade, dated March 1865, at Petersburg, a month before the end of the Civil War. It was a gift from Penn Brooks and his written message meant more to me than even the historic Grant dispatch. "I wanted you to have something to commemorate the campaign you have just been through. What would be more appropriate than this! I would like to think that you are as near the end of your war as Grant was his at City Point. With praise, admiration and affection, Penn." I do not often get a tear in my eye, but I did, then.

A final outburst on the campus remains vivid in my memory—the break-in and occupation of my office in January 1970. The grueling fall had left Betty and me both more than a bit tired. A friend had built a new house in Lost Tree, Florida, and telephoned me to propose that we use it for a week or so. A week was out of the question even during the independent activities period, but a few days sounded delightful and we invited Constantine and Betty Simonides to join us. We flew down in an afternoon, found the place, and prepared to take a deep breath. It was not to be.

The telephone rang. Jerry Wiesner was worried about the situation on campus. All kinds of grim demonstration plans were being considered, and the occupation of some site was being discussed. It turned out that we had finally given the radicals the incident on which they could mobilize their core group to dramatic action. It all stemmed from the aftermath of November Actions. Members of the student leadership, including Michael Albert, Katsiaficas, and others, had been involved in several nasty incidents. Albert had been admonished by the discipline committee, headed by historian Roy Lamson, on a charge of interference with some rightful activity on the campus. The admonishment did no good; Albert persisted and was again called before the discipline committee where he, in noisy open hearings, proceeded to insult the mild-mannered Lamson with regard to the committee's function. Lamson, who had served, with the rank of colonel, as chief historian of SHAEF after World War II,

With Michael A. Albert and Walter A. Rosenblith, 1969

voted, along with the entire committee, to expel Albert from the institute. Such disciplinary actions, however, required the approval of the president. I met with Albert who, although quite civil toward me, said that the whole rotten social and political system of the country was about to fall apart and MIT with it. He did not recognize the institute as having any authority. I also met with Albert's father, at his request, who pleaded that his son should be allowed to stay at MIT. His argument was that these "young Jasons," as he called them, were actually the hope of the country. They meant to build a nation, not tear it down; we at MIT should be more tolerant of the actions of young people. He showed me a photo of Albert at his high school graduation; he tearfully said that he and Albert's mother had sent the boy off to MIT as a well-mannered young man, and now we were responsible for his unmannerly outbursts. I heard what he was saying, but my duty was clear. Seeing no contrition in Albert, and weighing the likelihood of what any delay would do to our own overwrought judicial system, I accepted the discipline committee's recommendation and expelled him.

The radicals now had a cause, and they demanded Albert's readmission, with a threat of occupation of one or more sites on the campus. The matter was being discussed only in the tight inner circle of the SDS, and the target for occupation was unknown, but we knew it would come at some point. Shortly after I departed for Florida, John Wynne and Jerry realized it was imminent, and they wanted me to return to the campus. So, after being in Florida for less than a day, Constantine and I returned to Boston, arriving after 10 P.M. on a rather uneasy flight. The two Bettys would return the following day with our luggage. We were met at the airport by a worried Ken Wadleigh, now a vice president of the institute, and went directly to MIT. Near midnight, the academic council was still in session and showed the strain of waiting out a long day. A large demonstration was planned for the Student Center in mid-morning the following day. I spent an hour or two walking around the campus, talking with the people who were often there at that late hour. The situation felt more tense than usual. The next morning I went to my office and, after a brief time with Betty Whittaker, I and a few others met in our contingency office, where we often gathered in worrisome times. It was a back room in the Faculty Club, set up with an array of direct telephones to several sites on the campus. Close to coffee and the availability of a quick sandwich, it served admirably as a place for headquarters in times of trouble.

At about quarter to noon a telephone call warned me that the crowd was on its way to demonstrate in the president's office corridor. We often had such demonstrations, where our usual procedure was to lock the doors of the president's office and, typically, several of our top people—often Constantine, John Wynne, the dean on duty, and some quickly mobilized members of the faculty—would stand in front of our door to receive and respond to the demonstrators. That is the step that was put into effect on this occasion. The general feeling was that there would be a noisy demonstration and then, if sufficient fervor could be generated, the group would go to some other site and occupy it for a brief time, or, perhaps, hold another session of some kind. This time we were surprised.

Walter Milne, on the phone across the hall from the president's office, reported a group of 150 to 250 people noisily demonstrating in front of the president's door. Suddenly, a group of four ski-masked men carrying a pipe battering ram appeared at the edge of the crowd and worked their way to the side door of my office. This door was always closed and locked, having no outside doorknob, it was essentially a separate exit for my office. In two large crashing heaves, the door was splintered by the battering ram and my office was entered, followed by large clusters of demonstrators from the main crowd.

Betty Whittaker picked up as many papers as she could from her desk and, along with Betty Pigott, Jim Killian's longtime assistant, and Charlene Placido, the receptionist, was quickly ushered out of the office, by friendly forces, through the regular door. That door had now been opened from the inside and was admitting more and more of the crowd. Jerry Wiesner arrived quickly. Standing on a chair with a bull horn, he told the demonstrators to leave; they jeered him down. Since the whole affair was happening during a nonclass period the usual traffic down that hallway was not there, but the place was still crowded as the news was passed by word of mouth.

Walter Milne, my on-the-scene observer, went across the hall and quickly came back, his voice shaking and almost incoherent. He could not understand what had happened. Soon John Wynne was there, calm and organized, as always, but jarred to the core. In a surprise maneuver, the group had broken into the office and were now entering through both doors, I told John to take a deep breath and keep on top of the situation. The campus patrol had arrived in force and soon allowed no more entry, but a group of more than fifty stood in my office and in the adjoining two, including the reception room and Jim Killian's office. The barrier was still porous. Constantine and, later, Jerry were able to enter and get a good idea of who was there. Ski masks had disappeared, but the battering ram was still in the corner; Constantine said later that he could have picked it up but didn't.

Much later, we learned how the ram had been made. Tony Zona, an employee in the Metallurgy Shop, was approached by some students for help with what he thought was needed for a lab experiment. The device was essentially a six-foot length of six-inch steel pipe with two sets of handles welded on that served as the launching handles. Zona later made a miniature copy, which he presented to me. I still have it on my desk. The original has disappeared and may well be at the bottom of the Charles River.

The next morning newspapers all over the country carried headlines with, in some cases, banners across the top heralding "Mob Breaks into MIT President's Office." The question now was what to do. I, joined by the other key people, quickly decided to let them sit, after warning them as trespassers to leave. And there they sat. We had campus patrol on the outside. People could leave but could not reenter. At night, the lights in the president's office blazed all through the hours. So what else was new?

I had plenty of advice. Some alumni urged we attack, pull them out of there, and break a few skulls. But we sat and watched as groups met. The faculty passed a resolution supporting me. The bulk of the students, and an editorial in the *Tech*, decried the occupation. Petitions signed by the usual suspects urged me to be lenient and readmit Albert. We made contingency plans to enter if we had to, or if it went on too long. I will always remember Walter Rosenblith volunteering to lead the break-in if it were to come. It was soon clear to me, however, that the occupiers had little following among the students. Those students on the edge were disheartened by the action. I was sure that most of those inside were wavering. I intended to wait them out. Bob Sullivan, our able lawyer, made the only mistake he ever made with me; he urged me to negotiate with them and offer them a face-saving but "meaningless" victory. I said absolutely no, that the constituencies of alumni and friends on the out-side, not to mention the faculty and student body, would be appalled if there was any appearance, much less substance, of giving in to the mob.

On the evening of the second day, thirty-four hours after the occupation, we heard from some anonymous escapee that there were growing divisions on the inside; suddenly, at about midnight, the doors opened, cautiously at first, and the group ran out, shouting, to the student center. Paul Gray, on duty as always, entered the offices with our campus patrol. He said to me and then to the press, "It's a shambles." And so it was. Damage—dirt, mess, discarded debris, and minor vandalism—was every-where. But theft was limited to one fabric wall hanging, later rolled and wrapped and returned by mail. A silver Victorian letter opener was also returned, but it showed evidence of having been used to pry open my desk. There were no cigars for students to smoke posing for photographs while sitting at the president's desk, as had been the case at Columbia. We had removed our papers earlier; some items on the tape of Betty Whittaker's IBM typewriter were given some publicity but were of no importance.

I invited a few members of the faculty, including some inclined to sympathize with the occupiers, to see the debris in the office. They were aghast. With Paul Gray, John Wynne, and Jim Culliton leading the effort, twenty-seven of the break-in participants were identified. All were subject to disciplinary and civil actions. In the Cambridge district court in the following months, they were tried on the charge of criminal trespassing; all were found guilty and put on probation for a year, subject to jail terms if, during that following year, they committed additional crimes. Seven were expelled from the institute at the recommendation of the discipline committee. There were no attacks from that group again.

Most important, the radicals never again had an important following. The majority of students felt that the occupation was irresponsible and we could see that no strong support for the radical fringe remained.

Few events of any significance on the radical front occurred after this point, with one curious postscript. In October of 1971, after Wiesner had become president and I chairman, a bomb was exploded on the fourth floor of the Hermann Building, apparently originating in a ladies' rest room. It occurred in the predawn hours, and apart from modest damage to files, fixtures, and furniture, no real harm was done. It was the first and only time that a bomb threat was actually carried out at MIT. The culprits seemed to be an offshoot of the Weathermen. Once again, the campus was generally outraged by such a senseless and potentially dangerous act. After that, there were no more outbreaks.

This is not to say that the war's unpopularity had declined but the major battles at MIT were over. It had been at a high cost. Many members of the administration and faculty were worn out. Wadleigh, the dean for students, had resigned in 1969, to be followed by Dan Nyhart, who soon was worn down as well. The school deans had been bruised, and so were my close associates. Jerry Wiesner, Walter Rosenblith, Paul Gray, Betty Whittaker, John Wynne, Constantine Simonides, and Walter Milne all showed the effects. I do not think that most people appreciated the wear and tear and damage to individuals who were on the firing line. They had been working every day and every week with little respite. This was also true of the President's House, situated as it is close to the center of

The demonstrations wind down; Building 7, April 1970

the campus. By the spring of 1970, it seemed to me that one could breathe a great deal easier, and I began to hope for a respite. But there was none immediately on the job, for there was a full agenda to be completed at MIT.

As the campus began to calm down again, a surprising incident summed up the new tone. Jerry Wiesner and I, meeting at the end of a long afternoon, were asked if we could come to an emergency session of some faculty members. We dropped our discussion and got into a waiting car with Walter Rosenblith, speeding off to an unannounced meeting place. It seemed a little late in the term for such a meeting, and we were a bit puzzled, but Walter was not saying anything.

In a short time we were at Professor Isadore Singer's home in Newton, where we found ourselves surrounded by about twenty cheering professors. They represented the whole spectrum of opinion on the issues, from right to left and the center. I quickly scanned the faces: Bob Solow, Ithiel Pool, Kenneth Hoffman, Noam Chomsky, Sheldon Penman, Bob Mann, Jerry Lettvin, and many others. I saw Betty Whittaker, Constantine

Simonides, and Walter Milne. They were all there to celebrate the ending of another good year at MIT, an invigorating one but nonetheless a good one. They wanted to tell me, too, one said, that the entire ideological range of the faculty was represented there, by proxy at least. On top of that, they gave Jerry Wiesner and me small engraved clocks, which they paid for with their own money.

From time to time in the years that followed, people have asked me to describe the approach we used in dealing with the skirmishes and threats when so many other major institutions came away with serious scars. I usually respond by saying that we had a strong administrative group and kept a close and trusting relationship with the faculty and the staff. But that is not the whole story, of course. Some years after I retired, I came across a rough set of notes that I had used in a session with the academic council in one of our summer sessions. I reminded my colleagues of our point of view in the midst of upheaval and then made the following points. I am embarrassed by their brevity and tendency to overstate the obvious, but here there are:

1. Don't underestimate the opposition.
2. Deal seriously with the least radical and most stable group within the opposition.
3. Communicate honestly and continuously, especially with the faculty and its committees.
4. Listen, listen, listen!
5. Don't spend all your time reacting to what the opposition is doing. Concentrate on your own plan.
6. Don't be predictable in your tactics.
7. Don't let people get over-tired, including the opposition.
8. Keep a sense of humor. You have seen worse.

As I read these lines, I find them too simple, but they probably helped us at the time.

Betty, by late spring 1970, had proposed that we move out of the President's House, using it only for the normal round of campus occasions. We would be sorry to leave it but the times made it difficult to stay there. We had many pleasurable memories of the place and the guests who had stayed there. We looked at a few houses in our rare spare hours, and finally found a grand home in Wellesley Hills, which we were prepared to buy. Joseph Snyder and the executive committee, fully understanding the problem, came forward with a proposal to buy it for MIT and own it as an asset of the corporation, since there was no telling when it would be possible to live quietly in the President's House again. When school ended in June, we prepared to move our household goods to Wellesley Hills, and by mid-summer we were settled there. Two years later, when we moved back to the chairman's apartment on Memorial Drive, the institute sold the Wellesley house at a profit. Occasionally, I have thought how helpful it would have been had we owned that house ourselves. It was a great place, but we remained in "company housing," and it had its many compensations.

I remember the 1970 commencement season for many reasons. By that time, I began to feel that I had served long enough as president. Cecil Green once said to me, "Howard, I think each year of your presidency has been equal to three normal years." At least some were. There was another factor, secondary, but important nonetheless. Jim Killian announced at the Alumni Day gatherings of that year, that 1970–71 would be his last year as chairman. He had extended his normal term by a year at that point at my request and with the approval of the corporation, and now he was eager to move to some other tasks at the end of the 1971 academic year. He had told me, too, that he was increasingly worried about Liz's health and more than a bit about his own.

The chairmanship of the MIT Corporation is unusual, if not unique, in American higher education, and a word about it and its development may be useful here. The chairman of trustee bodies in the typical university structure is a part-time volunteer, usually senior in membership, who devotes considerable time and commitment to the tasks of leading the trustees and advising the president. The MIT Corporation essentially followed this pattern with minor exceptions until the post–World War II period. Then, both Compton and Bush, serving in turn as chairman, devoted increasing time to sharing these burdens designated by the president. Bush, as chairman, became strikingly helpful for the presidency, as well as the corporation, during Julius Stratton's acting presidency from 1957 to 1959. During Stratton's term as president from 1959 to 1966, first Bush and then Killian were increasingly visible. Killian's definition of the chairmanship began with his return from Washington in 1959. During his twelve years in this office and my own twelve years that followed, the office took on a new character. Duties related to MIT's increasingly heavy research funding, relationships with the learned societies and alumni bodies scattered across the country, fund-raising (especially during the fund campaigns), and steady and friendly advice during periods of difficulty were helpful to the president. The post had become full time and salaried, and it proved well worth the occasional ambiguities of the relationship between chairman and president. As Vannevar Bush once told me in response to my question about the duties of the chairman: the president runs the institute from inside looking out, and the chairman runs the institute from the outside looking in. That is a classic Bush epigram but, depending on the two collaborators, it essentially captures the closeness of the trust relationship of the two posts. Often, but not always, the chairman has previously served as president of the institute and is familiar with the territory. But new perspectives are also helpful and have served the institute well in the past. The president is always the chief executive, but reports to the corporation, through the chairman, which produces a certain useful tension, if also some ambiguity.

In 1971, there was not an apparent successor. Jay Stratton was older than Jim by three years and had been away at the Ford Foundation. Vannevar Bush could not be expected to return in harness. That weighed on my mind in those June days, and I began considering my own options. Did I want to assume the chairmanship myself were it to become available?

As I mulled it over that June, I often wished there was a way to take a short leave to recharge my batteries. In those Vietnam years, newspapers publicized that three years was the average span for college presidents. Three, or as a matter of fact five, were too short as a term, but there was no mechanism to permit a sabbatical. Two decades later, there were other ideas on the subject. At Wellesley, where I had been serving as a trustee, we gave Nan Keohane a year's sabbatical after five years on duty as president, and she went off for a change of pace and a change of geography for a full twelve months. She returned, as she has said, "fully charged with enthusiasm." That turned out to be a very constructive idea. That year's experience also was good for the acting president, Dale Rogers

Marshall. She went on to become president at Wheaton College. During the summer I discussed with John Wynne and Constantine my leaving the presidency, and they demurred more than a little. So did Jerry Wiesner, who worried about who might follow. He could not, he said.

In late June 1970, I concluded that it would be wise to leave the presidency in June 1971, and if the corporation were willing, to assume the chairmanship of the corporation. The second part of my hope was that Jerry Wiesner would become president. I was very positive about this step, as I was about the effectiveness and quality of our whole management group. Provost Walter Rosenblith, Associate Provost Paul Gray, Vice Presidents John Wynne and Constantine Simonides, were all stars. The deans were excellent, with Ray Bisplinghoff having replaced the retiring Gordon Brown. Stuart Cowen was a fine comptroller, and we were blessed with many strong individuals in department head posts. With Joe Snyder soon to retire, we had before us the challenge of finding a treasurer, but all in all, I was happy about the strength of our group. The Corporation had held together effectively, considering the pressures of the time. The executive committee of Mueller, Fisk, Coolidge, Murphy, and Thorn was superb even though, at the end, they, too, were getting tired. As Eleanor Roosevelt had said about her era, "It was no ordinary time." And it was an unforgiving time for university presidents and their close associates.

That summer's academic council retreat, which I had found such a useful way to get the group together for planning before the term began, was held again at Squam Lake in New Hampshire. On a rainy evening before the final day, I told the group of my intention to submit my resignation in the early fall, to be effective in June 1971. A gloomy silence followed this announcement, and later a lot of effort was expended asking me to reverse the decision. I told them I could not. Walter Rosenblith, with always a special poetic sense in difficult times, said something to the effect that we had all experienced Camelot at MIT in this administration. "Let us remember it that way," he said. Jerry was especially downcast, an unusual mood for him. By next day the weather had brightened, and we concentrated on what to do in these next few months.

I had earlier informed Jim Killian of my thinking, and he called a special meeting of the executive committee in New York City. There was essentially the same reaction. I reported my intention to the corporation at its meeting in October, and after a long pause, Crawford Greenewalt stood and introduced in his most serious way a resolution thanking me for my service and hoping it would be continued in another capacity. In general, the members were understanding, and many came to me at the conclusion of that meeting to say how positively they felt about my administration.

The announcement also surprised the faculty, but at the next regular faculty meeting, I was greeted with a strong show of support. I assured the faculty that I intended to work as I had right up to the end of my term. Someone asked me if there would be any new policies, and I answered that there would not.

The following months passed with swiftness except in the laboring process by which the new president was chosen. That seemed to drag on. We had a fine Corporation committee on the presidency, with James Fisk chairing it and strong members including Vannevar Bush, Paul Keyser, Carl Mueller, George Thorn, Julius Stratton, Jeptha Wade, and Uncas Whitaker. Serious and careful discussion marked the meetings, and faculty and student advisory groups were involved in the process, now standard procedure. The view I expressed to the committee was that the strongest candidate, by far, was Jerry Wiesner. I believe I was the key to carrying the day for Wiesner.

The committee went through all the usual steps, however, and outside candidates were reviewed. Inside, Paul Gray's name emerged often as a strong candidate. Paul had strong skills and special interests in budgetary matters, and clearly had grown a great deal. We were entering a time when the financing of the institute would be the first order of business. Faculty research support was weaker. We had been buoyed through the fifties and early sixties by large yearly increases in research, and that had effectively helped our budget. Now, partly because the federal departments and the congressional committees were not as pleased with their university associations, general federal support had flattened. After several years of good performance at MIT, we were feeling the pinch and pressure of shortfalls. Our reserves were strong, but belt-tightening was imminent, and it was important that administrations in the future be vigilant in cutting budgets. I felt that some combination of experience would be advantageous. In the end, Carl and his committee came up with an ingenious solution. Jerry was proposed as president, with Paul as chancellor, a post that had not been used since Stratton's time during the Killian administration. There was one more proviso attached. It was assumed, I was told, that I would become chairman. I agreed, but pointed out that I would need a little breathing room.

I had spent the years of my presidency absolutely immersed in my job, and I still was. I had turned down an occasional company suggestion regarding board membership, returning to my Federated membership on an agreement with Ralph Lazarus that included my condition that I be permitted to miss meetings when necessary. I had also accepted, in 1968, a membership on the board of the John Hancock Mutual Life Insurance Company, one of the Boston companies on which Karl Compton had once served as a board member. For the remainder, I had resigned my posts at Putnam and Hitchiner.

I had, of course, taken on some public posts that in a way went with the president's job. I was a member of some presidential committees, including the President's Advisory Committee on Labor-Management Policy, which I enjoyed enormously, and I was also appointed to Lyndon Johnson's National Commission on Productivity, which was not as productive as its name suggested. In 1968, I had also accepted a three-year term as a board member of the Federal Reserve Bank of Boston, and after a year, agreed to be chairman of that board for the last two years of my appointment. During my term, we selected a new president, Frank Morris, who went on to serve brilliantly for twenty years. The final choice had come down to Morris or Paul Volcker, and I am sure I made the right choice between those two able people. Volcker went on to distinguished service as chairman of the Federal Reserve System. We also selected a site for a badly needed new building for the Federal Reserve Bank of Boston. The old site had been downtown, but a directive from the Board of Governors that the regional banks should move to the outskirts of the cities—in our case to Route 495—created a problem for our board. We, in Boston, vigorously objected to that provision, and the governors finally allowed us to build the building opposite South Station, after the assembling of several acres to accommodate the new structure. It turned out to have been a sound decision. The old Federal Reserve Bank building eventually reincarnated as an upscale hotel where one can have a drink in a room called the Chairman's Office.

My other days away from the campus were largely during brief periods in the summer. MIT, under the sponsorship of the Ford Foundation and with the encouragement of the state department, had begun a relationship with the Technische Universität in Berlin during the last part of Jay Stratton's term. I was glad to continue that interest and worked with the MIT faculty group that was much involved. It was a constructive follow-up to a visit I had made to Berlin in 1961, in the planning days of the program, when I went there as head of a committee including Frank Reintjes and others to encourage the rapid expansion of computer use in the resurrected institutions in West Germany.

I agreed to go to Berlin in the summer of 1968 after our commencement to open the first German University Computer Convention, to be held at the university with IBM sponsorship, among others. This time, Betty and I were accompanied by the children, and we enjoyed the whole experience. Arthur Ippen, the distinguished civil engineer, himself born in Germany, agreed to translate into German the first pages of my keynote speech. Since I could read it well enough, it was warmly received. We had an opportunity to explore Berlin a bit; while much reconstruction had been done since the days of the war, it still showed signs of damage and destruction. IBM was obviously hoping, along with the mayor, to get some substantial renewal in that city, but the Berlin Wall was up and it was a gloomy and depressing place. In later visits, we came to know Berlin well, and came to respect the spirit and audacity of its people. After several days, our family went on to Frankfurt and, in a rented Mercedes, drove the Romantische Strasse and then on to Linz in Austria. There, we caught the riverboat to Vienna, and after a few days, ended up in Prague in the early weeks of the Dubcek regime.

It was an exciting time during the "Prague Spring." The citizens of Prague were virtually dancing in the streets with their new-found freedom. New newspapers and journals, new theaters and art works, and, especially, boisterous coffee-house conversations marked the days. Through a friend of Carroll Wilson—Josef Karvat, the dean of the Charles University Medical School—we had special glimpses of the times and toured the city with two young professors. We were sorry to leave

Prague, but it was just as well. A few days later in that first week of August, the Russians came in to occupy the country. By that time, we were back in Cambridge. We never saw Josef Karvat again, and apart from an impersonal Christmas card, never heard from him. Later, I learned that he died suddenly before his country's return to democracy. Imagine, having endured so much and then to die without glimpsing the freedom he so desperately sought!

Betty and I also traveled with a few other college presidents to Lima, Peru, for a few days in conference and, on another occasion, to Buenos Aires with Father Ted Hesburgh of Notre Dame.

Those few glimpses at the world beyond the campus and the Washington-Boston corridor made us hungry for a wider view of the world, and we looked forward to days of a little latitude—hence, my hope for some breathing room when I became chairman.

The children were growing up. Steve had finished Belmont Hill in 1970 and entered Lawrence University in Appleton, Wisconsin, that fall. It was not a happy or buoyant time on high school and prep school campuses, either. We attended his Belmont Hill graduation and had the disheartening experience of watching the graduates slouching in procession to get their diplomas in the school's assembly hall. They should have had a better time. But the smell of rebellion and disinterest in the status quo were surely in the air, and the high schools were not immune. The Vietnam war and its grim trappings were, in part, as visible there as on the college campuses.

Laura was looking forward to college, especially a coed one after all those years in Winsor, with some enthusiasm. A year later, she was admitted to Radcliffe. Bruce still had a year to go at Belmont Hill, and when he finished, was admitted to Harvard.

On occasional weekends in those years we went off to New Hampshire, often on Saturday to return to Cambridge on Sunday, and that place of refuge was a lifesaver for us. We had become close friends with our neighbors and with Leon Paquette, the cabinet maker, and Roger Leighton, the forester. Those visits provided happy hours and deepened our interest in the environment, in birds, and in old houses. Gradually, we put together there a tract of well over four hundred acres in scrub New Hampshire woods. On one occasion, we held a reunion of our whole family in

New Hampshire, and everyone came to enjoy two or three days at Christmas in the frozen New Hampshire woods.

The years 1970 and 1971 proceeded in relative quiet. The steam was out of the antiuniversity drive on the part of the strongest radical groups. Some had graduated, some had been expelled, some had disappeared. In those few years there were many departures from university presidential posts in the area The most notable was Nathan Pusey of Harvard, who left office to be succeeded by Derek Bok. We were sorry to see Nate and Anne leave Cambridge. Despite the near-disasters of the past few years, his long term had been very fruitful. In a short time Arland Christ-Janer resigned from B.U., Father Seavey Joyce resigned from Boston College, and Ruth Adams left Wellesley. John Silber arrived to take over the presidency of Boston University in my last year, as sure and scrappy then as he would prove himself to be in the coming years.

The smooth transition that has by and large characterized MIT was taking place. This was no season for parties for outgoing or incoming presidents, and certainly none of us wanted any. Jerry wanted a low-profile inauguration of the kind that was much in style with the rapid turnover of administrations in the sixties. The faculty produced a book of letters to me that I still treasure, and established a special faculty professorship, to be held by me for my working lifetime, which touched me deeply.

So the MIT presidency days ended on happy notes. The old academic council surprised me with a special lunch and speeches that I found very moving. In a way, the term did not end abruptly; I simply moved my office a short distance down the corridor to the chairman's office, which I had reestablished on the second floor of Building 5. I felt it was important for Jerry to have Killian's former office, originally Karl Compton's. As president, Stratton had kept his old office across the reception hall from Jim. It was that office that I occupied as president. Now was a good chance to switch back, and I insisted on doing so. This allowed Paul to move into the central space, and he remained there until Jerry's term ended.

As the student uproar and its faculty counterparts subsided, I had cause, in those last months, to think about the whole matter. What made the campus a battleground in such a vicious and self-damaging way is still difficult to comprehend fully. Although it was a situation of utmost significance and many educators—college presidents most of all—have thought and ruminated about it, few written or even spoken reviews have appeared. Unlike most revolutions, this one produced few accounts by survivors. The reason must be that clear-headed assessments are still very difficult.

The national upheaval that struck the college campuses so severely had no simple explanation. The central cause was the war, of course, and it should be said that the whole sorry episode would have ground on even longer had not the youth of America, so well typified by the best of the college youth, contested and demonstrated against it on such a large scale. But to say the war was the cause of the unrest is like saying slavery was the cause of the Civil War. It was much more complex than that.

The leaders of the young Turks, students and faculty alike, were not the pure idealists they thought they were. In some ways the principal leaders of the students thought of themselves as antifascists, but they frequently used fascist methods. They were often enmeshed in the notions of an extreme conspiracy theory to an extent hard to appreciate today. They credited the political and the military leadership with all the evils of postwar society. They saw conspiracy in everything. They saw it in the university. At MIT, the radical student leadership viewed the corporation as a giant capitalistic conspiracy. Many thought of their parents and professors as sellouts to the materialistic culture. They were willing to bring down the system, as most anarchists are, without a clear plan for the future. They were taken up with the sense that the country was sick and that, if necessary, annihilation was an appropriate remedy. Certainly, in their minds, damage to the college or university was a price that had to be paid for reform. In this, they were often encouraged, sometimes unwittingly, by members of the faculty. Some professors, although relatively few, failed the test of responsibility to their institutions in this way. I remember them now with more sadness than anger. They had let the institute down.

Most of the student rebels were bright and able young people. The leadership in time, predictably, became caught up in a celebrity mode of its own. As one told me in despair, "We have developed our own cult of personality." So they left the scene, disenchanted and still irresponsible—

a word they never accepted. But in their opposition to the war, they had a just cause.

The damage to many universities was real to both the institutions and the individuals close to them. At MIT, I believe we emerged as a stronger institution in many respects. I was often told in later years, as we entered the sixties, that we were divided in the faculty among many clusters of professional and technical expertise and interests. We finished the decade and began the seventies as one faculty, drawn together by the fire and stronger in many ways. We could feel that we had come through a storm, stronger in spirit if not in material resources.

In my last president's report, written for the year 1970–1971, I concluded by reexamining the way we had come through the difficulties:

For us at MIT we have had an opportunity to test our foundations. They are firm. In the most placid of times perhaps the best thing that an administration can do is to get out of the way and let the work proceed. These have not been placid times. The record is there to be examined. We have continued on our path of improving our pattern of education and we have sharpened our old sense of purpose. We are stronger in a sense than we were. But we will need every support we can muster in the future, and we must be bold in calling for that support. Created in a world that is above all a technological one, MIT has too important a calling to be content with less than a preeminent contribution through education, research, and service to the improvement of man's state.

The MIT professors holding named and endowed chairs, 1975

9
Chairing the MIT Corporation and Other Challenges

In late summer of 1971, I found I had a little more time—the first in quite a while—and Betty and I asked my mother to accompany us on a trip to a university presidents' meeting in Bristol, England. We added a few days in the Schleswig-Holstein area of Denmark and Germany, where she was able to experience the countryside of her mother's and father's birth, and where we stayed at a delightful inn, almost on the border, which she loved. At a small shop I overheard her try out a little of her schoolgirl German on a salesclerk. When she made her purchase, she said, "You see, I am not really German. I am an American." "Yes, I know," said the clerk, kindly.

She was to continue her unassuming and gentle style of living for the remainder of the decade, sharing an apartment in Chicago with my supportive sister, and enjoying her last years, secure in the love of her family. She died in June 1979 at age 86. My brothers and I went to Chicago during those final weeks when she lay dying in the hospital, to relieve my sister and to spend some time with my mother. Deathly ill, she spoke her last words to me during one of my hurried weekend trips to Chicago: "You had better run along and catch your train." She was going back forty years to my college days. To say that she was magnificent in her life and at her death is no overstatement.

In the early fall of 1971, Jerry Wiesner was inaugurated. His administrative team was a continuation, in many ways, of the previous five years. As president, he worked closely with me in the chairman's office, and we maintained our cordial and constructive partnership. The chancellor, Paul Gray, took on many administrative duties. Walter Rosenblith was appointed provost. John Wynne and Constantine Simonides completed

Jerome B. Wiesner and HWJ at Wiesner's inauguration, 1971

the old corps, and the rest of the team fell quickly into place. Wiesner had appointed Alfred Keil to succeed Paul in his post as dean of engineering. Bob Alberty in science, Bill Pounds in the Sloan School, Bob Bishop in humanities and social science, and William L. Porter in architecture and planning completed the deans' roster.

One of Jerry's first acts was to enlarge MIT's Committee for the Arts into a broader, more powerful Council for the Arts. We had already discussed this but in the uproar of the sixties, such a change seemed ill-timed. Jerry, wisely, moved to form the council early in his administration, when the timing was just right.

Over time that move stimulated a vigorous new interest in the arts at MIT. Among other things, there was a continuation of outdoor art—sculptures that added verve and quality to our campus landscape. The Great Court, which the corporation formally renamed Killian Court, became the setting for two important pieces. The first was a work by the

British sculptor Henry Moore. When Moore visited the MIT campus, Jerry and I showed him the Killian Court on a beautiful sunny day. As we walked through the court with him and his daughter, he began to show some interest as he gazed around that great space. When he saw the place we had in mind, on the edge of Du Pont Court, he became excited by the prospect. Nothing comes easily, especially in art, and his first choice for a sculpture to come to MIT proved impossible for us to acquire. The second, then situated in Berlin, was available and, with help from many people, we quickly arranged the transfer. The result was marvelous, even more so when we were given a second major work, the long-term loan from the Metropolitan Museum in New York of my own favorite piece of sculpture, Michael Heizer's *Guenette*. The loan of that work was arranged with timely help from Susan Hilles and Graham Gund, and it was placed at the edge of Lowell Court opposite the new Henry Moore. Other major pieces continued to come to the campus. In all these matters Wayne Andersen, then chairman of the Committee on Visual Arts, was of crucial help.

Another great addition to our life as a community was the advent and development of the MIT Museum. For the Wiesner inaugural, Richard Douglas, professor of history, had proposed to me that we have an exhibit of MIT historical objects, and this relatively small step grew over time into the museum. At the beginning, Douglas and I had asked Warren Seamans of the humanities department to work through this project, and the result interested many of us. I asked Seamans to assist me with a special effort in historical collections, and it soon became a full-time undertaking, with Richard Douglas's consistent and active support. First called the MIT Historical Collections and, later, the MIT Museum, the new unit, under Seamans, found, conserved, and exhibited in increasingly high professional style, the history of MIT and of technology in general. Portraits from the past, working models of equipment, and a whole range of historical objects, which had long lain unattended and unappreciated, were soon dug out of cellars and closets and other dusty places. As the repository became well known, new material poured in, and the museum became a favorite gathering place for faculty, staff, and especially alumni. By 1984, the MIT Museum was accredited by the American Association of Museums, unusually quickly for a collegiate museum. Although the present site of the museum is inadequate, I can clearly see the time when it will become more central, more engaged with the whole campus, and more attractive to its audience.

But the principal pressures of the seventies were the financial ones. Chancellor Paul Gray took the lead role in budget control and reduction plans, and over a period of years and with steady effort made good headway. It would turn out to be a never-ending effort. Inevitably, we had to mount a fund-raising campaign. Initial studies indicated that although the climate for raising money is never just right, we needed to consider a campaign that would have two central purposes: to shore up endowments supporting the teaching staff, as well as to build basic funding for the education program; and to complete some much-needed brick-and-mortar programs.

The Second Century Fund of 1961–1966, celebrating the institute's centennial, had concentrated almost entirely on building. Now it was important to emphasis endowment funds. We urgently needed additional staff support for such an effort and began to look for a new head of resource development. We found him in a somewhat unlikely place, the U. S. Army, and it was Jerry Wiesner who first heard of him. He was James Lampert, still on active army duty as a lieutenant general, and best known at the time as the U.S. high commissioner for the Ryukyu Islands of Japan, and as the American who had just officiated in the return of Okinawa to Japan.

Jim was bright and analytical, gregarious and likable, extremely calm under high pressures. He understood the process of organizing large campaigns, and he also held a master's degree from MIT. He was interested when we talked to him, and since his retirement from the army was imminent, he soon was able to come to us as vice president for development. He saw the campaign almost through with great effectiveness, but, sadly, he died before its end. I developed great trust in him, as well as deep affection. He was able to maintain the momentum for planning the campaign, and he pressed us hard to achieve its goals. For the corporation leadership post, we suffered a setback when Carl Mueller had to turn us down because of a critical workload in his home base at Loeb, Rhoades in New York. I was disappointed, and Carl certainly knew it, as he understood that on matters of importance to MIT I was not used to being turned down. Years later, when he volunteered to head the search effort in the mid-eighties to select my successor as chairman, he told me he had never forgotten his own sadness in having to say no to me earlier, and now he wanted to make up for it. He more than made up for it.

To chair the capital campaign of 1975–1980, I next asked Paul Hellmuth, a Boston lawyer of great capacity who knew MIT well, although he was not an alumnus. He was recommended by Jim Killian as someone who had a talent for fund-raising as well as a great admiration for MIT. His residence at 100 Memorial Drive made him a close neighbor, and I had known him through the Museum of Fine Arts. He now agreed to take the post at MIT, essentially a half-time commitment, if I would co-chair the campaign. I quickly agreed. The remainder of the organization soon fell into place, and we began to organize for the big effort, and a big effort it became.

During the month before we went public on the occasion of the regular meeting of the corporation development committee, three terrible things happened. Jim Killian, on whom we were relying for many parts of the fund-raising, and who had been quite active in the early planning, became desperately ill. The illness entailed substantial recovery efforts, including brain surgery to remove a subdural clot. Elizabeth Killian, Betty, and I waited several grim hours at the Mt. Auburn Hospital during the operation and its aftermath. Liz asked me to meet with the surgeon after the operation. He reported to me that he was hopeful about the results, but that we should be prepared for the worst. In time, Jim fully recovered, but he could never again proceed at his former pace.

Second, Uncas Whitaker, whom I had designated in my own mind as the lead corporation donor for the campaign, much as Alfred Sloan had been earlier, and who had indicated that we could count on him, fell dead of a massive stroke at his place on Swan's Island, Maine, as Jerry and I were heading up to see him to schedule the start-up session. Finally, in the fall of 1975, when we planned the campaign kick-off, there was a major stock market decline, and the economic climate proved to be tougher than expected. Nonetheless, we felt that our plan was a good one and that we had to go ahead. And so we did.

We set out to raise $225 million in two stages, and succeeded, by the end of five years, in raising $250 million. By today's standards those

With President Gerald R. Ford and James C. Fletcher, Administrator of NASA, November 6, 1974

preinflationary numbers seem modest, but it was a tough campaign, as all of them are, and it dominated my waking hours for five years. While not all of the designated and planned goals were reached, we did fund over fifty new endowed chairs, our chief objective, and that was a big lift. Along the way we also found some new sources, notably the Japanese. Thanks to Jim Lampert, who had various kinds of entry in that country, we rediscovered early Japanese roots at MIT in the person of Baron Takuma Dan of the class of 1878, who had gone on to found the modern Mitsui Company. Together, Jim Lampert and I sought funding for professorships from a number of Japanese companies beginning with our first visit there in 1973. As a result of our efforts, Japan became a continuing source of MIT funding as the years went on. Sadly for everyone, Jim Lampert died after a sudden onslaught of cancer in the summer of 1978, on the eve of another planned trip to Japan by the two of us. I missed him deeply.

We had the good luck to find his successor among the faculty of MIT. Samuel Goldblith, professor of nutrition and food science, had become an effective fund-raising volunteer on our faculty team, and he agreed, with enthusiasm, to take on Jim Lampert's post. By a twist of fate, Sam had been a newly commissioned second lieutenant after his graduation from MIT in 1940. Stationed in the Philippines when the war began, he spent, as he often put it, four years as a guest of the emperor in grim prison camps in the Philippines and in Japan. Sam was effective in his new post and began a second MIT career that flourished until his retirement many years later.

Carrying out a campaign to raise such a huge amount of money required a massive army of volunteers, and many new alumni and friends joined the effort. Along the way Paul Hellmuth asked to step down as his health problems became serious, but he continued to help MIT. It was he who first proposed the MIT weekends, efforts through which a cohort of potential large donors was brought to MIT for an intensive exposure and education about the institute and its needs. That system, which he adapted from Notre Dame's quite different sessions, continued to be effective in later fund-raising efforts at MIT.

Jerry and I found working together in our new roles to be most satisfying, and the welcome change from campus upheaval permitted travel in the company of Laya and Betty. Our trips outside the country occasionally had a special twist for both of us. In Spain, while attending a conference cosponsored by MIT, we were suddenly invited to see King Juan Carlos at his palace, where we had an unexpectedly serious conversation about the requirements for building an MIT-type of institution in Spain. That was nearly always the question presented to us outside the country: How can an MIT be developed in England, in Germany, in India, in Japan? We had to be cautious, even pessimistic, about the possible success of such a major venture. There was no point in underestimating the breadth and depth of the task. MIT, as has often been said, is sui generis. The form can be duplicated over time, but MIT springs, as we used to emphasize, from the character of the United States—entrepreneurial, inventive, risk-taking, and committed to a range of issues and disciplines that focused on science, technology, industry, and human affairs.

I had been to China with an Aspen Institute group in June of 1978, and in the course of our visit to Beijing, Paul Doty of Harvard and I met with the deputy chairman of the Chinese Academy of Science for general discussions. Out of those unofficial meetings and others came programs for greatly increasing the number of Chinese students who were coming to the United States, and especially to Harvard and MIT, for study. I proposed to the Chinese Academy that a group of MIT trustees and faculty make a trip to China to see the country and visit some universities. The academy responded with an invitation to come in 1980, and we organized a group of some twenty individuals, members of the corporation and the faculty, with their spouses.

After a brief stop-off in Japan, we spent three weeks in China, visiting several cities and attending meetings with government officials and education leaders, and, surprisingly, a group of surviving MIT alumni in Shanghai and again in Beijing. One of the first large delegations to be welcomed by the People's Republic, our group was dubbed "The Gang of Twenty and Chairman How," and the members of the corporation and faculty still remember it with pleasure.

Substantive in content and a wonderful travel experience, the trip was followed, two years later, by a similar trip to Cairo and its university. This occurred after an invitation from Anwar Sadat, with whom I had discussed the idea at a meeting of the Economics Club of New York. Sadat had met with President Reagan in Washington, and as part of his trip to the United States had been invited to address the Economics Club of New York. But complications developed at the last minute in the plans for his visit to New York and to the club. The mayor and the governor declined to attend because of the presumed negative impact on the Jewish vote. The corporate CEO designated to introduce President Sadat had also backed out at the last minute, and the executive director of the club had asked me if I would introduce Sadat at the meeting. Though I accepted with some uneasiness, I felt it was the appropriate thing to do. The meeting, extensively picketed, was held at the Waldorf Astoria Hotel, and businesspeople who filled the room wondered what Sadat would say.

I had the opportunity to spend the long evening with him at the head table, the curtain behind us barely concealing two of his secret service men, one with an Uzi at the ready. Sadat was a man of enormous personal

With Prime Minister Takeo Fukuda, Tokyo, Japan, 1978

magnetism, perhaps the most impressive famous personality I have ever met. During the course of our long conversation and preceding his speech, he expressed the hope that I and a few MIT colleagues would visit Egypt. He went on to address the club in a most engaging and straightforward way. Later he followed his invitation, quickly, by a letter inviting us to visit the University of Cairo, where MIT had a project, and to spend some time visiting the great historic sites in his country. I accepted on behalf of MIT after discussing the matter with the executive committee. Shockingly, Sadat was assassinated in Cairo soon after while reviewing a parade of his own troops. Hosni Mubarak, his successor as president, however, confirmed the invitation to MIT and proposed a similar program. To the

With President Hosni Mubarak and President Hassan Hamdi Ibrahim, Cairo University, February 1982

formal visits were added stops at the Aswan Dam, Abu Simbel, and the Valley of the Kings.

One related incident somehow stays with me. At the conclusion of our sessions at the university, President Mubarak asked about the visits on the Nile that we were about to undertake. I described them briefly and said we were especially looking forward to Luxor and Karnak, and I said, "I suppose you have been there many times." He looked at me and said, "You know, I have never visited those great places. I have often landed at the air field near Luxor, but have never had the time to visit those sites."

With these travels and others to which were often tied resource development objectives, we naturally attained a great sense of cohesion and high morale among the participants. The close friendships formed in those surroundings have endured and deepened to the present day. Although we have since lost several of the participating corporation members, the other comrades in travel have kept the warmth of those meetings much in mind.

On the MIT front during those years, a number of programs also made progress. The Joint Harvard-MIT Program in Health Sciences and Technology continued to evolve on its productive path. While the faculty and trustees at both institutions had separately approved all the organizational aspects of the program during my presidency including appointments and degrees, there were still large requirements to be met at MIT and Harvard. We needed a building to provide a home for Walter Rosenblith's ingenious idea of a college for these important medical activities. I found Helen Whitaker, Uncas's widow, to be deeply interested in the whole field, as her late husband had become over a period of years. Finally, in meetings held in Florida with the newly formed Whitaker Foundation, I asked Helen for $9 million to construct a Whitaker Health-Sciences Building, a gift I was quite sure by that time would be matched by the Pew Memorial Trust, with which I had had earlier talks. The Pew Foundation had been a constructive partner in other programs on the campus, including a major gift that completed the Ralph Landau Building for Chemical Engineering.

The whole amount for the health sciences was finally realized, and it made possible both the medical department building and the Whitaker Building, which housed Whitaker College. The addition of the medical building to the plan was a happy thought that has served the whole institute well. Previously, the MIT Medical Department and its Homburg Infirmary had been housed in a section of the main buildings, and over the years it became hopelessly inadequate for the requirements of the institute. Long-time medical director Dr. Albert Seeler, a quiet, understated professional of enormous quality and ability, had often mentioned to me the needs of the department. He frequently did so during my annual medical exam while pressing me with a stethoscope. When I became president, I assured him that I would seek to find a way to improve the physical surroundings and resources of that great department. Unfortunately, medical service was not as attractive, somehow, to potential donors as the medical research facilities that we had envisioned. The combination, however, of the Pew Foundation and the Whitaker Foundation made both parts of the joint structure possible. Both donors could then justify their support to the research facility, and both could accept the practical association with the medical services department. It was a great idea, as it was a great day when the two sections of the building were finally dedicated.

In the early days of my term as president, I adopted a new guideline for art as a part of new building construction at MIT. It was proposed by Lawrence Anderson, the dean of architecture and planning, and warmly supported by Wiesner, Stoddard, and Simha. We stipulated that one percent of the construction budget for any new building would hereafter be designated for art as part of the project. It took a while to get the process fully in play, but the new provision has added much to the quality of structures at MIT.

Among several building projects also completed in this period, two remain in mind, one ending in triumph and the other in disappointment. During my term, the visiting committee for chemical engineering had confirmed what we all basically knew: the Department of Chemical Engineering was in severe decline. After generations of path-breaking and creative domination of the field, which had been invented at MIT, the department lacked strong leadership, and its facilities were deficient and outmoded. The visiting committee, headed by Kenneth Jamieson, urged that we do something to correct both defects, and of course we accepted that recommendation and set out to act upon it. With first-rate help from the committee, composed of several CEOs from major petroleum companies who had once been students in the department, we appointed new leadership and reinvigorated the department. We built a new building, spurred by a lead gift from Ralph Landau, who while not an oil company CEO, had made his fortune in consulting businesses related to it. That plan for Landau's gift was hatched by Carl Mueller, who applied his usual creativity to devising the process.

The project that produced some disappointment was the sorely needed new major facility for the athletics department. The athletics and physical education program at MIT is one of its brilliant but unsung resources, used by a large proportion of the students, the staff, and the faculty. The program has been the necessary counterpoise to the rigorous academic program at MIT: the fulfilling of the sound mind-sound body concept of old. Pushed by a plan developed by Jim Smith, then the athletics director, and by his visiting committee, we had a fine building designed along with some additional facilities. The proposed project was to meet our need for a new covered hockey rink, and facilities for track and field, basketball, and field-house purposes in general. But money for athletics at MIT, and I understand at other universities, is not easy to raise. We had hoped at the outset that our alumnus Clint Murchison, an owner of the Dallas Cowboys, would provide a lead gift, and Clint had agreed, in principle, with Jim Lampert and me to provide that major amount. Indeed, he pledged it. But the financial upheavals of the late seventies ruined Clint, along with many other Texans, and drove that decent man to bankruptcy—perhaps even hastened his death. We managed, nevertheless, to build a structure with undesignated MIT funds from the campaign and some individual donations, and the new building has served conspicuously well. I am fond of it for several reasons, including the very personal one that, in the mid-eighties, after my retirement and during Paul Gray's term as president, the corporation, at Paul's request, voted to name the building after me. I remain touched and, on occasion, still astonished by their action. My old coach at Bowen High School would be amazed.

The buildings with which I was the happiest, however, were the dormitories and student houses, and we added several in my years. We had badly needed on-campus accommodations for undergraduates and graduate students, and the several new buildings along Memorial Drive, starting with the second McCormick Tower and MacGregor Hall and going west to Tang Hall, have made the life of the students somewhat more pleasant over the years. I had a lot of exposure to the problems of graduate and undergraduate student living and in developing decent living accommodations when I was dean of the Sloan School. I had seen the positive effect of providing quality living space for students, and I was committed to improving the situation at MIT.

One opportunity came at reunion time in 1967, when Reid Weedon of the corporation suggested I meet with a visitor among the returning classes: P. Y. Tang, class of 1923. Mr. Tang wanted to do something to show his appreciation to MIT for helping to make possible the development of his career in China and later, when he went to Hong Kong in 1949 to become a successful textile manufacturer there. In our conversation, I suggested a gift to provide a building with housing for graduate students, and we found a great space on the far west end of the campus. It became Tang Hall and has served generations of students. Tang had sent his son, Jack, to MIT, and later, a grandson, Martin, came to the Sloan School while I was dean. In 1994, the institute broke ground for the new Jack C. Tang Center for Management Education across Wadsworth Street from the Sloan Building. Parenthetically, I note that only the Du Pont, Green, and Whitaker buildings at MIT offer parallels in philanthropic family action at the institute. Ashdown House, named after Avery Ashdown, during my years also served as splendid renovated quarters for graduate students, and the remainder of the student residences down Memorial Drive form a fine riverfront facade for the institute's west campus.

The MIT years thus went on apace, with the usual rounds of federal funding problems that arose during Jerry's term. Between us and our colleagues, led by Paul Gray, the tight and narrow path between being in the black or slipping into the red was successfully negotiated. A key appointment in 1975 was our choice of Glenn Strehle as treasurer to succeed Joe Snyder. We looked at several strong candidates, but in the end settled with great good fortune on Strehle, who has served well and wisely ever since. Later, the growth of the endowment funds of MIT made it inevitable that MIT would finally put a major portion of the endowment in the advisory hands of an outside firm for investment management. With the direction of Glenn and Carl Mueller, the results have been solid, steady, and positive, which is the way that the best of the good endowment managers like to describe themselves.

One side action relating to the MIT financial situation during this time also fell in my lap. The problem was a threat of a major suit, and possibly a major loss, brought against MIT by NCR as an offshoot of a justice department action against IBM. Briefly, MIT owned the patent for the magnetic core memory that had been invented by Jay W. Forrester, which had made possible the fast modern computer; and as a result, MIT in the late fifties had negotiated an agreement with IBM for a royalty payment for each core memory unit the company used. That method of payment had netted MIT (and Jay Forrester) a very large return. Extending that agreement on royalty, in an equivalent sense, to all the additional users of the patent in computer and related applications had meant a steady stream of royalty income to MIT all through the sixties and into the seventies. Then, in the late sixties, the justice department, in its curious way, had brought suit against IBM for its dominance of the computer market and its presumed threat of a monopoly position. The suit named MIT and a few other universities as participants in the effort to make IBM dominant. While that proceeding droned on, contemporaneously with the Department of Justice's other blockbuster suit against AT&T, there was increasing resistance to MIT's pressing for its just claims against the last holdouts in the Forrester patent case. NCR was such a company, and with its tough new CEO, that company decided to bring suit against the institute, encouraged by the justice department action. We had legal help from the law firm of Herrick & Smith and other outside counsel, but I found the firm's chief lawyer on antitrust matters to be a very complicated man, with all kinds of torments about potential MIT guilt and potential MIT loss. He wanted to make a clean "confession" of our possible exposure, and Al Hill supported that plan at the outset. I didn't like the way the case was going.

Despite our lawyers' prediction that the NCR suit would be thrown out, the effort failed and I was reluctant to put Jim Killian, now ill, and an elderly Jay Stratton on the deposition list for the striped-suit lawyers representing NCR. I discussed the matter with Edward Hanify of Ropes and Gray, whom I had long admired. Hanify advised me that if we could settle out of court for MIT, we should do so. I called NCR's CEO, William S. Anderson, and found he was quite open to conversation because he, too, was weary of being pushed by his lawyers and law firms to fight MIT to the end. We met in New York near midnight in the Essex Hotel, and in one hour agreed upon the principle of settlement. NCR would pay a lump sum that was lower than the arithmetic calculation of our formula, which I felt was out of date in any case, and we would hold each other harmless. We settled, and later associations with NCR returned still more revenue to MIT.

Paul Cusick and the Herrick & Smith people felt that we should have gone to the mat, but Ed Hanify and the executive committee were relieved, as was I. Much later, Al Hill, with whom I had our one and only major argument over this issue, confirmed that I had probably done the right thing. As for me, I learned something about the law: Leaving the solution to the courts and to a jury in complex technical cases could produce an unpredictable result, and it should be avoided if negotiation is possible. I continue to hold that view in the light of other similar developments I have seen since.

Being a university president gave me the opportunity to fulfill major responsibilities in areas related to a broader citizenship. MIT presidents had found government service to be an appropriate avenue for this wider response, as did Jim Killian and Jerry Wiesner in Washington during their own active careers. Jay Stratton had become a foundation chairman after retirement as president. Both Jim and Jay had served on corporate boards. My interests tended to move me in other directions, although some government service was possible. I had served on presidential and defense service committees and commissions, but the commitment, except in the case of the Air Force Systems Command, had not been demanding.

Soon after my appointment as chairman at MIT, however, I was asked by the president of the National Academy of Sciences to take on the chairmanship of the Environmental Studies Board of the National Academies of Sciences and of Engineering, although I was not a member of either. The board, newly authorized by the academies, had been charged with choosing vital areas of the environment and setting standards for levels of toxins associated with them and, further, advising with government agencies, and especially the Environmental Protection Agency, on potential problems and possible regulations and legislation related to toxic chemicals. After discussions with several of our MIT colleagues, especially Walter Rosenblith, I accepted. The board was composed largely of academics and, after some delays in staffing, was able to enter an active role, especially in the areas of clean air and clean water. I found this service a wholly rewarding experience, and the patterns set by the board served the country well. I was also able to observe, once again, the remarkable willingness of private citizens in the United States to serve responsibly and with little or no compensation for substantial periods in government-requested service.

One of the members of the Environmental Studies Board was Donald Kennedy of Stanford University, who was to go on to a difficult presidency at that institution many years later. He was one of the brightest of the several very able board members, and his clear head, knowledge, and integrity, as well as his facility for writing and speaking about complex issues of toxic waste, pollution, and remediation, were extremely helpful to us. Listening to him over the many months of our work together, I saw in him an academic with a great future in setting science policy.

I also saw, amply on display, the highly competent but underrated staff persons who take those positions of trust in the government and quasi-governmental bodies. The board's executive officer was a great example of this species quite common in Washington. They were often men and women raised in the committee systems of Congress and the cabinet departments. They knew their way around the system and knew what would sell in Congress.

On a personal level, this experience broadened my understanding of the environment and the issues related to it. It was an even more controversial issue than I had believed earlier. Some problem areas, like point pollution traceable to individuals or organizations, could be handled if standards of evaluation were agreed upon. The broader horizon was more difficult. These problems are rarely within the purview of individuals or organizations and local governments, and as a result the federal government must often enter the picture. I also learned a new appreciation for the role of some private organizations involved in issues like the environment: The Nature Conservancy, the Audubon Society, the Wilderness Society, the Sierra Club, and dozens of regional organizations play an important role in these areas. I also learned about the complexities of testifying before agencies in Congress, and I rather enjoyed it. Most of all, I learned more about the precious and difficult interaction of factors that make up environmental issues. I had some exposure to these issues growing up as a Boy Scout in the big city, and the woodlands, lakes, and rivers had always occupied a magical place in my heart. Now, this experience, obviously broader in scope, gave me new appreciation of the scientific character of the natural surround. Human emotion, irrational reactions, and mendacity, however, still often dominate the discussion on environmental matters.

We were not so well served by staff some years later when I agreed to a different kind of assignment with the National Academies of Science and Engineering, but perhaps the task, coming before its time, was just too difficult. I was asked to serve as chairman of a committee of the academies to examine and make recommendations regarding whether advanced technology industries in the United States were unfairly threatened by Japanese competition. This still was very early in the day for this difficult and emotional topic, and it was one of the first interdisciplinary and public policy issues tackled by the academies. When I demurred at accepting, Frank Press, the president of the National Academy of Sciences, told me that I was the only person he knew he could count on to chair a commission so large and so varied in viewpoint and with members known to having opposing views; the ESB had gone so well and the new topic was so urgent, I simply had to take it on. The panel was indeed broadly composed, and its members included industrial leaders of many sectors and leading academics and public officials in the appropriate areas. We had a year in which to complete the task. We were not well prepared at the onset as far as staff resources were concerned. I was permitted to choose my own outside staff and consultant, and discussed with Bob Solow and others who might serve. They recommended Paul Krugman, who was just beginning his meteoric rise as a professor at MIT, later at Stanford, then back at MIT. But the results were not what I had hoped. Most of the economists who served in various capacities for the group felt that the problems largely arose from the monetary relationships between the countries; as soon as the two currencies reached appropriate levels opposite one another, competition would solve the seeming difficulties. I thought it was an incomplete solution then and although fifteen years later that line of argument is still being pushed, I have not changed my mind.

We were able finally to agree on many things. We concluded that U.S. high technologies were, and would be, seriously threatened by Japan's high tech industry, and that steps should be taken to ensure the strength of vital U.S. industrial segments, ranging from better management and more basic education to vocational training.

There was also agreement on a range of specific steps and, finally, the statement that if Japan continued to keep its markets closed, measures, including tariffs and other mechanisms, would be needed to induce Japan to be more open. We placed much emphasis on the fact that the trade deficit at levels then existing and surely coming would be unbearable, and the panel found it increasingly important that the trade deficit be reduced to manageable levels. Making the report acceptable to all members of the panel resulted in it being somewhat tepid.

The Japanese trade people were not pleased. I probably contributed to the problem by questioning my old friend Saburo Okita at a Harvard meeting on why he and I could not propose methods to bring the countries more closely together on competitiveness issues. He took the position that the market would solve these matters, and, of course, I had to disagree with him.

I have come away from my many associations and exposures to the Japanese with a fundamental and deep admiration for the competence of their industry and the quality of their people, and with a warm affection for those many I have known. I also come away with the strong sense that our two countries will be emotional competitors for a long time to come. I remember my close personal friendship with Yaichi Ayukawa, who had been the first Japanese doctoral student at MIT after the war, and who completed his Ph.D. in food science and nutrition under Professor Samuel Goldblith. Those two became close friends, as did Yaichi and I, and our families. I proposed him for membership on the MIT Corporation in the mid-seventies, and he eventually became a life member, where he served with great effectiveness until his death. I also remember my several meetings with Prime Minister Ohira, starting with his days as minister of agriculture, when he told me that it would be a great and positive thing for Japan to drop its heavy import duties on American agricultural products. He was unable to achieve this, and his untimely death during his term as prime minister was a blow to an earlier mediation of the trade deficit problem.

With the fiftieth anniversary of the end of World War II behind us, I think that still more time will be needed—perhaps time for this generation of veterans to disappear—to finally lay aside the memories of the war. We are now close allies with Japan and Germany, and it is vitally important that we remain so both politically and economically. But let an activity like the Hiroshima exhibit at the Smithsonian Institution arise, and we see that we are still not up to the point of forgetting or forgiving. It is hard to believe that those negative feelings still persist, especially when I am with old friends like the Ayukawas and the Karl Zanders of Berlin, friends and comrades for so long. Perhaps humans have far too long a memory; as Elie Wiesel has said, "We can forgive but we cannot forget." Our children and surely our grandchildren will have a better opportunity to do so.

Another side of my life was the expanded opportunity I had to join some private corporate boards. I had maintained my membership on the Federated and John Hancock boards, although, as I have noted, my attendance and attention to those businesses during the years 1968–1971 were far from perfect. The Federated chapter expanded quickly after 1971. Ralph Lazarus proposed that I become a part-time vice chairman of the board along with Harold Krensky, the former Bloomingdale's chairman and an executive vice president at Federated, with the expectation that we would become a two-man team taking on much of the overall policy management of the company. I felt a large debt to the Lazari and was glad to have some vista away from MIT after the days of the late sixties.

I agreed to spend half my time at this effort, the other half—the home half, so to speak—would be at MIT. Krensky, who was already a commuter from New York, and I, along with Maurice Lazarus, an old friend from Boston, were provided an apartment in a building overlooking the Ohio River in Cincinnati, and we had a great time over a period of two years commuting by Federated plane from Boston to Cincinnati. But it was not a durable solution to Federated's or Lazarus's problems. We made substantial headway in organization and management problems but we were not sufficiently visible, nor present frequently enough, for totally effective management. After a trial period of those two years, I decided to return full-time to MIT. With the campaign coming on, it seemed the best solution. I remained on the board of Federated, and as Harold Krensky became president, I played a somewhat larger role in board affairs, even as age and time began to erode the old structure. By the early eighties, with Ralph Lazarus and Krensky retired, I became less active on the board.

The company then went through the ultimate indignity of being taken over during the peak of the madness of the takeover eighties. This deed was led by a Canadian, Robert Campeau, from Toronto, who bid the price of the stock to such unreasonable levels that the board was unable to hold off the marauders. The takeover was successful, managed by all kinds of investment banker types, and the old board was, of course, fired by the takeover people. Campeau's victory was a hollow one, however. Although several members of the old board accepted Campeau's invitation to remain, I declined, and then watched with absolutely no satisfaction as the company, given its mountain of debt, eventually had to declare bankruptcy under chapter 11. A reorganized corporation under an old Federated hand, Allen Questrom, regenerated the surviving company and the future seems again on solid ground.

During my MIT presidency, I had been approached from time to time by outside companies and regularly declined invitations to join their boards. Now, with more time, I decided to accept three board memberships over a period of three years. Champion Paper, with nearly six million acres of timber in the United States and more in Canada, seemed a natural extension of my environmental interests, and I joined that board in 1970. The invitation came from Karl Bendetsen, who had been introduced to me by my old friend Dillon Anderson. After Bendetsen retired, we hired an outsider to be chairman, but within two years, we had to fire him. His successor as chairman was a young vice president of the company, Andrew Sigler, who went on to serve as chairman until well after I retired in 1993. A Harvard Business School doctoral candidate did her doctoral thesis on that board and its activities during several years. She presented the argument for having a chairman of a corporate board be an outsider. Later at General Motors and other companies, crisis times allowed for such an appointment.

Two other boards had much happier twenty–year-plus terms. I joined the J. P. Morgan Company board in 1971, after several meetings and visits with John Meyer, its chairman, and went on to serve under four more chairmen of that great bank: Pat Patterson, Walter Page, Lew

Preston, and Dennis Weatherstone. It was and is an outstanding banking company with which to be associated, and I learned much about the operations of a leading money center bank in the country. Apart from its quality business, the Morgan still reflects a sense of its history and its great forebears. On occasion, visiting the Morgan Library, once Morgan's home, I could readily imagine the old man sitting at his desk dealing almost single-handedly with the panic of 1907. I left the board after twenty-three years in 1994, and I can look back with intense satisfaction on my association with so many able and decent people. Few companies demonstrate so well the value of high integrity and competitiveness in the control of its business affairs.

Another company of the same stripe but in a different industry was E. I. du Pont de Nemours and Company, whose board I joined in 1972. Crawford Greenewalt had spoken to me from time to time about joining, and now, even though he had retired from the chairmanship and Brel McCoy had succeeded him, they came to me once again to propose membership. I agreed, and on the appropriate meeting day went down to Wilmington and the Du Pont Hotel, where I was to spend many a night over the next twenty-two years. At the appropriate hour the next morning, I entered the company's historic board room and was ushered to the one vacant seat at the table. Walter Carpenter, another former chairman, still active and wise, sat on one side of the vacant seat and said to me as I sat down, "That's the chair that Alfred Sloan sat in." I think I was struck speechless at the thought of sitting in the grand old man's chair, but I regained my voice over the next twenty-two years.

Du Pont was a great experience. I was among the first independent directors. The board members were typically Du Pont family members, active or retired heads of the several big businesses within Du Pont. For example, the head of the textile fibers division was an absolute baron in those days, and he sat on the board and its committees with great personal strength. Irénée Du Pont, our old MIT Corporation colleague, was the last of the Du Ponts to serve in a major management post in the company and also serve on the board.

Besides actively participating in the ongoing work of the Du Pont board, I was a member of the finance committee, the board's nerve center, and chaired the compensation committee for nearly twenty years.

Since the Incentive Compensation Plan had had common roots with General Motors dating back to the 1920s, the rewards for the top executive group were tied closely to corporate profit, and I enjoyed the heavily serious character of the meetings and its participants over the years.

The most important committee efforts were in still other directions. During his term as chairman, Ed Jefferson asked me to organize, and then to chair, a research advisory committee to guide and monitor the new life sciences and pharmaceutical group that he was developing. It was a decade of stirring work. I had decided to ask the deans of leading schools of medicine and other noteworthies in biology and pharmacy to join the committee, and arranged with Jefferson a fee package that was hard to refuse. Over the years, the deans at Harvard, Johns Hopkins, and Tufts, and the former heads of the Hughes Foundation, the FDA, along with Robert Weinberg, my colleague from MIT, Columbia's Cy Leventhal, and Floyd Bloom of Scripps, joined me in quarterly, and sometimes more frequent, meetings with the heads of the life sciences group at Du Pont. Eventually, Ed Woolard arranged to form a new joint enterprise with Du Pont and Merck that allowed Du Pont to capitalize on its considerable investment and at the same time escape with profit from a business that it really could not make into a leader in that period. It was a revelation to work with those able professionals, and some like Tosteson and Weinberg have remained close friends.

In the last several years at Du Pont, I was asked by Chairman Ed Woolard to chair a new environmental policy committee to oversee the concerns and activities of the Du Pont Company in the environmental field, where it was accused periodically of being the nation's number one polluter. The committee, composed of outside board members for the most part, took up its franchise vigorously, and I enjoyed leading the program. By the time of my retirement from the board in 1994, the committee, as well as the several managers who had reported to us over the years, felt that a lot had been accomplished. Committees of this type will be a part of many boards whose activities have a large effect on their environmental surround—and few companies in the natural resources field do not have such involvement and effort. I strongly recommended the creation of such committees in the years that followed.

Many accomplished people sat on the Du Pont board during the years of my tenure, people like Ed Jefferson, Ed Woolard, Hugh Sharp, George Edmonds, Ed Kane, and many others who are not common characters on typical board rosters. The star of the board's work, however, was Crawford Greenewalt, a superb business strategist and a sound technologist who had an uncommon touch with people, and whose wit and taste and wide-ranging interest in so many things around him from music to the photographic study of hummingbirds were amazing to me. He was a truly lovely man. When he died, he left a large gap at the company, which in my experience is a rare event in the history of organizations. At his funeral, the Mozart clarinet quintet was performed, a piece he had often played himself as a clarinetist. I came away from Du Pont with the sure sense that a great organization can keep its integrity and, in so doing, require a higher standard of performance from its people. I was fortunate in my association as board member with a number of excellent companies, but the Du Pont Company remains the high spot of these affiliations.

Close to it was the John Hancock Mutual Life Insurance Company. That experience started badly. The board, of which I was a very junior member, decided to oust its chairman for due cause, and I was asked to chair the committee to recommend a replacement. After this experience, which seemed to go well, my committee—the Committee on Organization—was made a permanent part of the board, and for the next twenty-four years I chaired it, choosing in succession a total of five CEOs. During most of that time, my associates were Richard Hill, Coleman Mockler, and Tom Phillips. Faced with the problem of dealing with a slow-growth insurance business, the company, especially under the long chairmanship of Stephen L. Brown, significantly advanced its standing as a financial services company.

Of a different scope entirely in corporate activities were the board posts on small, start-up companies. In some ways, they were more exciting and the board experience more exhilarating. The best of these later boards was Kenan Systems, the brainchild of a former student, Kenan Sahin. He entered the software field after years of teaching computer systems and management organization at MIT, Harvard, and the University of Massachusetts. He asked me to become an advisor to his firm beginning in 1986 and that role has remained my one active business role. The result of Kenan's focused and prodigious efforts was a successful company of strong potential in a specialized area of the software business. In time, several hundred bright young women and men found it a place to exercise judgment and innovative intelligence and at the same time get substantial experience. These young people, originally mostly graduates of MIT and Harvard but later graduates of many other institutions, created informal, eager, gifted, and energetic teams that were a tonic to watch.

In general, I came away from my associations with these entrepreneurs with a large respect for the contribution to our economic system that these people and their enterprises have made and seen through to success or, occasionally, to failure. I have enjoyed their company enormously, and I have learned much under their tutelage. May their ranks increase.

Along with the numerous corporate boards were many not-for-profit boards. One appointment had a humorous footnote. The secretary of the army had asked me to serve for a term as his civilian aide for the Commonwealth of Massachusetts. I strongly felt that the disappearance of ROTC from many campuses was a mistake and I accepted the post thinking I could speak out on that subject. I gave a few speeches and attended a few meetings to try to explain the colleges to the army and vise versa. After accepting I learned that I would hold the army's simulated rank of lieutenant general as a part of the unpaid assignment. It was to be used, of course, only in the event of some unnamed catastrophe. It was never noticed except when I was invited to Fort Devens in central Massachusetts to have lunch with the commandant. Fort Devens was the only army base left in New England and it served as the center for many U.S. Army activities. On the appointed date I drove up to the commandant's house, and there he was waiting at the head of the stairway of the broad veranda. He was the spit and polish image of General George S. Patton, and well he might have been, for he was Major General George S. Patton, son of the great general. He was trying very hard to look exactly like his father. He saluted smartly as I came up the steps and then extended his hand. His aide later explained to me that the general was well aware that my three stars outranked his two.

General Patton was also under the impression, for some reason, that I was the ice cream Howard Johnson. If Patton was disappointed in the lack of my restaurant heritage, he certainly did not show it. He was a most gracious host as we talked of education, the ROTC, and, surprisingly, the problems of NATO at the present time. We did not discuss our World War II experience. Within a month General Patton was assigned to Texas to command the Second Armored Division, "Hell on Wheels," as we used to call it. This explained his interest in NATO, for the division was soon assigned to American forces in Europe.

The bits of travel in connection with both my corporate duties and with MIT duties paled somewhat in comparison with the family's grand tour undertaken in 1975. June of that year found Steve, Laura, and Bruce all at some punctuation point in their college years, and for the first time we seemed to have some weeks that summer that were not occupied by other duties. Steve was in his last semester's work in graduate school in Wisconsin, Laura was close to the end of her undergraduate years at Harvard, and Bruce, having finished two years at Harvard, found them nearly finishing him and decided on a break before going on. It seemed like an excellent time to get everyone together for a round-the-world tour while we still could all manage the time. After careful planning, we assembled in San Francisco and headed for six weeks that would take us to the Hawaiian Islands, Japan, Taiwan, Hong Kong, Thailand, India, Iran, the U.S.S.R., Turkey, and the U.K.

There was a postscript to this period of my life that gave me much amusement. Over the years at MIT I had often had people say to me, upon meeting, "Are you any relation to the real Howard Johnson?" It was always a difficult question to answer, since the questioner almost always had in mind the ice cream-restaurant man. Sam Proger, physician-in-chief of the New England Medical Center—one of the grand old medical practitioners in Boston and a fellow trustee at Wellesley—brought Betty and me together with the other Howard Johnson and his wife Marjorie for dinner at the Ritz Carlton one evening, and we all enjoyed the experience so much that we repeated it from time to time, much to the delight of the restaurant staff who knew both of us. The other Howard Johnson turned out to be an affable and astute businessman who had a deep understanding of the American consumer and a strong penchant for

Commencement in Killian Court, 1979, the first outdoor commencement at MIT since 1927

sea travel. He and his wife, usually with his physician, Sam, sailed the oceans of the world on long voyages to remote places. The last time I saw him at one of our dinners was just after his return from still another voyage. He spoke to me, quietly and seriously, saying that he was troubled. On this last trip, he said several people came up to him and said, "Are you any relation to the Howard Johnson at MIT?" He burst into laughter, and so did I.

With I. M. Pei and Jan Fontein, planning the new wing of the Museum of Fine Arts, Boston, 1979

10

Boston's Museum of Fine Arts
in a New Era

MIT has enjoyed a variety of associations of different kinds with other institutions. One, of particular relevance to these memoirs, is a long-standing connection between MIT and the Boston Museum of Fine Arts. My own affiliation with the MFA started inconspicuously in the early seventies, and I certainly had no expectation that my role there would expand as it did. In the fall of 1971, I had become MIT's nominee as a member of the board of trustees of the museum, succeeding Jim Killian, who had been elected a trustee in his own right that year. Jim had been MIT's trustee, in turn, succeeding Jay Stratton in 1966. Betty and I had known the museum as members and visitors and occasionally had attended functions there in its rather stiff social atmosphere but we did not know it at all well. This was to change dramatically in 1975.

The Museum of Fine Arts was founded in 1871 as one of the first great art museums in the country, just ten years after MIT's beginnings, by agreement among Harvard and MIT and the Boston Athenaeum. Each institution had named four trustees for a new art museum, with our MIT delegation headed by William Barton Rogers, the founder of the institute. The trustee pattern varied since that time. The Lowell Institute and the Boston Public Library were also named trustees, and the board came to include the mayor of Boston, the Chief Justice of the Supreme Judicial Court of the Commonwealth, and the head, by whatever title, of public education in Boston. By 1966, a bylaws revision required the original founders to name only a single trustee, while the total trustee body grew to thirty-six, most elected by the trustees themselves.

My own exposure as a trustee, beginning in 1971, was strictly as a back-bencher. The president of the trustees at that time, George Seybolt, was a Massachusetts businessman who had succeeded the venerable Ralph Lowell a few years before. The board was composed largely of the Boston Brahmins who had served the museum faithfully and well, and whose families had often served for years along with a small sprinkling of outsiders who were collectors of one kind or another. Such names as Lowell, Gardner, Hilles, Osgood, Coolidge, and Cabot dominated the trustee list. In 1971, as they came to the end of an otherwise gala centennial celebration, the trustees and Seybolt were still smarting from being castigated by the government of Italy for the acquisition of an illegally smuggled painting, which had subsequently been returned to Italy by the chastened trustees. The incident resulted in the departure of a long-time and renowned director and his chief curator, and the museum was now struggling with a search for a new director. Despite these troubles, the museum and its staff and collections were magnificent. While the staff was naturally somewhat dispirited, I found them collegial as I made an introductory trustee indoctrination round.

But the troubles continued. A new director was hired, but he proved to be popular with no one—trustees or staff—and seemed to have little grasp of the problems of a major institution; it was soon proposed to the trustees that the new director be fired. Not wanting to leave, he hinted at legal action. The new president of the trustees, John Coolidge of Harvard, who had succeeded Seybolt, also was struggling; soon, in despair and overwhelmed by the job, he indicated that he, too, wanted to leave office following the annual meeting, after having served only two years. The problems at the museum soon came into public view through a series of highly critical articles in the *Boston Globe* written by its perceptive art critics Robert Taylor and Christine Temin. It was 1975 by this time and my seat was still decidedly in the second tier around the old board table. Nonetheless I occasionally talked with Jim Killian about the problems at the museum, and we wondered what the old guard could possibly do. I soon found out.

In August 1975, I had an unexpected visit in my office at MIT by a subgroup of the nominating committee of the MFA. Their question came after a discussion of the problems in the museum, and it was brief.

"Would I accept election as president of the museum?" I was surprised and not very enthusiastic, given my already jammed schedule, but I said I would consider the matter. Esther Anderson asked pointedly, "If you did take the job, what kind of time would you be able to give it?" They were looking around the chairman's office of the institute and could see that we had a lot going on. I told Esther that I would give it whatever it would require to do it right.

The reasons for my not accepting such a post were clear. We were about to launch a five-year fund-raising campaign at MIT. I was chairing the campaign, with Paul Hellmuth as a deputy. I was also relatively new at the MFA, scarcely knowing all the trustees by name, and not yet fully knowledgeable about the museum's great collections. Still, the proposal had appeal and offered an attractive challenge. Killian wondered whether it was a good idea, but felt that the honor involved would be good for MIT. He told me that the museum had several Harvard presidents over the years, but never one from MIT. Betty thought I should do it. It would be a great experience for me and good for the museum; she must have had second thoughts about it in later years when so many hours of commitment and time were required. Betty Whittaker said that she was willing to carry the extra load it would entail for her. Finally, I said I would accept the position if I were elected unanimously, and at the crowded trustees' meeting, which soon followed, I was so elected.

I addressed the trustees and proposed that, given our several pressing problems, the trustees now meet monthly, instead of quarterly. I welcomed working closely with Jan Fontein, the distinguished curator of Asiatic Art, who had just been appointed acting director. Within the year I nominated Fontein to be the director. He would serve effectively for the next decade. I also wanted full support from the trustees in settling with the former director. That problem was soon settled amicably. I took the following days off from MIT and went to the museum, meeting as many of the staff as possible, and had a long discussion lunch with the curators. I found myself very much at home with the curatorial staff.

The curators, some of whom had been at the MFA for years, reminded me of my fellow professors at MIT—deeply knowledgeable about their own fields and especially distrustful of administrators. They had reason to be. Their competence and commitment to their fields and to the MFA

With Edmund B. Gaither, Director, Museum Program; Elma Lewis, Director, National Center for Afro-American Artists; and Jan Fontein, Director, Museum of Fine Arts, Boston, 1976

were clear, but their morale was down to rock-bottom. The new acting director was one of them in every sense, but the curators now seemed to distrust him as if becoming an administrator had changed him in some fundamental way. The conversations also disclosed a common problem among people who have spent their lives learning about every facet of their own special fields: not understanding well enough the perspective of the whole institution.

The critics of the *Globe* and other regional newspapers were dubious about the new MFA president. They were so used to criticizing the leadership of the museum, perhaps rightly, that they had questions about what could be expected from an MIT president as president of the MFA. In print, several MIT professors, including Jerry Lettvin, came to a roaring defense. The *Globe* was soon to become a solid ally for the museum.

I was determined to find a way to build good administration into the leadership of the MFA, and there was not enough time for Fontein to learn everything on the job, just as there was not enough time for me to become knowledgeable about the artistic fields in any depth. An unexpected conversation with Robert Casselman, an old friend who had been the chief marketing executive for Edwin Land at Polaroid, gave me an idea and an opportunity. Bob had retired very early from Polaroid because of growing problems between him and Land, and I had hired him several years before as a part-time lecturer in marketing at the Sloan School. He was looking for a new challenge, and I proposed one: why not become associate director of the MFA, with responsibility for budgets, finance, planning, and physical plant? I arranged a meeting at our apartment at 100 Memorial Drive with Fontein and Casselman. After an hour, it was clear that we would get along well, and we had the beginnings of a team. It would become in time one of the best management teams in the museum field in the country. The trustees approved the new post and almost immediately things began to improve.

The system we devised—a director who concentrated on the artistic side of the museum, seconded by an administrative deputy—began to be called the Boston plan. It was copied often. We replaced a few key people, most notably the comptroller, and brought in a competent consultant, Ross Farrar, on plant and construction.

A project had been under discussion at the museum for some time to replace the decrepit auditorium, with its slivered seats and impossible acoustics. The MFA-retained architects had come up with dull ideas for such a replacement, and these inspired little interest and no money from the trustees or potential donors. Casselman, Fontein, and I agreed there had to be a creative way to achieve a new auditorium and, perhaps, get the other long-term additions that the museum badly needed. The building was underperforming, the museum shop was barely profitable, the restaurant was losing money and attracting mostly complaints, and the galleries themselves looked worn and shabby. The Huntington Avenue entrance, which had been architect Guy Lowell's inspiration in 1907, was now gloomy and unattractive. All these problems were seen against the backdrop of the museum losing almost $600,000 per year and heading deeper into the red. The endowment was weak and growing weaker. Attendance was declining. Relatively small amounts of money were being raised each year. Overlaying everything was the terrible state of humidity control and air handling in the building; the National Endowment for the Arts had indicated that the MFA was one of the worst museums in the country in this regard.

Could we develop a plan that could deal with some of these basic ills? The solution proposed by the architects hired by the museum was dreadfully prosaic and not responsive to our needs, and its estimated price was far too high. One of John Coolidge's legacies was a study that he had commissioned earlier from a Philadelphia fund-raising company that predicted an inadequate and pitiful response on the part of a large sample of prospective donors to an appeal for funds from the MFA. As I remember it, the total that could be raised in a campaign was estimated at under $10 million—discouraging news. In the meantime, the trustees were reacting positively to the new leadership at the museum: a more visible director, the beginnings of a more active program, and an effort to encourage the trustees to contribute, eager as they were for improvement in the museum. The staff was experiencing a new excitement as we talked to individuals and, more important, listened to them.

We needed a new architect, and I was going to New York for an architecture visiting committee session for MIT, which I. M. Pei was scheduled to attend. I knew Pei, of course, because of MIT building projects, and I wondered if he would be interested in our problem. I made sure to sit next to him, and I presented the idea: would he take a look at the MFA and come up with a plan for us? To my delight, he was much taken by the idea, and offered to change his schedule for the following day to join me in Boston. As it turned out, he knew the MFA well, having frequently spent hours in the Asiatic galleries during his years as an MIT undergraduate. He now wanted to make a contribution to the institution that had served him so well and so often during his youth. Fresh from his triumphs with the new East Wing of the National Gallery of Art in Washington, he was warmly received when I took him for a grand tour around the museum accompanied by Jan Fontein and Bob Casselman. He sparkled with ideas as he trotted from gallery to gallery. The trustees were delighted with the proposal to offer him an engagement, and I quickly fired the previous architect and his group; they were not at all happy, of course, but, then, we had not been happy with them either.

In time, Pei came up with a great set of ideas: a new wing adding a west entrance to the museum, great new space for a gallery, an audito-

The new west wing, Museum of Fine Arts, Boston, 1981

rium, increased storage space, a new restaurant and shop, the renewal of old spaces with more gallery footage, better climate control, and a plan to renovate the old entrance, which included opening, restoring, and making visible the great Sargent murals in the second floor domed entrance. The Huntington Avenue entrance would again be an important portal to the museum. Circulation of visitors would be vastly improved by completing the circle of galleries and reducing the number of dead-end corridors. Bob Casselman and Ross Farrar contributed mightily to this proposal, and finally we had a worthy plan. It was expensive, but I believed we could rally museum supporters around us. I pressed hard on the trustees, and suggested that contributions of one percent of net worth were not unreasonable. Almost all responded in that range.

If a few trustees left us, many more came forward. Helen Bernat, a trustee who had volunteered in the museum for years and who was, with her husband, Paul, a major donor, agreed to serve as cochair of the campaign along with Paul Hellmuth—her "other Paul," as she liked to say. Peabo Gardner—George Peabody Gardner—agreed to be honorary chairman of the campaign. A few days later, Harry Remis, not a trustee but very interested in the museum, came to Jan and me and said he was prepared to give us $1 million "cash on the barrel head," to pay for the new auditorium. I was elated and used the promise of that gift to generate more. Over a period of time, we raised almost $30 million for that effort.

But pledges are not paid off early in such a campaign, and we used the Massachusetts not-for-profit lending agency, MIFA, heretofore largely used for financing higher education buildings, for a ready draw so that we could go ahead. In succeeding administrations, without people like Helen Bernat, money-raising efforts declined and a sizable debt accumulated largely driven by new projects like the new Museum School building and a much-needed garage. Lesson one for not-for-profit institutions is to keep the fund-raising activity vibrant and deserving.

But those problems would emerge only later. From 1975 to 1980, when I served as president, the growing enthusiasm seemed permanent, The budget deficit declined each year, and our goal of breaking even by 1981 was achieved. We also dealt with the problem of the exhibit schedule. The MFA had lost its position on the national and international circuit in the first five years of the decade, and although we were now quickly readmitted, the lead-time for planning and scheduling major exhibits was three to five years. While we got back on track quickly, there was a dry spell that could not be avoided. In addition, the upheaval of the physical plant caused by renovation of the old building and the addition of the new wing made even the routine exhibits difficult. But soon, attendance figures improved. The long-vacant curatorship of paintings had been filled by the arrival of John Walsh, the former Metropolitan Museum curator, then a Columbia professor, who later became director of the Getty Museum. I liked John immediately when Jan Fontein invited him to visit the MFA, and I knew we had to get him. We did. He, in turn, recruited Theodore Stebbins, of Yale, who remained at the MFA as curator of American paintings and as a great force for scholarship, taste, and entrepreneurial endeavor. These two, along with the redoubtable Jonathan Fairbanks and several others like Cliff Ackley, who gradually replaced the legendary Eleanor Sayre, revitalized the program of the museum.

We had some new ideas for attracting visitors while many galleries were shut down for renovation. Clementine Brown, the MFA public relations head, contributed a particularly attractive idea. In the late seventies, a rebuilt and renewed Boston Faneuil Market was being completed under the architectural hand of Ben Thompson and the entrepreneurial and promotional genius of James Rouse. Rouse realized that the new marketplace could not flourish with only fast food restaurants and T-shirt shops, so he tried to upgrade the ambiance. Knowing this, Clem and I talked to him about a contribution of some free space, perhaps 10 to 20,000 square feet, for a museum branch or a satellite museum well positioned in Faneuil Hall. Jim liked the idea and proposed a great second floor space. A problem remained, of course, raising the money to make what was essentially warehouse space into a pleasant museum. I went to the Boston Foundation, which had decided to emphasize public education, and our idea appealed to their director. Their subsequent grant allowed us to redo walls, windows, floors, and skylights, and to deal with the major security and fire-prevention problems. We also needed program money; Andy Sigler and Champion International quickly provided $100,000. The experience so pleased Champion that, when the new headquarters for the company was developed in Stamford, Connecticut, the first floor of the building became a satellite of the Whitney Museum of New York; and art, through rotating exhibits and other programs, became a fixture in a city that was seeking to reclaim its urban interest.

The MFA Museum at Faneuil Hall flourished for three years and allowed our total attendance to stay close to the 900,000 level while restoration and construction at the main building went on. But costs were a problem, and when Rouse proposed to charge a hefty square-foot rental for the fourth year and beyond, in contradiction to his earlier proposal, the trustees voted to close the place. That was after my term as president, but I supported the cancellation. Still, the MFA was bringing art to the working men and women of the city, as well as to the crowds of visitors from the suburbs and tourists at the market. In retrospect, I think the idea was splendid in concept and quite good in execution. Our artistic and management staff had greatly improved.

One major force in the work of the MFA was the ladies committee, that talented group of women originally organized by Mrs. James

Lawrence and Perry Rathbone, and it glowed anew through all these adventures with enthusiasm and solid accomplishment. The committee, with the great help of Chuck Thomas of the museum staff, developed "Art in Bloom," and a spring week of flowers associated with art became a classic festival that has continued ever since. We expanded the membership of the museum, a step to which I gave great priority. It was helpful to talk to supporters and doubting Thomases alike about the 30, 40, and finally more than 50 thousand paying members who had a special interest in the museum's case. Even the leadership of the city of Boston, traditionally distant from what many perceived as an elitist organization, began to notice such numbers.

Paul Hellmuth and Helen Bernat had a great idea for a type of inner circle extension of the special givers of the museum. They proposed that we create a larger giver group of members, called patrons, who would give $1,000 each year for the privilege of belonging, and in return, get a ringside view of the museum. It seemed like a great deal of money, but the campaign to enroll patrons, with Helen's strong effort, greatly expanded. The patrons program is now a mainstay of the operating budget of that great museum.

Finally, by way of broadening our base and getting past the public impression that a small group of insiders ran the museum, I looked around for ways of having more diverse people get into the governance arena. Two groups were organized. The overseers, eventually a group of over 100, met twice a year to review the program and practices of the MFA. They elected the trustees and participated in the visiting committees and the many special programs of the museum. After a slow start, with enthusiasm sometimes waxing and sometimes waning, the idea went forward. While the overseers varied in their commitment to the museum, they provided a nurturing ground for potential trustees and an amplification chamber for the president and the director. It was a good idea and continues now, in a very strong way, to provide the best kind of support for the MFA.

The second group was one proposed by the indefatigable Kitty White. One did not have to study the trustees too closely to see that their average age was high, over sixty. It was very difficult to bring someone under forty into that relatively small group. Accordingly, we organized a new body, the museum council, that was made up of younger supporters, collectors, and doers in their thirties and forties, and even younger on occasion. The idea was to bring them into the museum and to let them develop a program that suited their youth and their interests. Because the council members turned over more rapidly than the overseers, the group had a natural self-renewal process, and it worked effectively for a time. It soon became clear, however, that better ways of engaging these museum supporters would have to be invented.

Events at the museum took on a special glow after what many felt had been several years of somnolence. With renovations of old galleries and a return to the national circuit for special exhibits, excitement returned to the museum. We initiated "free days" and "free evenings" to encourage families to come to the museum. General attendance at the museum continued to expand dramatically. Even more important, new groups were being reached. College students, for example, had always been welcome but admission prices and the cumbersome process of applying for student memberships inhibited many. We asked several universities in the Boston area to contribute an annual fee that would admit all of their students. MIT, I am pleased to report, was first to join, followed by many other schools. Special visitors often returned to see and, on occasion, be seen. One evening, Fontein and I found ourselves playing hosts to Jacqueline Kennedy Onassis, with a crush of people seeking to get a close look at her. I, too, was much aware of Jackie's knowledge of many of the notable works of art. I was taken, too, by her breathless, whispered conversation about the paintings. She certainly deserved her star reputation.

What impressed me most about the magnetism of the museum, however, was how it attracted individuals to work, study, and learn about the exhibits. One who came to work was Edwin Land, who had developed a large Polaroid lens that could function in a room-sized camera with room-sized film. By taking pictures on such a colossal scale, he could reproduce copies of the great museum works that showed the precise brush strokes of the original. We cooperated with him in developing the lens, and he produced many exciting works over a period of years. For a long time all seemed to go well. He would say to me, with his intelligent mind

With Jacqueline Kennedy Onassis and Jan Fontein at the Museum of Fine Arts, Boston, October 8, 1975

projecting fire through his eyes, "Howard, if we can make the exact art of Monet available to the average person just as authentic sound recordings are possible by the new stereo apparatus, we will have made a major contribution." He would in the end do so, and even the expert eye could not see the difference until one was within a few inches of the picture. But, alas, the public never bought the idea of the product on the scale that he had hoped. He was disappointed, but I do not think he ever gave up.

Nothing could mitigate the problem of space, which remained the chief difficulty until the new wing was finished. In the summer of 1981, it opened, a spectacular addition to the MFA. By that time, I had finished five years as president and had recruited Larry Fouraker, dean of the Harvard Business School, to succeed me. I became the chairman of the new board of overseers and planned to give it a strong effort.

I cannot leave the story of my five years as president, several more years as chairman of the board of overseers, and chairman of the executive committee without a comment about the portraits of George and Martha Washington, painted from life by Gilbert Stuart. The furor caused by the Smithsonian Institution's proposal to buy and take them from Boston in 1979 was front-page news and, unfortunately, occupied a lot of my time.

The portraits are icons of American history. Painted from life by Gilbert Stuart, they were copied again and again by Stuart, his daughter, and generations of copyists. The tight-jawed face of Washington represented on the one dollar bill is a copy of the Stuart portrait. The two great pictures belonged to the Boston Athenaeum and had come to the MFA in 1871 at the time of the founding of the museum as two of several "on loan" pictures from the Athenaeum. That venerable institution was now having severe financial problems and pressures, and new leadership on its board of trustees had embarked on a campaign to raise money for the Athenaeum by selling its paintings, one by one, as the financial wolves snapped at their heels. The MFA had managed to buy a few of these great paintings, but had been forced to pass on more than one major American work, including a great Trumbull.

It had been assumed by the MFA staff, wrongly it turned out, that the Stuarts, so much a part of Boston, would remain forever in the museum. Looking back on it now, it is clear that there had been a frightful lack of communication between directors and others at the two institutions, and the Athenaeum staff had been as much in the dark on the new program as the museum staff. Now, suddenly, an ultimatum was delivered in a most ungracious and un-Bostonian way: Did the MFA want to top an offer for the Stuarts of $5 million from the National Portrait Gallery of the Smithsonian? If so, it said in effect, please remit the check immediately. Fontein was dumbfounded when he called me, and so was I. The possibility that the portraits could be recalled had never been raised, to my knowledge, although much later my predecessor as president, John Coolidge, told me that the idea had been mentioned to him.

In response, I went immediately to Washington, D.C., and learned the truth from the ambitious director of the National Portrait Gallery and his deputy. They wanted to secure these treasures for the "nation's capital where they belonged rather than in a regional museum." I returned to Boston to discuss the situation with the MFA trustees. Most wanted to resist, but no one had any idea of where to raise the money. We were in the midst of the drive to build the new wing; that project clearly had to be a priority. Walter Muir Whitehill, a longtime major Athenaeum figure and the venerable secretary of the museum trustees, was horrified, and he counseled me to fight.

But the Athenaeum was adamant; "put up or shut up" was their message. While we had several crossover trustees, including James Ames and Susan Hilles, they seemed unable to influence the outcome. We leaked word of the problem to a few individuals outside the trustees, and soon the *Boston Globe* was on to the scrap. The *Globe*, of course, loved the story as it pitted Brahmins against each other. The mayor of Boston, Kevin White, decided it was good political smoke, and phoned me to talk about it. I minced no words, saying, "Kevin, Boston will lose the Stuarts and we need help." White jumped in with both feet. He held a news conference and likened the proposed deal as comparable to the Nazi plunder of European art during World War II. White's involvement made headlines and editorials all around the country, and evoked all kinds of countersuggestions. The Athenaeum and the Smithsonian were pictured as the villains, and the MFA was seen as a hapless and defenseless victim. A Herblock cartoon in the *Washington Post* depicting the Boston colonials defending the pictures against the big money Federals humorously described the situation.

But it was not funny to me. I proposed publicly that all who could help should contribute to a campaign to raise the $5 million. I also searched around for other possibilities, of which there were few. It was reported in the newspapers that Ross Perot had indicated that he might be able to help. Grasping at every straw, I called Perot. He said that he would consider buying the portraits to keep them from the Smithsonian, and I proposed that we could share them half time each over the years. "No," Perot said, "if I buy them, I will want them full time here in Dallas or in my offices." That quickly ended the conversation.

We proceeded to organize some kind of campaign. General James Gavin, the commander of the famed 82d Airborne during World War II, whom I had come to know well at that point, came forward and volunteered to lead the campaign against the takeover. The general, one of the authentic heroes of World War II, was furious about the proposed removal, and the "bureaucrats who dreamed it up." In the meantime I had negotiated informally with the Smithsonian's associate director to permit the MFA to have the portraits for a fraction of the time, if the Smithsonian succeeded in buying them. I wanted one year in each five. The Smithsonian, sitting with a strong hand, said they thought one year in ten was possible and, as a matter of fact, generous. When that idea was proposed, the Smithsonian trustees and the leadership of the Smithsonian wanted a complete victory and refused to accept even nine years out of ten as their fair share. That was the final straw for me.

Immediately, I went back to Washington, D.C., to a meeting arranged by a mutual friend there with the well-known director of the Smithsonian, Dillon Ripley. The meeting produced nothing. Ripley was overbearing and said Boston's gloomy corridors were no place for these American treasures. I found him difficult, despite his reputation and our common interest in birds and birding. He told me, speaking from a set of talking points prepared by staff at the Portrait Gallery, that they could expect up to two million people a year to view the portraits in Washington, whereas Boston could never have more than a million. Years later, on a television program featuring the presidential portraits in the National Portrait Gallery, a gallery official indicated that their attendance ranged up to four hundred thousand a year, and they thought that was quite good. So much for the earlier bureaucratic overstatement on the part of the Smithsonian!

During this period of turmoil, I was bombarded with phone calls, including one from an old friend, William Burden, the chairman of the Institute for Defense Analyses, and a regent of the Smithsonian. He said that it made no sense for Boston to have those portraits, and no part-time arrangement was acceptable. I remember his telling me, "We can't have those great paintings shuttling back and forth between Washington and Boston." Our relationship later healed, but for the moment the air between us was quite frosty.

Gavin and I decided that the only way we could win was to turn up the public relations heat, and we did. Public meetings in Faneuil Hall and around the city tried to drum up support for the "Washingtons Belong in Boston" campaign. We had broad support from many individuals, but the amounts contributed were relatively small. Boy scout troops gave dollars, tourists gave coins, and one remarkable lady gave $100,000. One or two local foundations helped. The John Hancock Mutual Life Insurance Company provided invaluable office and record-keeping support. Our concern about detracting from our main drive for the MFA, however, was a real handicap. In the end, we raised a substantial amount, but it was below the $1 million we sought as our minimum to play the game.

In the meantime, I kept in close touch behind the scenes with the Athenaeum. They had reluctantly given us a year to raise the money, and we still sought some accommodation. Finally, James Ames, who was a trustee of both the MFA and the Athenaeum, came to my office, and we hatched an idea of splitting the ownership 50–50 with the Smithsonian, with the paintings moving back and forth every three years. The three-year period helped ease the problem of conservation, and with the paintings beginning the alternate program with a Washington exhibition, we began to work out a further accommodation. I proposed that the Smithsonian should pay somewhat more than we, and ultimately the Smithsonian paid $2,750,000 and the MFA, $2,125,000; the Athenaeum took $125,000 less than the $5 million they sought. People on all sides said it was a fair and wise compromise, and even the mayor seemed mollified.

Fontein and I went down to Washington for the opening of the exhibit with the Stuarts in the National Gallery, and we managed to smile, stiffly, during the proceedings. I thought, in fact, that the arrangement was quite a good compromise. The museum kept significant ownership, the Athenaeum and its eager leaders got a little more money to deal with their budget problems, and the citizenry seemed happy. In a way, the museum appreciates the portraits all the more, and their periodic homecoming is a joyous occasion. Jim Gavin, whom we had elected to trusteeship at the museum by that time, gave a party at the MFA for all the volunteers, and he and I recited, together, unplanned and unrehearsed, the lines from Shakespeare's *Henry V*: "We few, we happy few, we band of brothers. . . ." The whole venture consumed a great deal of time, and it slowed our program at a critical moment. I will always regret that the situation developed as it did, but once thrust upon us, it was difficult to see how the MFA could have avoided the subsequent steps. The great not-for-profit institutions have more than enough outside opponents. They do not need to battle among themselves. In time, fortunately, friendships and close professional associations resumed between the MFA, the Athenaeum, and the Smithsonian.

Many other incidents took place along the way in my term at the MFA. We revitalized the museum presidents' association—a meeting every year of the presidents of the eight, and then the ten, leading general museums in the country, and this helped to keep us in touch and cooperate more effectively on a variety of matters. During one of the periodic assaults on the budget appropriation for the National Endowment for the Arts, I was designated to testify before Congressman Yates and his House budget subcommittee. Later, I. M. Pei and others told me that my testimony and that of Beverly Sills turned the tide, in that cycle at least.

I finished my term as president in September 1980, and the new wing was almost ready. In a final burst of effort, we had the exterior of all the old buildings cleaned, and the new structure looked magnificent. The wing was officially opened in July 1981, and Larry Fouraker, my successor, asked me to preside at the festive dedication party under tents on the back lot. The new wing opened as planned. There were speeches, music, and all the normal fanfare, creating a wonderfully festive atmosphere. All the usual local dignitaries attended, but one outside speaker stole the show. We had called on Barbara Bush, the wife of the new vice president, to represent the world outside Boston and New England. George Bush is the brother of an ardent Boston participant in the MFA, which is how the invitation was secured. Everyone was taken by Mrs. Bush, who remained with us the whole day.

The new wing and the subsidiary changes in the buildings and galleries changed for much the better the ways in which the museum functioned. Major exhibitions now came to us, and a great Renoir show seemed to demonstrate what could be done. The operating budgets of the museum were in solid condition. When Bob Casselman retired, Ross Farrar, who was a tower of strength, succeeded him. When Fouraker finished his term and Dick Hill his, the museum was in the black and had comfortable reserves with which to face the future. I agreed, at Hill's request, to serve as chairman of the new executive committee. When George Putnam succeeded Hill as president, it seemed to Jan and me that at last the MFA was on a sustainable roll.

Richard Hill had arranged for Fontein, who had led the museum so well for so many years, to return to a distinguished curatorship, which cleared the ground for a new director and a new chapter in the museum's history. The way now seemed clear for new and positive things. The museum, however, was to encounter difficult financial times once again. Fortunately, the tide again soon reversed. The museum, after a few years of difficulty, moved on to another chapter with a new director, Malcolm Rogers, and new trustee leadership. The museum has emerged with vitality, stability, and new momentum.

Having finished twenty years as a trustee in 1991, and since I had been the one to propose that trustees become "honorary" after twenty years, I felt obligated to follow the pattern. That tenure plan had been adopted as a guiding principle but not a requirement. I do not doubt, however, that the idea of retirement after a certain period, be it ten or fifteen or twenty years, is a good idea. It infuses the board with new blood and it helps deal with the problems of an extended tenure. The museum's old reputation had its roots in long membership terms, and I was intent on changing that.

In accord with the plan, I was elected an honorary trustee and president emeritus. I benefited so much from my involvement in the museum, and I enjoy seeing the museum move forward in many ways—its collections, its programs, its attendance. Recently at a dinner in Portland, Maine, a table companion commented on a friend of hers, saying with some awe, "You know, she is an overseer of the MFA and she is in on everything there." I nodded and thought how great it was that our little plan to expand the circle of involvement in the museum seemed to be working, in Maine at least.

The West Wing and all it symbolizes made the modern Boston museum possible, and I will be forever grateful for the opportunity to have played a role in building it.

There was a curious addendum to my museum chapter that puzzled me for a long time. In the winter of 1977, I had a telephone call from Douglas Dillon, the long-time chairman of the trustees of the Metropolitan Museum of Art in New York. I had met Dillon sometime before at the Council on Foreign Relations and also at the museum presidents meetings, but hardly felt that I knew him. He said he would like to meet with me on museum matters. Not knowing what the subject might be but assuming it was a general museum topic, I met with him in Boston, and later in New York, where he was accompanied by Richard S. Perkins of the Metropolitan board. The upshot of the meeting was a proposal that I become president of the Met—a new idea for a paid position to report to the trustees. The whole matter would have to go before the trustees, but Dillon assured me that he was quite confident of a positive closure to the proposal. They had decided that the added post of president and chief executive officer, a full-time position, was necessary to give the museum cohesiveness and help it deal with the realities of the modern world. The relationship between the president and the director of the museum, then Philippe de Montebello, was ambiguous, but they were sure that the details could be worked out. They were convinced that there would be few problems and much to be gained by the proposed arrangement. Issues of salary, living space, transportation, and so forth, had been addressed. I was, of course, fascinated by this proposal, but I also made it clear to Dillon and Perkins that I was unlikely to accept the offer. After giving the matter serious thought, I sent a declination letter within a few days. I concluded that I was too involved at MIT and leaving it would be too difficult. Dillon was courteously understanding. In time, they appointed a distinguished former diplomat to the job, and the new plan continued for the next twenty years.

I do not think the idea is a sound one, conceptually. Surely the management of complex art museums is a job that needs competent reinforcement of several kinds. To separate the artistic direction from the basic management functions also has some merit. But ambiguity at the top has special perils in the art world. I would prefer a chief executive officer who is the chief artistic officer and have at his or her side a deputy director for management who reports, as always, to the chief executive. The chairman of the trustee body is the overall policy head. Whether he or she is compensated or is a volunteer depends on the situation.

With Betty, 1998

11

MIT Goes On

In 1980, I was coming to the end of nine years as chairman of the corporation. I had found the years working with Jerry to be most rewarding. We had continued to enjoy a very close association, and I felt that we both worked well with the corporation, the faculty, and the staff. It had been a good fit and remains one of the best periods of my life and Betty's. As 1980 approached, with the campaign successfully concluded, it was time to plan for a successor to Wiesner as he reached age sixty-five. Jerry was more or less bound by the old rule of retirement, and he was ready for it. He wanted, of course, to continue his working association with MIT for some years, and he hoped that he could participate in major efforts toward improving relations with the Soviet Union and disarmament programs. I looked forward to working with him.

I appointed a search committee of the corporation, chaired by Carl Mueller, and we began that important process once more. Although there were serious looks at outside candidates, I do not believe that anyone in the executive committee was surprised when the recommendation came that Paul Gray should be the next president. There was a proviso, however, stipulated to me by a subgroup of the search committee, headed by Ralph Landau. I was asked to continue to serve as chairman for a minimum of three years. After brief discussion, it seemed reasonable to me to remain as chairman and work with Paul in the same way that I had worked with Jerry. Jerry was named Institute Professor, to be effective on his retirement, and he moved to his new life with great satisfaction.

The familiar step of the sedate yet happy corporation meeting at which Paul was elected MIT's fourteenth president now took place. Then, at a rather exuberant faculty meeting in Room 10–250, the announcement of Paul Gray's election was followed by great applause and the institute was off once again on a new chapter. The transition was predictably smooth and the work of the institute continued with Paul and Priscilla Gray comfortably assuming the roles of president and first lady.

The years from 1971 to 1980 had been important ones for our family's life. The years ahead, in a new partnership with Paul Gray as president, seemed a natural progression. During my years as chairman, we had moved from our temporary home in Wellesley Hills to the chairman's apartment at 100 Memorial Drive, on the MIT campus. That building, built on institute property as an investment by the New England Mutual Life Insurance Company in the early 1950s, was a self-contained village of its own. We lived in the penthouse, which had been constructed with housing for institute officers in mind. It had dramatic views of Boston, the Charles River, and the Boston skyline from Charlestown to Harvard. We had enough space to entertain, but it was not so large as to seem institutional. The one great defect in the apartment was its poor insulation and its heating system, which was not totally effective when temperatures hit the twenties and below, which they often did in Boston winters. We learned why the sitting room fireplace was so heavily used by our predecessors. Our wood supply from New Hampshire and Maine was vital to living comfortably in the apartment.

In 1978, Boston was hit with the "storm of the century"—up to two feet of drifting snow that throttled the city for a week. I made my way home from New York, walking the last distance through head-high drifts. On the thirteenth floor we felt snowbound, but the views of snow-covered Boston were magnificent.

We took on a whole new range of social responsibilities with the corporation post. Betty perfected the corporation lunch that followed the commencement in a way that became a tradition. As commencement took place in early June, she was able to prevail on the caterers to have Atlantic salmon, served cold with a dill sauce, a good white wine, and fresh strawberries for dessert. This was a pattern that pleased all of us after several hours of sitting and watching the graduates receive their degrees.

Since 1979, commencement takes place in Killian Court. The commencement speeches, which we reinstituted after a request from the graduates themselves, varied in their effectiveness, but I remember best the

With Virgilio Barco, President of Colombia, 1980

speeches of Helmut Schmidt, Virgilio Barco, Paul Tsongas, and Kay Graham.

The hours away from the institute for thinking, touring, and calling on a variety of our constituencies all over the country became more numerous and memorable during my days as chairman. We and the Wiesners often traveled together on business, but we also did so for pleasure. On the recommendation of Helen Whitaker, we visited the island of Sanibel on Florida's west coast. We returned several times and in 1977 bought a small condo on the island. It was a great lift to find a few days on the calendar and open the door to our place on Sanibel, even for just a long weekend.

It was not as dramatic as our earlier exposure to Costa Rica, which deserves its own footnote. In 1971 at a Harvard dinner with the Puseys, we met Donald Menzel, the Harvard astronomer. He urged us to visit Playa Flamingo, an isolated stretch of beautiful beach on the Pacific coast of Costa Rica. It was a small development by an enterprising Canadian who wanted to sell pieces of breathtaking land to a few people to ensure his own ownership of a much larger piece. On our first visit, we stayed for only a few days and then, after another visit, we bought a lovely piece of land overlooking three bays on the Golfo Papagallo, about fifty miles south of the Nicaragua border. Our plan was to join with a few other Americans in this new and beautiful community. A local architect and builder was quickly engaged, and he built a great house for us on the crest of a marvelous bluff overlooking the Pacific. Our few visits encouraged us, but the indelible fact of the lack of time to get to Costa Rica for more than a few days each year quickly became apparent, as it should have at the outset. We sold the house in 1974 to a Costa Rican friend who, in accordance with an old Costa Rican saying, promised to hang our hat on the rafter to ensure future visits. The saying didn't work in our case, and we never returned.

But the memory of that coastline, with its long white crescent of sand, its green jungle full of birds almost to the edge of the sea, with roseate spoonbills, parrots, and motmots, and its glorious sunsets, often returns to us. The recollection of that beach looking over the wild bay, as natural as it was when it was created, fills me still with a sense of beauty and nostalgia that made the whole venture worthwhile. I suppose it was an echo of that experience that made us turn to Fort Myers and Sanibel when the time came. Although it could not be compared as a physical setting to Costa Rica, it had some of the attributes, the birds and the natural beauty, that drew us back again and again.

Through all of these diversions and complementary involvements, MIT, of course, continued to be the abiding focus of my life as my term as chairman continued during Paul Gray's presidency. My pattern of working with Paul in the MIT structure from the executive committee of the corporation to the faculty was not wholly different from the pattern with Jerry Wiesner. After all, the three of us had developed the system. Gray and I were not as close as Wiesner and I had been, but we had a solid working partnership and the institute programs progressed well. Paul had appointed Francis Low, the distinguished physicist and a survivor of the 10th Mountain Division, as provost. When Low retired five years later, John Deutch, whom I had known well since he was appointed head of chemistry years before, succeeded him. John would go on later to key assignments in the Department of Defense and as head of the CIA. The strong line of provosts at MIT, which was to continue through Mark Wrighton and Joel Moses, moved forward the work of the institute.

MIT Corporation China visit, March 1980

One issue that had developed considerable heat and prolonged debate during my last three years was the proposal by Jack Whitehead to endow a major new enterprise in the molecular biology field at a suitable leading university, such as Stanford, Harvard, or MIT. The proposal had made an earlier appearance at MIT during Jerry's presidency. Jack Whitehead, who had made a fortune in health care technology, visualized an institute that would be *at* a university and receive the locational benefits, but would not be *of* the university. There was the rub. He wanted to make professorial appointments in the associated university, and he wanted those people under control of the new institute, which meant, of course, Whitehead's control. It was a condition that no university could stomach. He tried this proposal at Harvard and MIT, and when he came to Jerry and to me, we said a clear no, as Harvard had. As far as one could see, so did Stanford and a few others. Duke finally said yes when some changes were made, but the idea soon faltered, much to Whitehead's chagrin. To his credit, however, it must be said that he learned along the way.

In the meantime, he had found an individual in whom he had full confidence to direct the Whitehead Institute: Nobel Laureate David Baltimore of MIT. Whitehead said he would put the new institute and its accompanying dollars anywhere Baltimore wished. The conversations under the new plan were well under way with Wiesner, Rosenblith, and me before Paul came into office. But now the continuation of the discussion and a fleshed-out proposal became Paul's job and mine, as well as that of the Department of Biology. We were greatly enthusiastic about the idea of a plan that would bring major new resources to biology at MIT. Although we had strongly backed the new biology in the preceding years, we now needed more support, including facilities, if the full promise of this field were to be realized.

Gradually, the idea took shape in a way acceptable to us as well as Whitehead. The issue of appointments of professors at MIT was settled quickly. MIT would control the appointment process, as always. The director would be an MIT professor; the first would be David Baltimore, who was the main source of ideas for the new organization besides Whitehead himself. The governing body of the Whitehead Institute became broader than originally planned, and it included several MIT appointments. In total, $150 million would be invested in the Whitehead Institute and, in addition, MIT would receive endowment funds for professorships and fellowships. Jack Whitehead would have no direct role, although, obviously, he remained the major force behind the scenes. His children were to be appointed board members and this next generation has served impressively. I have often reflected on how well the process of passing responsibility to the next generation worked in this instance.

A satisfactory arrangement finally took form. In the process, we had many meetings with Whitehead at the offices of his law firm in New York. That firm had been founded by William Donovan, the American leader of the OSS during World War II, whose portrait presided sternly over the board room where the discussions were held. The actual negotiating team for Whitehead was headed by an able, tough-minded lawyer who reminded me of Federated's lawyers in times past. They approached the negotiations as though they were leasing a shopping center. On the MIT side, Paul Gray, David Baltimore, Bob Sullivan, and I gave as good as we got.

With the proposal ready, we now had the challenge of gaining the acceptance of the corporation and the faculty. We had kept the executive committee fully informed and involved, of course, and had reported the matter to the whole corporation at several quarterly meetings. There were understandable misgivings about this unique model, including the basic question "Why couldn't Whitehead just give his money like everyone else?" The answer lay in Whitehead's nature and the sheer amount of money involved. Jerry, Paul, and I had spent a lot of time going over the matter with Stratton and Killian. They were not persuaded, Jay for purest academic reasons, Jim because of his negative perception of the donor. In the end, all they would do was commit to not speaking or voting against it. I and the others were disappointed. It turned out to be somewhat worse than that; Jim rose in the next corporation meeting and said, rather stiffly, that he, as an emeritus member of the corporation, would not participate in the discussion on Whitehead. His tone spoke volumes. Members of the executive committee and several others in the corporation spoke enthusiastically for the proposal. In the end, John Wilson, a long-time friend, took a stand against the proposal, for reasons still unclear to me. Many members of the corporation of Wilson's generation, including Tom Cabot and Bill Coolidge, tried to point out the extraordinary benefits of the proposal to the field and to MIT. In the end, however, Wilson, along with Greg Smith and a younger member of the corporation, voted to defer the proposal. The rest of the corporation supported the Whitehead Institute idea, but it was the first real split that I had ever seen within the corporation, and I regretted that it came to that.

The faculty meeting was even more boisterous. Paul Gray did a masterful job of mobilizing support in a partly divided faculty. Although we had fully involved the biology department and the dean of science in our discussion, there were several vociferous opponents on the faculty, notably Bob Mann and Ascher Shapiro of mechanical engineering, and Anthony French of physics. During several meetings the debate raged, mostly around the issue of the control of appointments by the faculty and the corporation. In the end, the vote was overwhelmingly in favor of the proposal.

More than ten years later, the Whitehead Institute has proven its productivity and strength in the field, and its relationships with the Biology Department at MIT, while not without some tensions, are very solid and effective. We would not be the leaders in biology today were it not for the Whitehead Institute.

Jack Whitehead, ironically, died suddenly on the ski slopes within the decade, but I never saw any sign of his wavering from his substantial commitment. I concluded that there was no hidden agenda in Whitehead's mind. He really did want to give a large part of his wealth back to the system, and he saw the eventual plan for the Whitehead Institute as the vehicle. He stayed with this idea consistently, which I found admirable. David Baltimore served conspicuously well as the director of the new institute, and despite enormous pressures on him, he too never wavered in his effort to interlock the Department of Biology and the Cancer Research Institute with the new Whitehead Institute. In later years, he became, first, president of Rockefeller University, and later, president of the California Institute of Technology. His successors have carried on very well.

As the promised three years came to conclusion, I felt it was time to step back from full-time administration. I had spent seven years as dean, five as president, and now twelve as chairman, a total of twenty-four years at top administrative assignments, and it was time to step away. I informed the executive committee, after having told Carl Mueller and a few others earlier, that it would soon be time to start another serious fund-raising campaign and that it was important to prepare a chairman who would enlist for the whole effort. Further, Paul was now well experienced in the presidency, so it was clearly time for a new chairman. The corporation was agreeable as long as the new candidate to do the job was found, and I agreed to carry on until that condition was met.

There was a timing problem. With the exception of Vannevar Bush, who served as chairman in the late fifties, the chairman had always been a former president. Jerry was the logical candidate now, but he had said earlier that he was not cut out for that post and, besides, he was now sixty-eight. The bylaws stipulated that the chairman had to be a member of the corporation and that gave us a wide field. Paul Gray suggested that David Saxon, an alumnus with three MIT degrees, just completing his final year as president of the University of California Statewide System, and with a few years' experience as an MIT corporation member, was an obvious candidate. Paul met with David, and I talked to him at some length. Yes, he was interested, and in the end he accepted. I finished my term in June 1983 and was succeeded by David Saxon, who served for the next seven years in harness with Paul Gray.

Leaving the chairman's job involved a few formalities, all of them pleasant. The corporation had a grand evening for Betty and me, and in addition to Jerry and Carl Mueller, Paul Gray, I. M. Pei, and others spoke. I was moved by all of their words, and even more by the sincerity and sense of comradeship. The post was my most satisfying job, and I had a feeling of sadness in leaving it.

I became a life member and honorary chairman of the corporation. I also returned to teaching, occupying the post of faculty professor, which the faculty had established some years earlier, uniquely for me during the remainder of my life. That unprecedented step was taken by the faculty in 1971 at the last meeting of that body over which I presided. The chairman and the secretary called on Robert Solow, my old colleague, to present a resolution establishing the new chair. When the body stood and applauded, I was deeply moved. As I looked at that assembly in Huntington Hall, I saw many individuals with whom I had campaigned so often in the past. MIT always had been an institution of high standards, but it was fair to say that it was often a loose alliance of professional cohorts. Now, still independent as always, the faculty had stood together and, while often disagreeing, cohered as a community of scholars under the most intense pressure. I will always remember the faculty that way— resolute and together.

Each year for the next three years I taught a management seminar in the Sloan School. I required the course participants to be undergraduates with an interest in management, and limited the class size to twenty or a few more. I covered a series of topics from organization to ethics. It was a great experience for me and, I believe, for most of the students. I also had a group of freshman advisees each year, several of whom have gone on to major careers. I was struck by how advanced these students were in areas like computers and mathematics, music and languages, and how much they had traveled and accomplished. At the same time, they seemed to me naive and inexperienced about the world in general. The lack of life experience showed. After three years of this activity, I felt I had accomplished most of my purpose in getting a sense of what the current student was like. For the first time in more than twenty years, I had gone back to the classroom, and I found I still enjoyed it.

By 1990, I was ready to slip the bonds of a strict regular schedule, and I quickly adjusted to the less restricted life of a former president and chairman. I had plenty to do. I had been a trustee of the Alfred P. Sloan Foundation since 1983, and in 1987, when Tom Murphy retired as chairman, I was asked to assume the chairmanship. Most of my predecessors

Bruce, Stephen, and Laura, 1986

had been former General Motors chairmen. Sitting in Mr. Sloan's old conference room, I could not help thinking of the days thirty years earlier when I, somewhat unsure and uneasy, would come to the very same office in Rockefeller Center to call on Alfred Sloan and his colleagues on behalf of the management school at MIT.

A first task as Murphy's term came to an end was to find a new president, since Albert Rees, my old Chicago classmate and colleague, was retiring from that post. We sought out Ralph Gomory, whom I had known when he was the head of research of IBM. He was retiring from IBM at age sixty and we persuaded him to join the foundation as president in the second year of my term as chairman. I continued for the next seven years, presiding over the board of the foundation, overseeing and supporting Gomory's administration. The grants program was the core of the activity, and it was exciting to see it develop. I also enjoyed seeing the endowment grow substantially over this period. We accomplished this with the help of a strong market, but the decision we took to reduce the levels of General Motors stock held by the foundation was also sig-

With Harold Edgerton, Media Laboratory, 1990

nificant. I was sure of the wisdom of this move both for fiduciary and diversification reasons. I retired as chairman at the required age of seventy-two in 1995 and turned the gavel over to Harold Shapiro, the president of Princeton, feeling that I was closing the loop with Alfred Sloan that had begun forty years before.

When I retired from the Sloan Board, I could see my more formal organizational involvements coming to an end. This was not stressful to contemplate. I was ready for a little more space on the canvas, and in this regard, I was always grateful that MIT provided office room and secretarial support for former presidents. I was especially fortunate in this sense. The incomparable Betty Whittaker had gone on to become associate secretary of the corporation and had been succeeded by, first, June Ferracane, and for the past ten years by Muriel Petranic. At one point, Killian, Stratton, Wiesner, and I had active offices. Then, in a relatively short time, the other three were gone—Jerry and Jay within months of each other. I miss their conversation and their collaboration. Each of the former presidents was different from the others, but our experience and commitment to MIT made us a special band. I was especially close to Jerry, having worked with him for nearly thirty years. He and I each had an office in E-15, the Media Laboratory, at the invitation of Nicholas Negroponte, and I never had more hospitable surroundings. Later, shortly before his death, the building was named in honor of Wiesner. I still miss him.

Paul Gray's years as president came to an end in 1990 as he completed ten years in that office. His decade had passed very constructively for MIT. The choice of a successor was once again before the institute, and once again, the corporation committee was chaired by Carl Mueller. This time, however, in full recognition of the times and of the system, a faculty advisory committee, chaired by Robert Solow, worked in tandem with the corporation committee. It was a constructive development with wise chairmen and strong committees. In due course, Charles M. Vest of the University of Michigan was elected president, and Paul Gray, the chairman of the corporation. Vest had served as provost of Michigan, having previously served as the dean of engineering at that institution. Once again, it was a fitting choice. In 1997 Alex d'Arbeloff would become chairman of the corporation when Gray retired from that post.

New problems and new issues coexist with the verities of university administration: providing continued high-quality education and research under increasing financial pressures. The opportunities have never been better, and the responsibilities never heavier.

Retirement from the relatively unbending daily schedule has given Betty and me a chance to travel more and to enjoy two homes—one in Florida on the Gulf of Mexico, and the other on the Atlantic Ocean in New Hampshire. We have enjoyed our little grandsons—now three in all—and are grateful to have seen them develop personalities of their own.

I recall now a dinner staged by the XVI Military Region in France to which my old commanding officer, Bill von Seggern, and I were invited in March of 1945, as one could see the war in Europe grinding to a close. My table companion on one side was a cynical French major from the staff of the military region in Montpellier. We had seen a lot of each other the previous months, sometimes under difficult circumstances, and I told him how happy I was that we would soon see the end of this war— the last on a world scale. He violently disagreed and drank some more. He said that he had served in "la guerre de quatorze," and now in the sec-

With Paul E. Gray and Jerome B. Wiesner, October 1979

Aerial photograph of MIT, 1996, with Kendall Square beyond

ond, and he knew that the nature of man was to nationalize, to develop hatreds, and then to fight. We disagreed strongly that evening, with my argument based largely on my belief that man, forced by the threat of grim new technologies, had an ability to learn. How does that argument look fifty years later? I know that I was too optimistic. While we have escaped a global war for all these years, there are constant savage and regenerating regional wars with no signs of letup. The cost of competing armaments still remains horrendous. With the cold war ended, however, there are some positive signs. I am optimistic that the new century, about to dawn, will provide a time for large-scale improvement in prospects for peace around the world and that society can fully concentrate on other global issues.

Once again, I am in a personal time of adventure and change. Change is always a stimulator, and if it doesn't occur too frequently, it is good for the soul as well as the mind. I have always looked ahead with a kind of curiosity and excitement to what awaited me around the next bend in the road. I find I have that outlook now. That is the way I expect to look at the next chapter, however long or short. For me, at the close of the day, I am grateful to have lived my life in the twentieth century and to have lived most of it at MIT.

Coda: A Note for Students on Leadership

I think about the careers of our students whose working lifetimes will stretch fifty years into the future. Technology and politics will change dramatically and so will the venues, the economics, the methods, and even the character of work and the workplace. But the satisfactions that human beings derive from working together will not change. Work interactions will still be among the first satisfiers for average citizens during their lives. Trust, confidence, participation, and the opportunity to learn and be rewarded will still be goals to be achieved.

Students, understandably, have always had a deep interest in career paths. During this last decade, because the organization of work has changed so rapidly, that interest is sharper than ever. They have occasionally come to me and asked two questions: First, how does one become president of a university; and second, what things should be kept in mind in leading or guiding this kind of organization?

In my case, I concentrated on an academic career after I completed a good part of my graduate work. I enjoyed teaching and working with students. I felt an exhilaration seeing students grow, just as I found satisfaction in discovering new knowledge and new ideas. I found, however, I needed to enter the real world from time to time to verify the life of the mind. I soon found that, given the opportunity, I also enjoyed managing an academic group. It echoed experiences that I had earlier in my life. As the groups grew larger, the tasks grew in difficulty but also in satisfaction. One needs the opportunity to learn these new skills and approaches, learning from success but also learning from failure.

Trying to understand a working group is fascinating, and it is satisfying to choose people and see their growth, and feel a sense of cohesion develop within the group. I urge students to stay out of management if this does not appeal. As I went on, I found it was important to understand the informal as well as the formal structure. I was fortunate to have some great counselors along the way, and I had great good fortune in my working partners. Trust and competence and a common wave length to facilitate communication are critical in this process.

At a relatively early age I was offered new and more complex responsibilities, and I welcomed them. It helped enormously that I also had the never-failing support of my wife. Without that, nothing would have been worth the effort.

When I came to MIT, my only goals were to become a professor and to be the best in my field. The administrative posts that came to me later were the result of unpredictable events. They represented major risks on the part of those who made the appointments. Had I failed, I was well aware that they, too, would have been disappointed.

I have told students that the only part of a career path that they can control in large part is their own preparation. I have always been lifted by the statement attributed to Abraham Lincoln, "I will study and get ready and, perhaps, some day my chance will come." That is a statement of hope justified occasionally by reality. But the preparation process is, in itself, worthwhile regardless of the outcome. Beyond preparation, a student can assess the quality of the organization and the people within it, and then stay away from, or plan to change, those of doubtful quality.

People have often told me sympathetically that I was unlucky to be elected MIT's president just before the storm of protest and unrest broke across the country and across the world. I never felt that way. One cannot control the times of one's own life in any case. They are the only times one will have, and the problem is to optimize every opportunity. True, I had high hopes of accomplishing certain goals at MIT. So does every president; so did the corporation and, certainly, so did the faculty. Then the storm came, but I was probably a better president in terms of accomplishment during times of adversity than during prosperity. I left the presidency without regret except for the work still undone. Fortunately, the MIT system allowed some continuity.

But the students ask: When you get the chance and you have the opportunity, how do you manage a large organization? These are complex matters, difficult to imagine without being immersed in the situation. I counsel students to spend a lot of time thinking about the nature of the job and what they want to accomplish. The prime need at an early point is to set high standards and to build a special society of accomplishment, responsibility, and purpose. Gone are the days when one can assume that people in the organization will follow a leader automatically at a highly productive level. It is important to understand fully the nature of the place and its technology, and where it should go. People need to trust; they need examples of high competence; they need mentors, and they need an opportunity to contribute and belong.

The method and the point of view are clear in outline, difficult to do well in practice, but worthy of the effort. At MIT, the pace of learning is often likened to getting a drink from the fire hose. Okay, as they say in the new world, here is a drink from the fire hose on leading in difficult times:

• Assess the situation, the constituencies, and the history; understand them in depth. Take time to think. Believe in your goals. Include in the process enough personal reconnaissance so that the data become trustworthy and alive. A word about *personal reconnaissance:* The words are Penn Brooks's, learned as a young lieutenant. One understands a situation by seeing the people firsthand, listening to what they say, and, most important, studying the process. Listen to everybody. It is amazing how many good ideas one gets from the least likely sources. Incidentally, the much advertised "open door" is excellent policy in tranquil times, but it tends to favor the bold and the chronic responders. I prefer to get out into the field and see and hear the other people.

• Surround yourself with a top team. Delegate fully and expect information in a timely way. Give the team all the credit.

• Develop the goals using all the knowledge and information possible, but remember that, in the end, the leader is not one who averages the opinion and strikes the median, or mediates the extremes, but is one who sets high goals that inspire by quality and reach. All depends on the quality of the decision. Be sure you have it right, but be prepared to make adjustments along the way. Then, act in a timely way.

• Be inclusive in thinking about the scope of participation by members of the organization. Do not be exclusive. Management is not a secret society. Be visible, not only on the lofty dais, but in the work place.

• Communicate clearly and often what is being done, and why. This includes communicating with the entire organization from trustees and directors to the outer reaches of the organization.

• In times of trouble, the leader really earns his or her pay. Expect opposition and try to learn from it. Few people get the kind of battle they expect. Do not engage your opponents on their ground if you can possibly help it. Stay flexible and stay cool. Never panic. Keep your sense of humor.

• Stay connected with the broad world and the broad economy. Keep your perspective.

• Be worthy of the trust of the organization. In the end, it is the only reward worth having.

The goals of different organizations will vary, but these points are constructive in most of them. In a university, for example, the faculty must maintain its own independent commitment to education and intellectual development. The members of the organization have a right to expect efficient governance. They do not need blandness in leadership; they need encouragement to deal with the difficulties. But, in return, the members of a faculty carry a large responsibility for the students and for the institution.

The changes in the academic landscape since World War II are vast and striking. New factors reinforce the older model that so aptly characterizes this most focused of American universities. MIT is broader in its definition of technological problems, broader in the fields it requires and nurtures, broader in its view of the universe, and more diverse from the viewpoint of gender, race, and place of birth of its people. We take pride in our increased international responsibility and reputation. The institute values its role as an intrinsically American institution that responds not to class structure but to merit and accomplishment. MIT and other institutions of higher learning will be asked to play an even greater role in the society of the twenty-first century. We will all be diminished if they do not.

The changes in the business landscape are probably even more far-reaching. Reorganization and restructuring are the order of the day for the competitive firms' world. But let no one assume that the verities of human satisfaction—trust, confidence, and fairness—are less important. The task of management in the new century is to make it possible for employees to achieve these important goals as well as to drive the business in terms of productivity and profit. Will it be possible to meld these two sets of goals? I believe so, but only time will tell. That is how I conclude this note on leadership. I have a sure sense that the years ahead will provide challenges enough and rewards enough for those who seek the responsibility for holding the center.

Sources

In writing these memoirs, I relied on my own memory of the events and times and on the indispensible help of Elizabeth J. Whittaker and Muriel A. Petranic. Where we could, we drew on our own files. We were helped immensely by the MIT libraries and archives, Elizabeth Andrews and Donna Webber, the MIT Museum, Michael Yeates, the files of MIT's Tech Talk, and Loretta H. Mannix. I also used the services of the public libraries in Rye, New Hampshire, and Sanibel and Fort Myers, Florida.

Apart from massive coverage in periodicals of the time, there are few eye witness accounts by observers and administrators of the late nineteen sixties and early seventies. For those who may want to consult other accounts, I recommend these publications: William J. McGill, *The Year of the Monkey* (McGraw-Hill, 1982); Robben W. Fleming, *Tempest into Rainbows: Managing Turbulence* (University of Michigan Press, 1996); Roger Rosenblatt, *Coming Apart* (Little, Brown, 1997); Douglas Knight, *Street of Dreams: Nature and Legacy of the Sixties* (Duke University Press, 1989); Warren G. Bennis, *An Invented Life* (Addison Wesley, 1993); and Richard M. Freeland, *Academia's Golden Age* (Oxford University Press, 1992). The following articles are cited in this book: "Come Squeeze or Bust, in Ho-Jo We Trust," *Fortune*, May 1970; "MIT: New President Will Pursue Broadened Goals," *Science* 151 (March 25, 1966); "Universities: The Man Who Cooled MIT," *Time*, November 21, 1969; and "Art and Money," *New England Monthly*, October 1987.

For the reader who would like more background on the World War II chapter, Civil Affairs, and the invasion of the south of France, I would recommend: Phillipe Burrin, *France under the Germans: Collaboration* and *Compromise* (The New Press, 1997); Ian Ousby, *The Ordeal of France, 1940–1944* (New York: St. Martin's Press, 1998); *La Libération de Montpellier, Août 1944* (Aristide Quillet, editeur, Paris, 1945); Tzvetan Todorov, *A French Tragedy: Scenes of Civil War, 1944* (Hanover, N.H.: University Press of New England, 1996); Geoffrey J. Clark and Robert Ross Smith, *Riviera to the Rhine* (Washington, D.C.: U.S. Army Center for Military History, 1993); Harry L. Coles and Albert K. Weinberg, *Civil Affairs: Soldiers Become Governors* (Washington, D.C.: U.S. Army Center for Military History, 1986); Robert Zaretsky, *Nîmes at War: Religion, Politics and Public Opinion in the Gard, 1938–1944* (University Park: The Pennsylvania University Press, 1995).

Registry of Names

Below are brief identifications of many of the individuals mentioned in the text. The information provided is intended to help the reader identify these individuals and does not represent a complete biographical history.

Ruth M. Adams (1914–)   President, Wellesley College, 1966–1972. Vice president, Dartmouth College, 1972–1988.

Morris A. Adelman (1917–)   Joined the faculty of the MIT Department of Economics, 1948; professor, 1969–1987.

Robert A. Alberty (1921–)   Dean, University of Wisconsin Graduate School, 1963–1967. Professor of chemistry, MIT, 1967–1991; dean, MIT School of Science, 1967–1982.

Sidney S. Alexander (1916–)   Assistant professor of economics, Harvard University, 1946–1949; with International Monetary Fund, 1949–1952. Economic adviser, Columbia Broadcasting System, 1952–1956. Professor, MIT Sloan School of Management,** 1956–1986.

*Theodore M. Alfred (1925–)   Held faculty/staff positions, MIT Sloan School of Management,** 1955–1967; visiting associate professor, Indian Institute of Management, Calcutta, 1963–1965. Professor of management policy, Weatherhead School of Management, Case Western Reserve University, 1967–. Associate, then acting dean, 1968–1972; dean, 1972–1984.

Wayne Andersen (1928–)   Joined faculty of MIT Department of Architecture, 1964; professor of architecture, 1968–1986.

Dillon Anderson (1906–1974)   With law firm of Baker and Botts, Houston, Texas, from 1929; partner from 1940. Special assistant to U.S. president for national security affairs, 1955–1956.

Esther D. Anderson (Mrs. E. Ross Anderson) (1915–)   Volunteer, Museum of Fine Arts, Boston, 1964–; trustee, 1971–1990; vice president, 1973–1990; honorary trustee, 1990–; (honorary) governor of the Museum School; MFA Benefactor, 1984.

*Lawrence B. Anderson (1906–1994)   Faculty member, MIT Department of Architecture, 1933–1965; named professor, 1944; department head, 1947–1965; dean, MIT School of Architecture and Planning, 1965–1972.

*Martin C. Anderson (1936–)   Faculty member, Graduate School of Business, Columbia University, 1962–1968. Special assistant to U.S. president, 1969–1971; assistant to U.S. president for policy development, 1981–1982. Senior Fellow, Hoover Institute on War, Revolution and Peace, Stanford University, 1971–.

*W. Gerald Austen (1930–)   Named chief of surgery, Massachusetts General Hospital, 1969; surgeon-in-chief, 1989. Professor of surgery, Harvard Medical School, 1966–1974; Churchill professor of surgery, 1974–. Life member, MIT Corporation, 1982.

David F. Austin (1898–1986)   With US Steel Corporation, 1934–1958; vice president, 1934–1954; executive vice president, 1954–1958.

*Yaichi Ayukawa (1923–1991)   Held research managerial positions in several leading Japanese companies before becoming the founding president of Techno-Venture Company, Ltd., in 1975. Life member, MIT Corporation, 1987.

David Baltimore (1938–)   Joined faculty of MIT Department of Biology, 1968; named professor, 1972. Nobel Prize in medicine, 1975. First director, Whitehead Institute for Biomedical Research, 1982–1990. President, Rockefeller University, 1990–1991; professor of biology, 1992–1994. Returned to MIT as Cottrell Professor of Molecular Biology and Immunology, 1994; named institute professor, 1995. President, California Institute of Technology, 1997–.

Pietro Belluschi (1899–1994)   Professor of architecture and dean, MIT School of Architecture and Planning, 1951–1965. National Medal of the Arts, 1991.

*Warren G. Bennis (1925–)   Professor, MIT Sloan School of Management,** 1959–1967. Provost, State University of New York, 1967–1968; vice president, academic development, 1968–1971. President, University of Cincinnati, 1971–1977. Distinguished professor, business administration, University of Southern California Business School (Los Angeles) 1980–1988; University professor, 1988–.

*William B. Bergen (1915–1987)   With the Martin Company (aerospace division, Martin Marietta Corp.), 1937–1967; executive vice president, 1955–1959; president, 1959–1967. With North American Aviation (later Rockwell International), 1967–1978; group president, aerospace division, 1971–1978.

Helen Bernat (Mrs. Paul Bernat)   Volunteer at the Museum of Fine Arts, Boston, from 1956 until her death in 1993; trustee, 1966–1993; vice president, 1978–1983; vice chair, board of trustees, vice chairman, board of overseers, 1984–1986; honorary trustee, 1986; and great benefactor, 1989.

Aneurin Bevan (1897–1960)   Leader of the Welsh miners in the 1926 General Strike in Britain. Labour member of Parliament from Wales, 1929–1960. Minister of Health, 1945–1951; held major responsibility for developing and implementing National Health Service.

Robert L. Bishop (1916–) Joined MIT faculty of economics, 1942; professor, 1957–1986; department head, economics and social science, 1958–1965. Dean, MIT School of Humanities and Social Science, 1964–1973.

Raymond L. Bisplinghoff (1917–1985) Faculty member, MIT Department of Aeronautics and Astronautics, 1946–1968; named professor, 1953; on leave 1962–1966 serving as associate administrator, National Aeronautics and Space Administration (NASA); head, MIT Department of Aeronautics and Astronautics, 1966–1968; dean, MIT School of Engineering, 1968–1970; chancellor, University of Missouri at Rolla, 1974–1977.

Fischer Black (1938–1995) Professor, Graduate School of Business, University of Chicago, 1971–1974. Professor of finance, MIT Sloan School of Management, 1975–1984. With Goldman, Sachs and Co., 1984–1995.

Floyd E. Bloom (1936–) Chief, laboratory for neuropharmacology, National Institute for Mental Health (NIMH), 1968–1975. Professor, Salk Institute, 1975–1983. Director, division for preclinical neuroscience and endocrinology, Scripps Research Institute, 1983–1989; chairman, department of neuropharmacology, 1989–.

Derek Bok (1930–) Joined faculty of Harvard University Law School, 1958; named professor, 1961; dean 1968–1971. President of Harvard University, 1971–1991. 300th Anniversary University Professor, Harvard University, 1991–.

*Welles Bosworth (1868–1966) Architect who created the plan for the MIT Cambridge campus and designed the first buildings dedicated in 1916. Other achievements included the reconstruction of the Palace of Versailles following World War I and the Egyptian Museum in Cairo.

*Rodrigo Botero (1934–) Economist, served in several government posts in Colombia, including special assistant for economic affairs to the president, 1966–1970; minister of finance, 1974–1976.

*Edward L. Bowles (1897–1990) Joined MIT faculty of Electrical Engineering, 1921; professor, 1937–1963. During World War II consultant to Secretary of War Henry Stimson. Consulting professor, MIT Sloan School of Management,** 1963–1969.

*Edward H. Bowman (1925–1998) Joined faculty of MIT School of Management,** 1952; professor of management, 1964–1966, 1969–1974. Dean, Ohio State University College of Administrative Science, 1974–1979. Professor of management, MIT Sloan School, 1979–1983.

Kingman Brewster, Jr. (1919–1988) Provost, Yale University, 1961–1963; president, 1963–1977. U. S. Ambassador to Great Britain, 1977–1981. Master, University College, Oxford, 1984–1986.

*William S. Brewster (1917–) Executive with USM Corporation, 1939–1976; chairman and CEO, 1968–1976. MIT Corporation member, 1970–1975.

*Edward Pennell Brooks (1895–1991) With Sears, Roebuck in several executive positions, 1927–1951, director, 1941–1951; MIT Corporation member, 1941–1946; first dean, MIT School of Industrial Management, 1952–1959.

Douglass V. Brown (1904–1986)   Joined faculty of MIT Department of Economics and Social Science, 1938; named professor of industrial relations, 1943; Alfred P. Sloan Professor of Industrial Management, 1946, serving in MIT School of Management** until 1974. Chairman of MIT faculty, 1949–1950.

E. Cary Brown (1916–)   Economist, U.S. Treasury Department, 1942–1947. Joined faculty, MIT Department of Economics, 1947; professor, 1958–1986; department head, 1965–1983.

*Gordon S. Brown (1907–1996)   Joined faculty MIT Department of Electrical Engineering, 1939; named professor, 1946; first director of Servomechanisms Laboratory, 1939–1952; department head, electrical engineering, 1952–1959; dean, MIT School of Engineering, 1959–1968; Dugald C. Jackson Professor of Electrical Engineering, 1968–1973; institute professor, 1973; institute professor emeritus, 1974.

Stephen L. Brown (1937–)   With John Hancock Mutual Life Insurance Company, 1958–; senior vice president, treasurer, 1977–1981; executive vice president, 1981–1987; president, COO, vice chairman of the board, 1987–1992; chairman, CEO, 1992–.

McGeorge Bundy (1919–1996)   Dean, Faculty of Arts and Sciences, Harvard University, professor of government, 1953–1961. Special assistant to U.S. President for national security affairs, 1961–1966. President, Ford Foundation, 1966–1979. Professor of history, New York University, 1979–1989.

William P. Bundy (1917–)   With law firm Covington & Burling, Washington, D. C., 1947–1951. With CIA, 1951–1961. Held several secretarial posts, U.S. Department of Defense, 1961–1964. U.S. assistant secretary of state for East Asian and Pacific Affairs, 1964–1969. Visiting professor, MIT Center for International Studies (CIS), 1969–1970; senior research associate, 1970–1972. Editor, *Foreign Affairs*, 1973–1984.

*George M. Bunker (1908–1985)   Vice president of manufacturing, Kroger Co., 1942–1949. President, Trailmobile Inc., 1949–1952. President, general manager, director, The Martin Co., 1952–1959; chairman, 1952–1961; merged into Martin Marietta, 1961; chairman, Martin Marietta Corp., 1961–1977. Chairman of executive committee, director, Bunker-Ramo, 1975–1985.

*John E. Burchard (1898–1975)   Joined MIT faculty in 1938 as director of Albert Farwell Bemis Foundation with rank of professor. Appointed director of libraries of the institute, 1944 (on leave 1940–1945 serving on several military-scientific missions). First dean, MIT School of Humanities and Social Science, 1950–1964. Visiting professor, University of California, Berkeley, 1964–1967.

William A. M. Burden (1906–1984)   In charge of aviation research, Scudder, Stevens & Clark, NYC, 1932–1939. Special aviation assistant to the secretary of commerce, 1942–1943. Assistant Secretary of Commerce for air, 1943–1947. Partner, William A. M. Burden & Co., beginning 1949. U.S. ambassador to Belgium, 1959–1961. Board chairman, Institute for Defense Analyses, 1959–1991.

Eugene W. Burgess (1898–1972)   Executive with General Mills, 1941–1951. Visiting professor, MIT School of Industrial Relations, 1954–1955. Lecturer, University of California at Berkeley, 1955–1965

Robert K. Burns (1909–1990)   Joined the staff of University of Chicago School of Business and Division of Social Sciences, 1946; executive officer, Industrial Relations Center, 1946–1974; professor of business and social science, 1948–1968; professor of business administration, 1968–1974.

*Vannevar Bush (1890–1974)   Faculty member, MIT Department of Electrical Engineering, 1919–1932; first dean of newly organized MIT School of Engineering, 1932; dean and vice president, 1932–1938; president, Carnegie Institution, 1938–1955. As science adviser to President Roosevelt during World War II, directed activities to organize U.S. science and technology for the war effort and served as director, Office of Scientific Research and Development, 1941–1947. Life member, MIT Corporation, 1939; chairman, 1957–1959; Honorary chairman, 1959–1971.

Thomas D. Cabot (1897–1995)   Beginning in 1922, spent entire career with family business, originally focused on gas and carbon black. President, Cabot Corporation, 1954–1960; chairman, 1960–1969; honorary chairman, 1969–1995. Life member, MIT Corporation, 1951.

*Robert C. Casselman (1918–1985)   Following twenty-two-year career with Polaroid in engineering production and marketing, served as associate director, Museum of Fine Arts, Boston, with responsibility for administration, development, and finance, 1976–1979.

Eduardo F. Catalano (1917–)   Professor of architecture, MIT, 1956–1977. Works include Julius A. Stratton Student Center and Grover M. Hermann building, both on the MIT campus.

Noam A. Chomsky (1928–)   In 1955 joined faculty of MIT Department of Modern Languages (renamed the Department of Modern Languages and Linguistics, 1965, and the Department of Foreign Literatures and Linguistics, 1969); named professor, 1961; Ferrari P. Ward Professor, 1966; institute professor, 1976.

Arland F. Christ-Janer (1922–)   President, Cornell College, Mt. Vernon, Iowa, 1961–1967. President, Boston University, 1967–1970. President, Stephens College, Columbia, Missouri, 1975–1983.

Milton U. Clauser (1913–1980)   Director, MIT Lincoln Laboratory, professor of aeronautical engineering, 1966–1970; provost, academic dean, U.S. Naval Postgraduate School, Monterey, California, 1970–1974. NASA Space Program Advisory Council, 1971–1974.

Clark M. Clifford (1906–1998)   Special counsel to U.S. President, 1946–1950. Senior partner, Clifford & Miller, Washington, D.C., 1950–1968. Secretary of Defense, 1968–1969. Senior partner, Clifford & Warnke, Washington, D.C., 1969–1991.

John R. Coleman (1921–)   Carnegie Institute of Technology Department of Economics, 1955–1963; professor, department head, 1960–1963. Dean, Division of Humanities and Social Science, 1963–1965. President, Haverford College, 1967–1977. President, Edna McConnell Clark Foundation, 1977–1986.

John F. Collins (1919–1995)   Mayor of Boston, 1960–1968. Beginning in 1968, MIT visiting professor affiliated with urban studies in the Departments of Political Science, Civil Engineering, and the Sloan School of Management, and later as consulting professor at the school. Retired in 1981.

Karl T. Compton (1887–1954)   MIT's ninth president, 1930–1948, and chairman of the corporation, 1948–1954. Member, National Defense Research Committee, 1940–1945, which in 1941 became part of the Office of Scientific Research and Development. Chairman, Joint Research and Development Board, which oversaw military scientific research efforts in the postwar period, 1948–1949.

William A. Coolidge (1901–1992)   Founder, Enterprise Associates, 1940, and New Enterprises, Inc., 1946, which later became National Research Corporation. Philanthropist. Life member, MIT Corporation, 1953.

Stuart H. Cowen (1921–1994)   MIT: Director of fiscal planning, 1964–1970; comptroller, 1970–1973; vice president for financial operations, 1973–1984.

Archibald Cox (1912–)   Professor, Harvard Law School, 1946–1961. Solicitor General, U. S. Department of Justice, 1961–1965. Williston Professor, Harvard Law School, 1965–1976. Carl M. Loeb University Professor, Harvard University, 1976–1984.

James J. Culliton (1937–1996)   MIT: Assistant to the vice president for administration and personnel, 1970–1984; director of personnel, 1973–1984; vice president for financial operations, 1984–1994; vice president for administration, 1994–1996.

Paul V. Cusick (1917–1982)   Joined staff of MIT Division of Industrial Cooperation, 1946; later served in Division of Defense Laboratories. Assistant treasurer, 1954–1957; comptroller, 1957–1970; vice president for business and fiscal relations, 1970–1978.

*Alexander V. d'Arbeloff (1927–)   Co-founder, Teradyne, Inc. 1960; CEO, 1961–1997. Life member, MIT Corporation, 1994; chairman, 1997–.

*John M. Deutch (1938–)   Joined faculty of MIT Department of Chemistry, 1970; named professor, 1973; department head, 1976–1977. With U.S. Department of Energy, 1977–1980, undersecretary, 1979–1980. Named Arthur C. Cope Professor of Chemistry, MIT, 1981; dean of science, 1982–1985; provost, 1985–1990. Undersecretary, U.S. Department of Defense, 1993–1994; deputy secretary, 1994–1995. Director of Central Intelligence, 1995–1996. MIT institute professor, 1990–.

*Bradley Dewey (1887–1974)   Co-founder, Dewey & Almy Chemical Company, 1919; president, 1919–1952; chairman, 1952–1954. Life member, MIT Corporation, 1936.

*William R. Dickson (1935–)   Joined MIT Department of Physical Plant, 1960; director, 1971–1980. MIT vice president for operations, 1980–1982. Senior vice president, 1982–1998.

Paul H. Douglas (1892–1976)   Joined industrial relations faculty, University of Chicago, 1920; professor of economics, 1925–1949. U.S. senator from Illinois, 1949–1967.

Richard M. Douglas (1922–)   Professor of history, MIT, 1962–1991; head, Department of Humanities, 1962–1972; chairman, the history section, 1988–1989.

*Charles Stark Draper (1901–1987)   Faculty member, MIT Department of Aeronautics and Astronautics, 1935–1966, named professor, 1939; head of department, 1951–1966; named institute professor, 1966. Director of MIT Instrumentation Laboratory, 1935–1969. In 1973 the laboratory became independent of MIT and was renamed the Charles Stark Draper Laboratory. Under his direction the technology for inertial navigation was invented and brought into operational use.

John T. Dunlop (1914–)   Faculty member, Harvard University Department of Economics, 1938–1985; Lamont University Professor, 1970–1985; dean, Faculty of Arts and Sciences, 1970–1973. U.S. Secretary of Labor, 1975–1976.

*Irénée du Pont, Jr. (1920–)   Joined E. I. du Pont de Nemours Company, 1946; retired as senior vice president, 1978; director, 1959–1988. Life member, MIT Corporation, 1968.

Robert H. Ebert (1914–1996)   Founded Harvard Community Health Plan, 1969. Dean of faculty of medicine, Harvard University, 1965–1977; Caroline Shields Walker Professor of Medicine, 1973–1977.

*Harold E. Edgerton (1903–1990)   Joined faculty of MIT Department of Electrical Engineering, 1932; professor, 1938–1966; institute professor, 1966–1968. Pioneer in strobe and underwater photography. Co-founder and partner, Edgerton, Germeshausen & Grier (EG&G).

Douglas Ensminger (1910–1989)   Ford Foundation representative in India, 1951–1970.

Ross W. Farrar (1938–)   Consultant, Museum of Fine Arts, Boston, 1971–1978; director of operations, 1978–1980; associate director of the museum, 1980–1986; deputy director, 1986–1989. Executive director, Palmer & Dodger (law firm, Boston, Mass.), 1989–.

*James B. Fisk (1910–1981)   With Bell Laboratories, 1939–1974, serving as president, 1959–1973, and chairman, 1973–1974. Served on three MIT presidential search committees, chairing two of them. Life member, MIT Corporation, 1963.

*Carl F. Floe (1908–1998)   In 1939 joined the MIT Department of Metallurgy (renamed Metallurgy and Materials Science, 1967); named professor, 1950; assistant provost, 1952–1956; assistant chancellor, 1956–1959; vice president for research administration, 1959–1969.

Jan Fontein (1927–)   Curator, Asiatic Art, Museum of Fine Arts, Boston, 1966; museum director, 1976–1987; Matsutaro Shoriki Curator for Research, 1987–1992.

*Jay W. Forrester (1918–)   Co-founded MIT Servomechanisms Laboratory, 1940; division head, Lincoln Laboratory, 1951–1956; founded Digital Computer Laboratory, director, 1951–1956; inventor of magnetic core memory for computers. Professor of management, MIT Sloan School,** 1956–1972; Germeshausen Professor, 1972–1989; head, Sloan School** Systems Dynamics Group, 1960–1989.

Ralph E. Freeman (1894–1967)   Professor of economics, MIT, 1931–1960; head, Department of Economics and Social Sciences, 1934–1958.

Milton Friedman (1912–)   Associate professor of economics, University of Chicago, 1946–1948; professor, 1948–1962; Paul Snowden Russell Distinguished Service Professor, 1962–1982. Nobel Prize in economics, 1976.

Paul M. Fye (1912–1988)   With U.S. Naval Ordnance Laboratory, Washington, D.C., 1948–1958; associate director for research, 1956–1958. Director, Woods Hole Oceanographic Institution (WHOI), 1958–1977; president, WHOI corporation, 1961–1986; president emeritus, 1986–1988.

George P. Gardner (1917–)   Executive with Paine, Webber, Jackson & Curtis, (later Paine Webber Incorporated), 1952–. Life member, MIT Corporation, 1963.

James M. Gavin (1907–1990)   Enlisted as private in U.S. Army, 1924; commissioned 2d lieutenant following graduation from West Point, 1929; advanced through grades to lieutenant general; retired, 1958. U.S. Ambassador to France, 1961–1963. Chairman, Arthur D. Little, Inc., 1964–1977.

Peter P. Gil (1922–)   Director, executive development programs, MIT Sloan School of Management,** 1962–1966; associate dean, 1966–1982. Professor, dean, Graduate School of Management, Clark University, Worcester, Mass., 1982–1987. Senior lecturer, MIT Sloan School, 1987–1994.

Robert F. Goheen (1919–)   Member of Princeton University faculty in classics, 1948–1957; president of the university, 1957–1972. Chairman, Council on Foundations, 1972–1977. President, Edna McConnell Clark Foundation, 1977. U. S. ambassador to India, 1977–1980. Senior Fellow, Woodrow Wilson School, Princeton, 1981–.

*Samuel A. Goldblith (1919–)   Joined MIT Department of Food Science and Technology, 1949; named professor, 1959; director, Industrial Liaison Program, 1974–1978; vice president for resource development, 1978–1986.

Ralph E. Gomory (1929–)   With IBM, 1959–1989; director of research, 1970–1986; vice president, 1973–1984; senior vice president, 1985–1989; member, corporate management board, 1983–1989. President, Alfred P. Sloan Foundation, 1989–.

*Paul E. Gray (1932–)   After serving nearly twenty-five years in academic and administrative posts at the institute, including professor of electrical engineering, associate dean for student affairs, dean of the School of Engineering, and chancellor, served as the institute's fourteenth president, 1980–1990, and then chairman of the corporation, 1990–1997. Professor, Department of Electrical Engineering and Computer Science, 1997–. Life member, MIT Corporation, 1997; honorary chairman, 1997–.

*Cecil H. Green (1901–) Joined Geophysical Service, Inc., 1930; president, 1950–1955; chairman, 1955–1959. Co-founder, Texas Instruments, Inc., 1950. Life member, MIT Corporation, 1961.

*Crawford H. Greenewalt (1902–1993) Entire career spent at E. I. du Pont de Nemours Company, 1922–1973; president, 1948–1962; chairman of the board, 1962–1967; and chairman of the finance committee, 1967–1973. Government service during World War II included participating as a consultant on the Manhattan Project. Life member, MIT Corporation, 1951.

Robert K. Greenleaf (1904–1990) With AT&T, 1929–1964; director, management research, 1957–1964. Consultant, Ford Foundation, 1962–1971. Consultant, R. K. Mellon Foundation, 1962–1972. Founder, Center for Applied Ethics, Inc., now Robert K. Greenleaf Center, Indianapolis, IN.

Alfred M. Gruenther (1899–1983) Following graduation from West Point advanced through grades to general; retired 1956. Military service included chief of staff, Fifth Army, 1943–1944; chief of staff, 15th Army Group. 1944–1945; chief of staff, SHAPE, 1951–1953; supreme allied commander in Europe, 1953–1956.

Dzherman M. Gvishiani Citizen, USSR, later Russia. Deputy chairman, State Committee for Science and Technology, 1962–1976. Director, Systems Analysis Institute of the USSR (now Russia), 1976–. Professor, Prague Foreign Economy School, 1979–1989.

*Elias P. Gyftopoulos (1927–) Faculty member, MIT Department of Nuclear Engineering, 1958–1996; Ford Professor of Engineering, 1970–1996. Chairman, MIT Faculty, 1973–1975.

Edward B. Hanify (1912–) Admitted to Massachusetts bar, 1936; joined Ropes & Gray, Boston, Mass., 1936; partner, 1947–1985; of counsel, 1985–.

*Edward J. Hanley (1903–1982) Allegheny Steel Company, 1936–1951. CEO, Allegheny Ludlum Steel Corporation, 1951–1968. Life member, MIT Corporation, 1961.

Frederick H. Harbison (1912–1976) Professor of economics, executive officer, industrial relations section, University of Chicago, 1945–1955. Professor of economics, director, industrial relations section, Princeton University, 1955–1967; Roger W. Straus Professor of Social Sciences, professor of economics, 1967–1976.

George R. Harrison (1898–1979) In 1930 joined MIT Department of Physics as professor and director of the Research Laboratory of Experimental Physics; dean, School of Science, 1942–1964.

*William R. Hawthorne (1913–) MIT faculty of Mechanical Engineering, 1946–1951. Professor of Applied Thermodynamics, University of Cambridge,

England, 1951–1980; head of engineering department, 1968–1973; Master of Churchill College, 1968–1983. Visiting institute professor, MIT, 1962–1968, 1973–1978. Member, MIT Corporation, 1969–1973.

*Harold L. Hazen (1901–1980)   Joined faculty, MIT Department of Electrical Engineering, 1925; named professor, 1938; department head, 1938–1952; dean of the graduate school, 1952–1967; foreign study adviser, 1967–1972.

Paul F. Hellmuth (1918–1986)   With Boston law firm Hale & Dorr, 1947–1976; partner, 1952–1956; senior managing partner, 1956–1976. MIT Corporation member, 1974–1979.

Grover M. Hermann (1890–1979)   Founder, president, director, American Asphalt Paint Co., 1913–1940; named changed to American Marietta Co., 1940; president, director 1940–1950; chairman, director, 1950–1961; merged into Martin-Marietta, 1961; chairman, 1961–1965; honorary chairman, 1965–1966.

Theodore M. Hesburgh, (1917–)   Ordained Roman Catholic priest, C.S.C., 1943. Chaplain, University of Notre Dame, 1947–1949; executive vice president, 1949–1952; president, 1952–1987. President, Rockefeller Foundation, 1977–1982.

Albert G. Hill (1910–1996)   Joined faculty of MIT Department of Physics, 1937; named professor, 1947. Staff member, MIT Radiation Laboratory, 1941; director, Research Laboratory of Electronics, 1949–1952; director, Lincoln Laboratory, 1952–1955; deputy head, physics department, 1967–1973; vice president for research, 1970–1975; director, Plasma Fusion Center, 1976–1978. Chairman, Draper Laboratory board of directors, 1970–1982.

Thomas M. Hill (1914–1977)   Joined MIT School of Management,** 1946; named professor, 1963; associate dean, 1969–1975; head of Sloan School group that helped to establish Indian Institute of Management, 1961–1963.

Kenneth M. Hoffman (1930–)   Faculty member, MIT Department of Mathematics, 1956–1996; named professor, 1963; head of department, 1971–1979.

Jerome H. Holland (1916–1985)   President, Delaware State College, 1953–1960. President, Hampton Institute, 1960–1970. U.S. Ambassador to Sweden, 1970–1972. MIT Corporation member, 1969–1979.

Houlder Hudgins (1900–1963)   Beginning in 1927 served in executive positions with several U. S. business organizations including Montgomery Ward Co. before joining the faculty of the MIT School of Management** in 1955 with the rank of professor.

*Robert I. Hulsizer (1919–)   Professor, physics, MIT, 1964–1986; director, Education Research Center, 1964–1968; chairman, MIT faculty, 1977–1979.

Herold C. Hunt (1902–1976)   Superintendent, city schools, Chicago, IL, 1947–1953. Professor of education, Harvard University, 1953–1970; Charles W. Eliot Professor of education emeritus, 1970–1976. Undersecretary, U.S. Department of Health, Education, and Welfare, 1955–1957.

Arthur T. Ippen (1907–1974)   Joined MIT Department of Civil Engineering in 1945; named professor, 1948; first director of the institute's hydrodynamics laboratory, 1951–1973; named Ford professor of engineering, 1965, and institute professor, 1970.

Stanley M. Jacks (1916–) Instructor in economics, MIT, 1946–1950. Associate professor, economics, Simmons College, 1951–1958. Associate professor, MIT School of Industrial Management,** 1959–1964; senior lecturer, MIT Sloan School of Management,** 1964–1980.

***Shirley A. Jackson (1946–)** Member technical staff, AT&T Bell Laboratories, 1976–1991. Professor of physics, Rutgers University, 1991–1995. Chairperson, Nuclear Regulatory Commission, 1995–. Life member, MIT Corporation, 1992.

***J. Kenneth Jamieson (1910–)** Executive vice president, Exxon Corporation (formerly Standard Oil of New Jersey), 1964–1965; president, director, 1965–1969; chairman, CEO, 1969–1975. Life member, MIT Corporation, 1975.

Edward G. Jefferson (1921–) With E. I. du Pont de Nemours and Company, 1951–1986; senior vice president, 1973–1980; president, COO, 1980–1981; chairman, CEO, 1981–1986.

John E. Jeuck (1916–) Joined faculty of School of Business, University of Chicago, 1946; dean, professor of marketing, director of executive program, 1952–1956. Professor, business administration, Harvard Graduate School of Business Administration, 1955–1958. Professor, business administration, University of Chicago, 1958–1991.

Howard Johnson (1896–1972) Began in business as owner of a drug store in Wollaston, Mass., in 1924; expanded into the ice cream business in 1928, which led to a chain of restaurants in many sections of the United States. Before retiring in 1959 had served as president, treasurer, chairman, director of Howard Johnson Enterprises.

Frank S. Jones (1928–) Senior lecturer, executive director, MIT Urban Systems Laboratory, special assistant, Office of the President, 1968–1969; named professor of urban affairs, 1969; Ford Professor of Urban Affairs, 1970–1992. Director, Community Fellows Program, 1971–1992.

Thomas W. Jones (1949–) From 2d vice president to senior vice president and treasurer, John Hancock, 1982–1989. Executive vice president, CFO, TIAA, 1989–1993; president, COO, 1989–1997. Vice chairman, Travelers Group and vice chairman and CEO, Salomon Smith Barney Assets Management, 1997–.

Vernon E. Jordan, Jr. (1935–) President, National Urban League, 1972–1981. Partner, Washington law firm Akin, Gump, Strauss, etc. MIT Corporation member, 1975–1980.

W. Seavey Joyce (1913–) Ordained Roman Catholic priest, S. J., 1943. Joined faculty of Boston College as chairman, Department of Economics, 1949, and served additionally as dean, College of Business Administration, 1952–1966; vice president for community affairs, 1966–1968; president, 1968–1972.

Michael A. Kane (1943–) Physician, MIT Medical Department, 1974–; associate director, 1980–1995. Associated with Mount Auburn Hospital since 1974 and with the Massachusetts General Hospital since 1995. Clinical instructor, Harvard Medical School, since 1977.

Alfred A. H. Keil (1913–)   Professor and head, MIT Department of Naval Architecture and Marine Engineering (later renamed Ocean Engineering), 1966–1971; dean, School of Engineering, 1971–1977; Ford Professor of Engineering, 1977–1978.

Donald Kennedy (1931–)   Joined faculty, Stanford University, 1960; professor, biological sciences, 1965–1977; department chairman, 1965–1972; university provost, 1979–1980; president, 1980–1992; Bing Professor, Environmental Science, 1992–.

Nannerl O. Keohane (1940–)   Political science faculty, Swarthmore College, 1967–1973; Stanford University, 1973–1981. President, Wellesley College, 1981–1993. President, Duke University, 1993–. Member, MIT Corporation, 1992–1997.

*James R. Killian, Jr. (1904–1988)   After more than twenty years in administrative posts at MIT, served as its tenth president, 1949–1959. On leave from MIT as the first full-time science adviser to a U.S. president, 1957–1959. Chairman, MIT Corporation, 1959–1971, life member and honorary chairman, 1971–1979, life member emeritus, 1979–1988. Was a major influence in the establishment of the nation's space program and in the founding of public television.

Charles P. Kindleberger (1910–)   Faculty member, MIT Department of Economics, 1948–1976; named professor, 1951; Ford International Professor of Economics, 1972. Chairman, MIT Faculty, 1965–1967.

Grayson L. Kirk (1903–1997)   Faculty member, Columbia University, 1943–1972; Bryce Professor of History and International Relations, 1959–1972; provost, 1949–1950; vice president and provost, 1950–1951; president, trustee, 1953–1968.

*Malcolm G. Kispert (1923–1975)   Assistant to MIT presidents Compton and Killian, 1946–1956; administrative vice chancellor, 1957–1961; vice president for academic administration, 1961–1971; institute secretary, 1971–1975.

Douglas M. Knight (1921–)   President, Lawrence University, 1953–1963. President, Duke University, 1963–1969. President, Questar Corporation, 1976–. Member, MIT Corporation, 1965–1970.

Harold Krensky (1912–1994)   Vice president, Bloomingdale's, 1947–1959; chairman, managing director, 1967–1969. From executive vice president to president, chairman, Filene's (Boston), 1960–1966. With Federated Department Stores, Inc. (parent company), 1965–1982; president, 1973–1980; director, 1969–1982.

*Paul R. Krugman (1953–)   Joined faculty of MIT Sloan School of Management, 1980; professor of economics, 1984–1994. Professor of economics, Stanford University, 1994–1996. Professor of economics, MIT, 1996–.

Edwin Kuh (1925–1986) Joined MIT School of Management** faculty, 1955; named professor of finance and economics, 1962; director, Center for Computational Research in Economics and Management Science, 1978–1986.

*James B. Lampert (1914–1978) U.S. Army career included service as superintendent of West Point Academy 1963–1966, high commissioner of Ryukyu Islands, 1969–1972; retired as lieutenant general, 1972. Vice president for resource development, MIT, 1972–1978.

Roy Lamson (1908–1986) Visiting professor, MIT Department of Humanities, 1957–1958; professor, 1958–1973; named Class of 1922 Professor, 1971. Director, Humanities, Science and Engineering Program. Assistant to MIT president for the arts, 1971.

Edwin H. Land (1909–1991) Founder and chief executive officer of Polaroid Corporation, 1935–1980; inventor of instant photography. Named visiting institute professor at MIT, 1956.

*Ralph Landau (1916–) Cofounder, Scientific Design, 1946. President, Halocon International, Inc. 1963–1982. Consulting professor of economics, Stanford University, 1982–. Life member, MIT Corporation, 1976.

William H. Lane (1914–1995) Trustee, Museum of Fine Arts, Boston, 1982; honorary life trustee, 1986; Great Benefactor (with his wife Saundra), 1986.

Frances Lawrence (Mrs. James Lawrence) Founder and chair, Ladies Committee, Museum of Fine Arts, Boston, 1956; honorary trustee, 1977–.

Fred Lazarus, Jr. (1884–1973) With F & R Lazarus & Co., 1903–1957; president and CEO, 1945–1957. Chairman, CEO, Federated Department Stores, Inc. (parent company), 1957–1967; chairman, executive and finance committees, 1967–1971; chairman, executive committee, 1971–1973.

Maurice Lazarus (1915–) With Foley's (Houston, Texas), 1945–1958; executive vice president, 1948–1958. President, treasurer, Filene's (Boston, Mass.), 1958–1964; chairman, 1964–1965. Vice chairman, Federated Department Stores, Inc., 1965–1970; chairman, finance committee, 1971–1982.

Ralph Lazarus (1914–1988) General Merchandise Manager, F & R Lazarus Co., 1935–1951. Executive vice president, Federated Department Stores, 1951–1957; president, 1957–1967; CEO, 1966–1981; chairman, 1982–1984.

Richard Leacock (1921–) Photographer, producer, director of documentary films. Professor of cinema, head of the film section, MIT Department of Architecture, 1969–1988.

Timothy Leary (1920–1996) Assistant professor, psychology, University of California, Berkeley, 1950–1955. Director, psychological research, Kaiser Foundation (Oakland, CA), 1955–1958. Lecturer, Harvard University, 1959–1963. First guide, League Spiritual Discovery, 1964–1996. President, producer, Futique, Inc. (electronic books), 1985–1996.

Jerome Y. Lettvin (1920–) Joined MIT as research assistant holding a joint appointment in the Research Laboratory of Electronics and the Department of Biology, 1951. Professor of communications physiology (Departments of Electrical Engineering and Biology), 1966–1988.

Edward H. Levi (1911–)   Joined faculty of University of Chicago Law School, 1936; named professor, 1945; dean, 1950–1962. Provost, University of Chicago, 1962–1968; president, 1968–1975. U.S. attorney general, 1975–1977.

*Norman Levinson (1912–1975)   Joined faculty of MIT Department of Mathematics, 1937; named professor, 1949; department head, 1968–1971; institute professor, 1971.

Irving M. London (1918–)   Professor, chairman, Department of Medicine, Albert Einstein College of Medicine, 1955–1970. Professor of biology, MIT, 1969–1989. Director, Harvard-MIT Division of Health Sciences and Technology, 1969–1985. Director, Whitaker College of Health Sciences, Technology, and Management, 1978–1983. Professor of medicine, Harvard Medical School, 1972–1989.

Francis E. Low (1921–)   Professor of physics, MIT, 1957–1967; Karl Taylor Compton Professor, 1968–1985; institute professor, 1985. Provost, 1980–1985. Institute professor emeritus, 1992.

Salvador E. Luria (1912–1991)   Professor, MIT Department of Biology, 1959; founded the MIT Center for Cancer Research and served as director, 1972–1985. Nobel Prize for medicine, 1969.

Donlyn Lyndon (1936–)   Head, Department of Architecture, University of Oregon, 1954–1967. Professor of architecture, MIT, 1967–1978; head of department, 1967–1975. Private practice, Berkeley, Calif., 1975–.

*Margaret L. A. MacVicar (1943–1991)   Joined MIT Department of Physics, 1969; named professor, 1980; appointed first dean for undergraduate education 1985; founder of the Undergraduate Research Opportunities Program (UROP), 1969. Vice president, Carnegie Institution, 1983–1987.

Boris Magasanik (1919–)   On the faculty of the Harvard Medical School Department of Bacteriology and Immunology, 1951–1959. Professor of microbiology, MIT, 1960–1977; head, Department of Biology, 1967–1977; Jacques Monod Professor of Microbiology, 1977–1990; senior lecturer, 1990–.

*Robert W. Mann (1924–)   Joined faculty, MIT Department of Mechanical Engineering, 1953; named professor, 1963; Germeshausen Professor, 1972–1974; Whitaker Professor of Biomedical Engineering, 1974–1992; Whitaker Professor emeritus and senior lecturer, 1992–.

Donald G. Marquis (1908–1973)   Joined faculty, Department of Psychology, Yale University, 1933; associate professor, 1938–1945; department chairman and director, psychology laboratory, 1941–1945. Professor of psychology, department chairman, University of Michigan, 1945–1947. Professor of management, MIT School of Management,** 1959–1973.

William Ted Martin (1911–)   Member of faculty, MIT Department of Mathematics, 1936–1943; professor, 1946–1976; head of department, 1947–1968. Chairman, MIT faculty, 1969–1971.

*James J. McCormack (1910–1975) U. S. Army and U. S. Air Force, 1932–1955; retired as major general and director of research and development, U.S. Air Force, 1955. President, Institute for Defense Analyses, 1956–1959. Special adviser to MIT president, 1955–1957; vice president for industrial and governmental relations, MIT, 1957–1965. Chairman, COMSAT, 1965–1975.

*Katharine Dexter McCormick (1875–1967) S. B. in biology, MIT, 1904. National Treasurer of the Woman Suffrage Movement. A founding officer of the League of Women Voters. Early supporter of Margaret Sanger. Major MIT benefactor, providing funding for Stanley McCormick Hall, on-campus residence for MIT women students.

Victor K. McElheny (1935–) Science reporter, *The Boston Globe*, 1966–1972; *The New York Times*, 1973–1978. Director, MIT's Science Journalism Fellowships, 1982–1998.

Douglas M. McGregor (1906–1964) Joined MIT faculty of economics and social science, 1937; named professor of psychology, 1948. A founder of the industrial relations section in the School of Industrial Management,** served as its executive director, 1943–1948. President, Antioch College, 1948–1954. Returned to MIT as professor of industrial management, 1954; Sloan Fellows Professor of Industrial Management, 1962–1964.

Robert N. McMurry (1901–1985) Headed Chicago office of Psychology Corporation, 1935–1943. Robert N. McMurry & Co. (consulting service for personnel, industrial relations, and market research), 1943–1953. McMurry, Hamstra & Co., 1953–1958; named changed to McMurry Co., 1958.

Robert S. McNamara (1916–) Executive, Ford Motor Company, 1946–1961; president, 1960–1961. Secretary, U. S. Department of Defense, 1961–1968. President, World Bank, 1968–1981.

*Robert C. Merton (1944–) Joined MIT faculty as instructor in economics, 1969; began teaching finance, MIT Sloan School of Management, 1970; named professor, 1974; J. C. Penney Professor of Management, 1980. George Fisher Baker Professor of Business Administration, Harvard University, 1988–. Shared 1997 Nobel Prize in economic sciences with Myron S. Scholes.

John M. Meyer, Jr. (1905–1996) President, Morgan Guaranty Trust Company of New York, 1965–1969. Chairman and CEO, J. P. Morgan & Co. Incorporated, 1969–1971.

*Charles L. Miller (1929–) Faculty member, MIT Department of Civil Engineering, 1955–1977; named professor, 1961; department head, 1961–1970; associate dean, MIT School of Engineering, 1970–1971; director, Urban Systems Laboratory, 1968–1975.

Max F. Millikan (1913–1969) Joined faculty of MIT Department of Economics, 1949. On leave from MIT, Assistant Director, CIA, 1951–1952. Professor of economics and first Director of MIT Center for International Studies, 1952–1969.

Walter L. Milne (1922–) Joined MIT News Office, 1951. Named Assistant to the President, 1957; served additionally assistant to the chairman, 1959–1990.

Responsibilities included oversight of MIT's community and governmental relations.

Franco Modigliani (1918–)   Joined faculty of MIT School of Industrial Management** as professor of economics, 1960; professor of economics and finance, 1962–1970; institute professor, 1970–1988. Nobel Prize in economics, 1985.

David G. Moore (1918–)   Faculty member, sociology, industrial relations, and business administration, University of Chicago, 1950–1956; director, executive program, 1955–1956. Dean, New York State School of Industrial and Labor Relations, Cornell University, 1963–1971. Senior then executive vice president, Conference Board, 1971–1979. Chairman, Department of Business Administration, University of North Florida, 1979–1986.

Francis D. Moore (1913–)   Surgeon in chief, Peter Bent Brigham Hospital, Boston, 1948–1976. Joined teaching staff of Harvard Medical School, 1934; Moseley Professor of Surgery, 1948–1976; Elliott Carr Cutler Professor of Surgery, 1976–1980. Moseley Professor Emeritus, 1980.

Elting E. Morison (1909–1995)   From assistant professor to Sloan Fellows Professor of industrial management, MIT School of Management,** 1946–1967. Professor of history, Yale University, 1967–1972; master, Timothy Dwight College, 1968–1972. Killian Professor of Humanities, MIT, 1972–1995.

Frank E. Morris (1923–)   Assistant to secretary for debt management, U. S. Treasury Department, 1961–1963. Vice president, Loomis Sayles and Co., Boston, 1963–1968. President, Federal Reserve Bank, Boston, 1968–1985.

*Richard S. Morse (1911–1988)   Organized and served as president, National Research Corporation, 1940–1959. Director of research, assistant secretary of the Army, 1959–1961. Senior lecturer, Sloan School of Management,** MIT, 1963–1977; president, MIT Development Foundation, Inc. 1972–1977.

*Joel Moses (1941–)   Joined MIT Department of Electrical Engineering and Computer Science, 1967; named professor, 1977, department head, 1981–1989; D. C. Jackson Professor, 1989–; dean, MIT School of Engineering, 1991–1995; provost, 1995–1998.

Daniel P. Moynihan (1927–)   Director, Harvard-MIT Joint Center for Urban Studies, 1966–1969; served as adviser and counselor to U.S. president in several capacities, 1969–1973; U. S. ambassador to India, 1973–1975; U.S. permanent representative to UN, 1975–1976. U.S. senator from New York, 1977–.

*Carl M. Mueller (1920–)   Partner, Loeb, Rhoades & Company, 1960–1977; managing partner, 1973–1977. Vice chairman, Bankers Trust Company, 1977–1985. Served on three MIT presidential search committees, chairing two of them. Named honorary lecturer, MIT, 1990. Life member, MIT Corporation, 1976.

*Clint W. Murchison, Jr., (1923–1987)   With his brother, assembled commercial empire including insurance, banking, publishing, professional sports. Life member, MIT Corporation, 1977.

William Beverly Murphy (1907–1994)   Started with Campbell Soup Company in 1938; retired as President and CEO in 1972. Life member, MIT Corporation, 1965.

Thomas A. Murphy (1915–) With General Motors Corporation from 1938; elected comptroller, 1967; treasurer, 1968; vice president, 1970; vice chairman, board of directors, 1972; chairman and CEO, 1974; retired, 1981; continued as director until 1988. Chairman, Alfred P. Sloan Foundation, 1982–1988.

Charles A. Myers (1913–) Joined MIT faculty of economics, 1939; professor, industrial relations, 1949–1964; joint appointment Department of Economics and Sloan School of Management,** 1964–1967; Sloan Fellows Professor of Management, 1967–1978.

John W. O'Neill (1918–1977) Commissioned 2d lieutenant U. S. Army, 1940; advanced through grades to lieutenant general, U.S. Air Force, 1967. Military service included commander, Electronic Systems Division, Air Force Systems Command, Bedford, Mass., 1964–1967.

Thomas P. O'Neill, Jr. (1912–1994) Member, Massachusetts State Legislature, 1936–1952. Representative from Massachusetts to U.S. Congress, 1952–1986; majority whip, 1971–1973; majority leader, 1973–1977; Speaker of the House, 1977–1986.

Walter H. Page (1915–) Joined J. P. Morgan & Co., then a private partnership, 1937 (firm incorporated and became known as J. P. Morgan & Co. Incorporated, 1940). President, J. P. Morgan & Co. Incorporated, 1971–1978; chairman and CEO, 1978–1979.

Ellmore C. Patterson (1913–) Joined J. P. Morgan & Co., than a private partnership, 1935 (firm incorporated and became known as J. P. Morgan & Co. Incorporated, 1940). President, J. P. Morgan & Co. Incorporated, 1969–1971; chairman and CEO, 1971–1977. Life member, MIT Corporation, 1983.

*I. M. Pei (1917–) Architect whose works include National Gallery of Art East Building, Washington, D.C.; West Wing, Museum of Fine Arts, Boston; expansion and modernization of the Louvre Museum, Paris. MIT Corporation member, 1972–1977, 1978–1983.

Sheldon Penman (1930–) Joined faculty of MIT Department of Biology, 1962; named professor, 1971.

James A. Perkins (1911–1998) Vice president, Swarthmore College, 1945–1950. Vice president, Carnegie Corporation, 1950–1963. President, Cornell University, 1963–1969. Chairman, International Council for Educational Development, 1970–1990.

Ithiel de Sola Pool (1917–1984) Joined MIT faculty of political science, 1953; named professor, 1958; Ruth and Arthur Sloan Professor of Political Science; head, Division of, then Department, of Political Science, 1959–1968. Also associated with MIT Center for International Studies.

William F. Pounds (1928–) Joined faculty of MIT School of Management,** 1961; professor, 1966–1998; dean, 1966–1980. Senior adviser to Rockefeller Family, Associates, 1981–1991.

Frank Press (1924–) Professor of geophysics, California Institute of Technology, 1955–1965. Professor of geophysics, head, Department of Earth and Planetary Sciences, MIT, 1965–1977; institute professor, 1981. Science adviser to U.S. president, director, Office of Science and Technology Policy, 1977–1980. President, National Academy of Sciences, 1981–1993. Life member, MIT Corporation, 1992.

Lewis T. Preston (1926–1995)   In 1951 joined J. P. Morgan & Co. (merged with Guaranty Trust Co., named Morgan Guaranty Trust Co., 1959). President, J. P. Morgan and Morgan Guaranty Trust Co., 1978–1980; chairman and CEO, 1980–1989.

Nathan M. Pusey (1907–)   President, Lawrence College, 1944–1953. President, Harvard University, 1953–1971. President Andrew W. Mellon Foundation, 1971–1975.

Charat Ram (1918–)   Leading Indian industrialist known for management expertise and public service record. From 1936 to 1985 associated with DCM Ltd., parent company for a range of successful manufacturing and engineering ventures including sugar, fertilizers, and chemicals.

*John S. Reed (1939–)   With Citicorp/Citibank since 1965; chairman, CEO, 1984–. Life member, MIT Corporation, 1985.

Albert Rees (1921–1992)   Joined faculty of economics at the University of Chicago, 1948; named professor, 1961; department chairman, 1962–1965. Member of the faculty of economics, Princeton University, 1966–1979; director of Industrial Relations Section, 1968–1971; chairman, Department of Economics, 1971–1974; provost, 1976–1977. President, Alfred P. Sloan Foundation, 1979–1989.

*Edward B. Roberts (1935–)   In 1958 joined the staff of Systems Dynamics Group, MIT School of Management**; named professor of management, 1970; David Sarnoff Professor of Management, 1974–.

Hartley Rogers, Jr. (1926–)   Joined faculty of MIT Department of Mathematics, 1955; named professor 1964. Chairman, MIT faculty, 1971–1973. Associate provost, 1974–1980.

Walter A. Rosenblith (1913–)   Joined faculty, MIT Department of Electrical Engineering, 1951; named professor, 1957; institute professor, 1975. Chairman, MIT faculty, 1967–1969; provost, 1971–1980. Foreign Secretary of the National Academy of Sciences, 1982–1986.

*John Ross (1926–)   Professor, MIT Department of Chemistry, 1966–1980; department head, 1966–1971. Chairman, MIT faculty, 1975–1977. Professor of chemistry, Stanford University, 1980–; chairman, Department of Chemistry, 1983–1989.

Walt W. Rostow (1916–)   Professor, economic history, MIT, 1950–1960; staff member MIT Center for International Studies, 1951–1960. Counselor, chairman, Policy Planning Council of U.S. Department of State, 1961–1966. Special assistant to U.S. president, 1966–1969. Rex G. Barker, Jr., professor of political economy, Department of Economics and History, University of Texas at Austin, 1969–.

Jack P. Ruina (1923–) Professor of electrical engineering, MIT, 1963–1994; vice president for MIT Special Laboratories, 1966–1970. President, Institute for Defense Analyses, 1964–1966.

(David) Dean Rusk (1909–1994) Held several secretarial posts, U.S. Department of State, 1946–1951. President, Rockefeller Foundation, 1952–1960. U.S. Secretary of State, 1961–1969. Sibley Professor of international law, University of Georgia Law School, 1970.

*Kenan E. Sahin (1941–) After many years of teaching and research at the University of Massachusetts at Amherst, the Harvard School of Public Health. the MIT Department of Electrical Engineering, and the Sloan School, founded Kenan Systems Corporation, a software company, 1982; president, 1982–.

Paul A. Samuelson (1915–) Member of faculty, MIT Department of Economics, 1940–1985; named professor, 1947; institute professor, 1966–1986. Nobel Prize in economics, 1970, and National Medal of Science, 1966.

*Francis W. Sargent (1915–1998) Chairman, Massachusetts Water Resources Commission, 1956–1959; chairman, Massachusetts Department of Public Works, 1965–1966; governor of Massachusetts, 1969–1974.

*David S. Saxon (1920–) Joined faculty, department of physics, University of California at Los Angeles, 1947; named professor, 1958; dean of physical sciences, 1966; vice chancellor, 1968. Provost, University of California Statewide System, 1974–1975; president, 1975–1983. Member, MIT Corporation, 1977–1982; chairman, 1983–1990; honorary chairman, 1990–1995. Life member, 1990.

Edgar H. Schein (1928–) Faculty member, MIT School of Management,** 1956–1993; named professor, 1964; Sloan Fellows Professor of Management, 1978–1990; undergraduate planning professor, 1968–1971; chairman, Organization Studies Group, 1972–1982.

*Erwin H. Schell (1889–1965) Joined faculty of business and engineering administration (then part of MIT's Department of Economics), 1917; professor, 1929–1955. First head of the course in business and engineering administration when it was established as a separate department in 1930. Initiated MIT executive development program, 1931.

Francis O. Schmitt (1903–1995) Joined MIT Department of Biology, 1941, with rank of professor; department head, 1942–1955; named institute professor, 1955. Chairman, Neurosciences Research Foundation, 1962–1974; trustee, 1974–1995.

Myron S. Scholes (1941–) Faculty member, Sloan School of Management, MIT, 1968–1973. Faculty, University of Chicago, 1973–1983. Frank E. Buck Professor of Finance, Stanford University Graduate School of Business, 1983–1996. Shared 1997 Nobel Prize in economic sciences with Robert C. Merton.

Warren A. Seamans (1935–) MIT personnel officer, 1964–1966; administrative officer, MIT Department of Humanities, 1966–1971; founding director, MIT Museum, 1971–1996.

Albert O. Seeler (1915–1976)   Joined MIT medical department as a physician, 1956; physician in chief, 1959; professor of medicine, head of the medical department, 1960–1976. Physician in chief, Harvard Medical Service, Boston City Hospital, 1959–1973.

*Donald P. Severance (1916–)   Assistant to MIT registrar, 1938–1941; assistant registrar, 1941–1949; secretary and treasurer, MIT Alumni Association, 1949–1962; executive vice president, 1962–1974.

James A. Shannon (1904–1994)   Director, Squibb Institute for Medical Research, 1946–1949. Associate director in charge of research, National Heart Institute, 1949–1952; associate director, National Institutes of Health, 1952–1955; director, 1955–1968. Assistant surgeon general, U.S. Public Health Service, 1952–1968. Professor, biomedical sciences, Rockefeller University, 1970–1975.

Eli Shapiro (1916–)   Professor of finance, University of Chicago, 1946–1952. Professor of finance, MIT School of Industrial Management,** 1952–1962; associate dean, 1954–1957. Professor of finance, Harvard Business School, 1962–1971; Alfred P. Sloan Professor of Management,** MIT, 1976–1984.

*David A. Shepard (1903–1983)   With Standard Oil Company (New Jersey)1927–1966; named executive vice president, 1949, director, 1951, and executive committee member, 1959; retired in 1966. Life member, MIT Corporation, 1955.

*George P. Shultz (1920–)   Member, MIT faculty of industrial relations, 1949–1957. Professor, industrial relations, University of Chicago Graduate School of Business,1957–1968; dean, 1962–1968. U.S. secretary of labor, 1969–1970. Director, Office of Management and Budget, 1970–1972. U.S. secretary of the treasury and assistant to the president, 1972–1974. With Bechtel Corporation, 1974–1981; president, 1975–1977, vice chairman, 1977–1981. U.S. secretary of state, 1982–1989.

Abraham J. Siegel (1922–)   Joined MIT faculty of economics, 1954; professor of economics, MIT Sloan School of Management,** 1964–1993. Associate dean, Sloan School, 1967–1980; dean, 1980–1987.

Andrew C. Sigler (1931–)   Began career with Champion Papers Co., 1957; named president, 1972. President and CEO, Champion International Corporation (parent company), 1974–1979; chairman and CEO, 1979–1996.

*O. Robert Simha (1931–)   Planning officer, MIT Planning Office, 1960–1973; director of planning, 1973–.

Constantine B. Simonides (1934–1994)   MIT: assistant to director of summer session, 1960–1962; assistant director, international programs, Sloan School, 1962–1966; assistant to dean, 1963–1966; assistant to the president, 1966–1970, vice president, 1970–1985; vice president and secretary of the corporation, 1985–1994.

Arthur L. Singer, Jr. (1929–)   Administrator, MIT, 1955–1963. Executive associate, Carnegie Corporation, 1963–1966. President, Education Development

Center (EDC), (Newton, Mass.), 1966–1968. Vice president, Alfred P. Sloan Foundation, 1968–1994.

Irwin W. Sizer (1910–) Joined MIT science faculty, 1935; named professor of biochemistry, 1956; head, department of biology, 1956–1967; dean of the Graduate School, 1967–1975. President, Whitaker Health Sciences Fund, Inc., 1974–1984.

***Alfred P. Sloan, Jr. (1875–1966)** President, General Motors Corporation, 1923–1937; chairman, 1937–1956, honorary chairman, 1956–1966. Founder, Alfred P. Sloan Foundation, 1934.; cofounder, Sloan-Kettering Institute for Cancer Resarch, 1945. Life member, MIT Corporation, 1932.

***Gregory Smith (1907–1994)** With Eastman Kodak, 1932–1972; president and general manager, Eastman Gelatine Corporation, 1957–1972. Life member, MIT Corporation, 1977.

***Louis D. Smullin (1916–)** During World War II, staff member, MIT Radiation Laboratory. Helped plan and establish Lincoln Laboratory through Project Charles studies, 1952. Named professor of electrical engineering, MIT, 1960; Dugald Caleb Jackson Professor of electrical engineering, 1973; head of department, 1966–1973.

Benson R. Snyder (1923–) Psychiatrist in chief, MIT, 1959–1969; dean for institute relations, 1969–1973; professor of psychiatry, 1967–1975; director of the MIT Division for Study and Research in Education (DSRE), 1975–1985.

Joseph J. Snyder (1907–1995) Became assistant treasurer of MIT in 1945, treasurer and corporation member *ex officio*, 1950; treasurer and vice president, 1951–1972, treasurer, 1972–1975; treasurer emeritus and financial consultant, 1975–1995.

Robert M. Solow (1924–) Joined faculty of MIT Department of Economics, 1950; named professor, 1957; institute professor, 1973–1995. Received Nobel Prize in economics, 1987.

***Robert C. Sprague (1900–1991)** Founder and CEO, Sprague Electric Company 1926–1971; honorary chairman, 1971–1991. Life member, MIT Corporation, 1955.

Theodore E. Stebbins, Jr. (1938–) Associate professor, art history and American studies; curator, American painting and sculpture, Yale University, 1969–1977. John Moors Cabot Curator, American Paintings, Museum of Fine Arts, Boston, 1977–.

J. E. Wallace Sterling (1906–1985) Faculty member, Department of History, California Institute of Technology, 1937–1948; named professor, 1942; Edward S. Harkness Professor of History and Government, 1945. President, Stanford University, 1949–1968.

J. Paul Sticht (1917–) Executive with Campbell Soup Company, 1948–1960. With Federated Department Stores, Inc., 1960–1972; president, 1967–1972. With R. J. Reynolds Industries, Inc., 1972–1984; chairman and CEO, 1979–1984. MIT Corporation member, 1979–1984.

*Philip A. Stoddard (1917–)   Joined administrative staff at MIT Instrumentation Laboratory, 1947; held positions in several MIT administrative departments, 1948–1956; assistant treasurer, 1956–1957; vice treasurer, 1957–1961; vice president for operations and personnel, 1961–1970; vice president for operations, 1970–1980.

*Julius A. Stratton (1901–1994)   After more than thirty years in a variety of academic and administrative posts at MIT including professor of physics, director of the Research Laboratory of Electronics, provost, vice president, and chancellor, served as the institute's eleventh president, 1959–1966. Life member, MIT Corporation, 1966. Chairman, board of trustees, Ford Foundation, 1966–1971.

*Glenn P. Strehle (1936–)   Named treasurer of MIT and *ex officio* member of the corporation, 1975; served additionally as vice president for resource development, 1986–1994; treasurer and vice president for finance, 1994–1998; treasurer emeritus and advisor to the president and chairman, 1999–.

Robert E. Sullivan (1935–)   Joined Herrick, Smith, Donald, Farley & Ketchum (later Herrick & Smith), 1960; partner, 1970–1985. Partner, Palmer & Dodge, 1985–1995; founder and partner, Sullivan, Weinstein & McQuay, 1996–. (All three law firms in Boston, Mass.)

*Ping Y. Tang (1898–1971)   In 1924 founded major industrial complex in Shanghai, China, concerned with the manufacture of textiles, flour, and cement. Following a change in the political situation in mainland China, moved to Hong Kong and established the South Sea Textile Manufacturing Co., Ltd., with operations throughout southeast Asia. First of three generations of MIT graduates.

Lewis Thomas (1913–1997)   NYU School of Medicine: professor, chairman, Department of Pathology, 1954–1958; professor, chairman, Department of Medicine, 1958–1966; dean, 1966–1969. Yale University School of Medicine: professor, chairman, Department of Pathology, 1969–1972; dean, 1972–1973. President, CEO, Memorial Sloan Kettering Cancer Research Center, 1973–1980; chancellor, 1980–1983; president emeritus, 1984–.

George W. Thorn (1906–)   Physician in chief, Peter Bent Brigham Hospital, Boston, 1942–1972. Hersey Professor of Theory and Practice of Physic, Harvard Medical School, 1942–1972, professor emeritus, 1972–. Pioneer in organ transplants. Life member, MIT Corporation, 1975.

Lester C. Thurow (1938–)   Joined MIT faculty of economics and management, 1968; named professor, 1970. Dean, MIT Sloan School of Management,** 1987–1993.

Daniel C. Tosteson (1925–)   Caroline Shields Walker Professor of Cell Biology and dean of the Faculty of Medicine, Harvard University, 1977–1997.

Charles H. Townes (1915–)   Provost and professor of physics, MIT, 1961–1966; institute professor, 1966–1967. Professor of physics, University of California, Berkeley, 1967–1986. Nobel Prize for physics, 1964.

*George E. Valley, Jr. (1913–)   Staff of MIT Radiation Laboratory, 1941–1945; faculty member, Department of Physics, 1946–1974; named professor, 1957. Assistant director, Lincoln Laboratory, 1950–1953; associate director, 1953–1957. Undergraduate planning professor, 1965–1968.

Charles M. Vest (1941–)   Joined faculty of University of Michigan (Ann Arbor) Department of Mechanical Engineering, 1968; named professor, 1977; associate dean for academic affairs, College of Engineering, 1981–1986; dean, 1986–1989; Provost, vice president for academic affairs, 1989–1990. Fifteenth president, MIT, 1990–.

Felix M. H. Villars (1921–)   Faculty member, MIT Department of Physics, 1952–1991. Named professor, 1960. Chairman, MIT faculty, 1981–1983.

William E. von Seggern, Jr. (1913–1988)   U.S. Army captain, infantry, during World War II. After the war worked for the U.S. Department of Agriculture for many years. Buried in Arlington National Cemetery.

*Emily V. Wade (1925–)   Long active in public service programs and institutions relating to conservation and animal care. Life member, MIT Corporation, 1990.

*Jeptha H. Wade (1924–)   With Kenway, Jenney & Hildreth, 1953–1956. Joined Choate, Hall, and Stewart, 1956; partner, 1960–1990. Both law firms in Boston, Mass. Member, MIT Corporation, 1969–1979.

*Kenneth R. Wadleigh (1921–1994)   Joined faculty, MIT Department of Mechanical Engineering, 1946; named professor, 1961; dean for Student Affairs, 1961–1969; vice president, 1969–1975; vice president and dean of the graduate school, 1975–1984.

*Mary Frances Wagley (1927–)   Headmistress, St. Paul's School for Girls, 1966–1978; director, Episcopal Social Ministries of Diocese of Maryland, 1979–1984. Life member, MIT Corporation, 1988.

John Walsh (1937–)   In curatorial positions associated with department of European paintings, Metropolitan Museum, New York, 1970–1975. Professor, art history, Columbia University, 1975–1977. Mrs. Russell W. Baker Curator of Paintings, Museum of Fine Arts, Boston, 1977–1983. Director, J. Paul Getty Museum, Malibu, Calif., 1983–.

Dennis Weatherstone (1930–)   President, J. P. Morgan & Co. Incorporated, 1987–1990; chairman and CEO, 1990–1995.

James E. Webb (1906–1992)   Director, U. S. Bureau of the Budget, 1946–1949. Undersecretary of State, 1949–1952. President, general manager, Republic Supply Co., 1953–1958; chairman, 1958. Administrator, National Aeronautics and Space Administration (NASA), 1961–1968. Private law practice, Washington, D.C., 1968–1978.

*D. Reid Weedon, Jr. (1919–)   Joined firm of Arthur D. Little, Inc., 1946; senior vice president, 1962–1991; chairman, Arthur D. Little Management Education Institute, Inc., 1978–. Life member, MIT Corporation, 1980.

Arnold N. Weinberg (1929–)   Joined faculty of Harvard Medical School, 1962; named professor of medicine, 1971; professor in health sciences and technology,

Harvard-MIT, 1987. Physician with the Massachusetts General Hospital since 1962. Medical director, MIT medical department, 1986–.

*Robert A. Weinberg (1942–)   Joined faculty, MIT Department of Biology, 1973; named professor, 1982; American Cancer Society Professor of Biology, 1985. Member, Whitehead Institute for Biomedical Research, 1982. National Medal of Science, 1997.

Victor F. Weisskopf (1908–)   Joined MIT Department of Physics as professor, 1946; department chairman, 1967–1973; institute professor, 1966–1974. Manhattan Project at Los Alamos, 1943–1946. Director-general, European Center for Nuclear Research (CERN), 1961–1965.

Helen F. Whitaker (1906–1982)   Life member, MIT Corporation, 1979. (See Uncas A. Whitaker.)

*Uncas A. Whitaker (1900–1975)   Founder, AMP Incorporated. In partnership with his wife, Helen F. Whitaker, provided resources that made possible MIT's expansion of basic research in biology and health sciences. Life member, MIT Corporation, 1966.

Katharine S. White (Mrs. John W. White)   Member, ladies committee, Museum of Fine Arts, Boston, 1957–1962, 1964–1968; chair, 1965–1967. Member, board of trustees, 1974–1990; honorary trustee, 1990–. Vice chair, board of overseers, 1983–1985; chair, 1985–1990.

Edwin C. Whitehead (1919–1992)   In 1939 with his father founded Technicon Corporation for the design and manufacture of scientific and clinical equipment. In 1982, provided the funding for the Whitehead Institute for Biomedical Research, affiliated with MIT. Life member, MIT Corporation, 1989.

Elizabeth J. Whittaker (1929–)   Assistant to director, MIT summer session, 1963–1966; administrative assistant to Howard W. Johnson, 1966–1983; assistant secretary, MIT Corporation, 1982–1987; associate secretary, 1987–1993.

*Sheila E. Widnall (1938–)   Member of faculty, MIT Department of Aeronautics and Astronautics, 1964–1993; chair, MIT faculty, 1979–1981; associate provost, MIT, 1992–1993. Secretary of U.S. Air Force, 1993–1997. Abby Rockefeller Mauze Professor of Aeronautics at MIT, 1986–1998; institute professor, 1998–.

Jerome B. Wiesner (1915–1994)   After more than twenty-five years in academic and administrative posts at MIT including professor of electrical engineering, director of the Research Laboratory of Electronics, dean of the School of Science, and provost, served as the institute's thirteenth president, 1971–1980. On leave from MIT, 1961–1964, special assistant for science and technology to U.S. presidents Kennedy and Johnson. Named MIT institute professor, 1962. Life member, MIT Corporation, 1980.

Kathryn A. Willmore (1943–)   Joined MIT Sloan School, 1965; executive assistant to MIT president, 1981–; additionally director of public relations services, 1986–; secretary, MIT Corporation, and secretary to its executive committee, 1994–; vice president and secretary of the corporation, 1998–.

*Carroll L. Wilson (1910–1983)   Assistant to MIT president Karl T. Compton, 1932–1936. First general manager of the U.S. Atomic Energy Commission, 1947–1950. Joined the faculty of the MIT School of Management,** 1959; named professor, 1961. Director, MIT Fellows in Africa Program, 1960–1967. Served as Mitsui Professor in Problems of Contemporary Technology, 1964–1983.

*John J. Wilson (1907–1985)   Business executive and industrial entrepreneur, focusing especially on the development of companies growing out of emerging technologies; secretary of the MIT Corporation, 1959–1979; life member, MIT Corporation, 1962.

Everett M. Woodman (1916–)   Held teaching posts in educational psychology in several U. S. universities, 1946–1952. In India in positions with the U. S Information Agency, the U. S. Embassy (New Delhi), and the Ford Foundation, 1952–1962. President, Colby Junior College (New London, N.H.), 1962–1972. Country director, Peace Corps, Morocco, 1975–1977.

Edgar S. Woolard, Jr. (1934–)   With E. I. du Pont de Nemours and Company, 1957–1997; executive vice president, 1983–1987; president and COO, 1987–1989; chairman and CEO, 1989–1997.

John Wulff (1903–1985)   Member of the faculty of the MIT Department of Physics, 1931–1937; the Department of Metallurgy, 1937–1968; named professor, 1946. First holder of the Class of 1922 Professorship, established in 1962 to recognize outstanding teachers at the institute.

Francis E. Wylie (1905–)   In reportorial and editorial positions with Louisville, KY, *Herald-Post,* 1928–1936 and *Courier-Journal,* 1937–1944. Bureau chief, Boston office, *Time* magazine, 1944–1954. Director of public relations, MIT, 1955–1970.

*John M. Wynne (1920–)   MIT Sloan Fellow, 1955–1956. Director, Sloan School Executive Development Program, 1958–1961; associate dean, Sloan School, 1961–1967; on leave 1963–1964 as head of MIT faculty at the Indian Institute of Management at Calcutta. Vice president, organization systems, MIT, 1967–1970; vice president for administration and personnel, 1970–1980.

Whitney M. Young, Jr. (1921–1971)   Dean, School of Social Work, Atlanta University, 1954–1960. Executive director, National Urban League, 1961–1971. MIT Corporation member, 1970–1971.

Jerrold R. Zacharias (1905–1986)   MIT Radiation Laboratory, 1940–1945; Manhattan Project, Los Alamos, 1945–1946. Named professor of physics, MIT, 1946. Director of Laboratory for Nuclear Science, 1946–1956. Named institute professor, 1966. Chairman, MIT faculty, 1962–1963.

*MIT degree
**The MIT School of Industrial Management began operation in 1952. In 1964 it was renamed the Alfred P. Sloan School of Management.

Index

Italic page references indicate photographs.

A. B. Dick & Company, 70
A-bomb (World War II), 54
Abram, Morris, 158–159
Ackley, Clifford S., 250
Adams, Margaret, 119
Adams, Ruth M., 161–162, 211
Adelman, Morris A., 94
Advanced Management Program (Harvard), 81
African Fellows Program (MIT), 99, 104, 106
Air Force Electronics Systems Command, 109, 230
Alhambra Victory, 64
Albert, Michael A., 196, *197*
Alberty, Robert A., 127, 216
Alexander, Sidney S., *86*, 104
Alfred, Catherine C., 72, 81
Alfred P. Sloan Foundation. *See* Sloan Foundation
Alfred P. Sloan School of Management. *See* Sloan School (MIT)
Alfred, Theodore M., 70, 72, 81–83, 105
All-India Management Association, 89
Allen, Roger, 70
Alsop, Joseph W., 191–192
American Association of Museums, 217

American Legion, 56
Ames, James B., 256, 258
Andersen, Wayne, 217
Anderson, Dillon, 121, 235
Anderson, Esther D. (Mrs. E. Ross), 245
Anderson, Lawrence B., 100, 127, 142, 177, 226
Anderson, Martin C., 95
Anderson, William S., 229
Annapolis (U.S. Naval Academy), 161
Apartheid, 161
Apollo Program, 129, 169
Armour Tech (Illinois), 16
Army Enlisted Reserve Corps, 19
Army General Classification Test, 20
Army Specialized Training Program (ASTP), 23–24
Arts at MIT, 216–217
Ashdown, Avery A., 228
Ashdown House (MIT), 228
Assassinations
  Kennedy, Robert 172
  King, Martin Luther, Jr., 172
Association of American Universities, 154–155
AT&T, 229
Athenaeum in Boston, 255–256, 258–259

Athletics at MIT, 226–227
Atomic Energy Commission, 98
Audubon Society, 231
Austen, W. Gerald, 133
Austin, David F., 94–95
Austin, James M., 140
Austria, 209
AWOL soldier, 166–167, 182
Ayukawa, Yaichi, 233–234

Bad Hamburg (Germany), 50, 52–53
Baehr, Melanie, 70
Baker, George, 111
Balbo, Italo, 7
Balch, D. E., 72–73
Ball, George W., 156
Baltimore, David, 267–268, 270
Barco, Virgilio, 106–107, 264,
    265
Barrett, Charles, 116
Battle of Britain, 15
Battle of the Bulge, 50
Bavelas, Alex, 75–76
Bell, Charles, 73
Belluschi, Pietro, 93
Bemis, William, 160
Bendetsen, Karl R., 235
Bennis, Warren G., 87, 135
Bergen, William B., 102
Berlin (Germany), 209, 217
Berlin Wall, 109, 209
Berman, Milton S., 121
Bernat, Helen (Mrs. Paul), 249–250,
    252
Bernat, Paul, 249–250
Bevan, Aneurin, 28–29, 31, 60, 62
Biarritz Beach Walk (Sorolla), 146
Big Sail (Calder), 138
Bishop, Robert L., 93, 100, 128, 189,
    216
Bisplinghoff, Raymond L., 128, 206
Black, Fischer, 94
Black Student Union (Cornell), 158
Blanchard, Elwood P., Jr., 84
Block, Herbert L., 256
Bloom, Floyd E., 237

Board of Visitors of the Air Force
    Electronics Systems Command,
    109
Bok, Derek, 211
Boston Athenaeum, 255–256, 258–
    259
Boston College, 167
Boston Foundation, 251
Boston Globe, 179, 194, 244, 246,
    256
Boston Public Library, 243
Boston University, 167
Bosworth, Welles, 147
Botero, Rodrigo, 106–107
Bounin, Jacques, 42
Boutry, Hubert, 40
Bowen Arrow, The, 9
Bowen High School, 8–10, 227
Bowles, Edward L., 95
Bowman, Edward H., 87, 105
Boy Scouts of America, 10–12
Boyle, George, 9
Brewster, Kingman, Jr., 155, 158
Brewster, William S., 136
Bronfenbrenner, Martin, 17
Brooke, Edward W., III, 150, 162
Brooks, C. Wayland, 67
Brooks, Carol W., 92
Brooks, Edward Pennell, 75–76, 79–
    80, *83,* 85–86, *86,* 88, *90,* 91–
    93, 97, 116, 149, 196, 279
Brossman, Charles, 61
Brown, Clementine M., 251
Brown, Douglass V., 75–77, 81, *83,*
    86, 87–88, 94, 105, 116–118
Brown, E. Cary, 79, 94
Brown, Gordon S., 93, 111, 116,
    127, 130–131, 142, 206
Brown, Jean A., 116
Brown, Mary N., 116–117
Brown, Stephen L., 238
Buchanan, James M., 66
Building 7 (MIT), *152, 202*
Building 20 (MIT), 80
Bundy, McGeorge, 155, 191
Bundy, William P., 155

Bunker, George M., 102
Burchard, John E., xviii–xix, 93, 128
Burden, William A. M., 257
Burgess, Eugene W., 88
Burns, Gertrude E., 95
Burns, Robert K., 17, 60, 64–70, 72–73, 77
Bush, Barbara P., 259
Bush, George H. W., 259
Bush, Vannevar, 80, 86–87, 96, 98, 100, 113, 115, 117, *122*, 136, *160*, 173, 204–205, 207, 270

Cabot, Lewis P., 244
Cabot, Thomas D., 269
Caffrey, Jefferson, 48
Calcutta Management School, 99, 105
Calder, Alexander, 138
California, University of, Berkeley, 165
California Institute of Technology, 191
Cambridge Chamber of Commerce, 151
Camp Bowie (Texas), 23
Camp Grant (Illinois), 19–20, 59, 64
Camp Myles Standish (New England), 25
Camp Robinson (Arkansas), 20–22, 24, 172
Campbell Soup Company, 70–71, 84, 88, 112
Campeau, Robert, 235
Cape Kennedy, 129
Carmichael, Stokely, 157
Carnegie Institute of Technology, 92
Carpenter, Walter S., Jr., 236
Carson Pirie Scott and Company, 70
Carter, James E., Jr., 222
Casals, Pablo, 40
Casselman, Robert C., 247–249, 259
Catalano, Eduardo F., 101–102, 104
Catholic Church (in France), 37

Center for International Studies (MIT), 89
Center for Management Education (MIT), 228
Central College (Chicago) (now Roosevelt University), 15–17, 19, 60
Centre d'Etudes Industrielles (Switzerland), 105
Champion International, 235, 251
Chemical Engineering Department (MIT), 225–226
Chicago
  Democratic National Convention in, 172–173
  Democratic political machine, 15
  in Great Depression, 6–7
  Memorial Day parades in, 56
  neighborhoods of, 1–2
  steel industry, in 1930s and 1940s, 2–3, 15
  World War II and, 15
Chicago Daily News, 9
Chicago Tribune, 9, 15
China, 222
Chinese Academy of Science, 222
Chomsky, Noam A., 167, 192, 202
Christ-Janer, Arland F., 211
Churchill, Winston L. S., xviii–xix
CIA, 188
Civil rights movement, 157–159
Clark, W. Van Alan, *83*
Clark, William Ramsey, 175
Clauser, Milton U., 128
Clifford, Clark M., 155–156
Clinton, Hillary Rodham, 162
Co-op Program at Armour Tech, 16
Coeducation, 161–162
Coleman, John R., 66, 75, 77, 87, 104
Coleman, Mary I., 66, 77
Collins, John F., 94–95
Colomb de Daunant, Gilbert, 41–42, 47–50
Colombia management program, 106–107
Columbia University, 165

Commission on MIT Education, 188
Committee for the Arts (MIT), 216
Committee on Engineering and Living Systems, 130–131
Communists (French), 36–37, 43–44
Compton, Karl T., 98, 204, 208, 211
Compton, Margaret H., *130*
Connolly, John B., III, 108
Conrad, Paul, *184*
Coolidge, John, 244, 248, 255
Coolidge, William A., 136, 206, 269
Cordier, Andrew W., 165
Cornell University, 158, 172
Corporation Committee on Succession, 111
Corporation Joint Advisory Committee (CJAC), 183
Costa Rica, 265–266
Coughlin, Robert, 70
Council of the Arts (MIT), 216
Council on Foreign Relations, 260
Cowen, Stuart H., 141, 206
Cox, Archibald, 166
Creanza, Joseph, 17
Cuban missile crisis, 109
Culliton, James J., 201
Cunningham, Ross M., *83*, 108
Cusick, Paul V., 141, 229
Czechoslovakia, 209–210

Dan, Takuma, 220
Dana, Richard, 55–56
d'Arbeloff, Alexander V., 274
Dartmouth College, 167
de Gaulle, Charles A., 34, 37, 42, 48
de Klerk, Frederik W., 161
De Lattre de Tassigny division, 35
de Montebello, Philippe L., 261
Death camps (World War II), 54
Decision-making, development of, xi–xii
Democratic National Convention (Chicago), 172–173
Department of Defense (DOD), 128, 168, 170–171, 194
Department of Justice, 228–229

Detachment D3 L1, 42
Deutch, John M., 266
Dewey, Bradley, 96
DeWitt, William, 9–10
Dickson, William R., 141
Dillon, Douglas, 260–261
Donovan, William, 268
Dormitories at MIT, 227–228
Doty, Paul M., 222
Douglas, Paul H., 66–68
Douglas, Richard M., 217
Dow Chemical, 188
Drake University (Iowa), 16
Draper, Charles Stark, 129, 169–173, 177–178, 191–194
Draper Laboratory (MIT), 171, 177–178, 193–195
Draper Manufacturing Company, 84
Driscoll, Frances, 146–147
Drug abuse, 163
Du Pont Court, 217
du Pont, Irénée, Jr., 236
Dubin, Robert, 66
Dufty, William, 28, 31
Duke University, 267
Dunlop, John T., 166
Durand, David, *86*

E. I. du Pont de Nemours and Company, 236–238
Earth Day, 164–165
Ebert, Robert H., 131–132
Eder, Harold H., 106–107
Edgerton, Harold E., *273*
Edmonds, George P., 238
Educational Policy Committee, 186
Edward Coles Elementary School, 7
Edward Pennell Brooks Center, 83
Egypt, 222–224
Eisenhower, Dwight D., 53, 72, 86–87
Electrical power outage of 1964, 109–110
Emanuel, Robert, 53
Empress of England, 31
Endicott House, 81–82, 174

Engineering, management and, xii
Ensminger, Douglas, 88–89
Environmental issues, 164–168, 230–232
Environmental Protection Agency, 230
Environmental Studies Board (National Academy of Sciences), 230
ETH (Zurich), 191
Experimental Studies Program (MIT), 186

Faculty Advisory Group (FAG), 172
Faculty Club (MIT), 198
Faculty meetings (MIT), 144
Fairbanks, Jonathan L., 250–251
Faneuil Hall (Boston), 185
Farben, I. G., 53
Farrar, Ross W., 247, 249, 259
Federal Bulldozer, The (Anderson), 95
Federal Reserve Bank of Boston, 208–209
Federal Reserve System, 208
Federated Department Stores, 112–115, 119–121, 123, 144, 183, 234–235
Feininger, Lyonel C. A., 146
Fellows in Africa Program, 99, 104, 106
Ferracane, June, 273
Fetter, Robert, 87
Fields, Edward, 146–147
First European Civil Affairs Division, 27, 29, 42
Fisher, Archie, 7
Fisk, James B., 111, 115, 136, 206–207
Fletcher, James C., *220*
Floe, Carl F., 93
Florida University (Miami), 140
Fluegge, Bruce B., 10, 12
Fontein, Jan, *242*, 245–248, *246*, 250, *254*, *255*, 258–260

Food and Agriculture section (Germany), 53
Ford Foundation, 89, 104, 111, 118, 133, 209
Ford, Gerald R., *220*
Ford, Horace S., 100
Forrester, Jay W., *86*, *95*, 228
Fort Devens (Massachusetts), 239
Fortune magazine, 182
45th Division, U.S. Army, 32
Fouraker, Lawrence E., 254, 259
France
  Alès, 47
  Beaucaire, 35
  Béziers, 38
  Cannes, 32
  Carassonne, 38–39
  Catholic Church in, 37
  Cerbere, 39
  Communists in, 36–37, 43–44
  De Lattre de Tassigny division in, 35
  Delta Base Headquarters in, 34
  Dunkirk, 15
  Languedoc Roussillon departments in, 34–35, 40, 42
  Marseilles, 32–34, 40–42, 50–51
  Montpellier, 37–40, 42–52, 54–55
  Nîmes, 47
  Palavas, 55
  Paris, 48
  Perpignan, 39–40
  Port Vendres, 39
  Prades, 40
  resistance heroes, 36–39, 44–45
  Sète, 39–40
  Tarascon, 35
  Toulon, 32
  Vichy French and, 35–39, 44, 47
Frankfurt (Germany), 53, 209
Freeman, Ralph E., 88, 91, 94
French, Anthony P., 269
French language camp (Vancouver Island), 17–18
Friedman, Milton, 66
Fukuda, Takeo, *223*

Fulmer, Vincent A., 117
Fye, Paul M., 133–134, *134*

Gaither, Edmund B., *246*
Gardner, George P., 136, 250
Gardner, John L., 244
Gavin, James M., 256–258
General Edmund Alexander, 26
General Electric Corporation, 168–169, 188
General Mills Corporation, 72–73, 88
General Motors Corporation, 120, 189, 235, 237, 271–273
Geneva Convention, 44
German POWs, 44, *44,* 55
German University Computer Convention (1968), 209
Germany, 50, 52–54, 109, 209, 217
GI Bill, 65–66, 69
Gil, Anita, 105
Gil, Peter P., 105
Glasgow Herald, 61
Glasgow University (Scotland), 59–63
Glenn, John H., Jr., 129
Glielmi, Alfred, 23
Globalization, xii–xiii
Goetz, Billy E., *86*
Goheen, Robert F., 155
Goldblith, Samuel A., 221, 233
Gomory, Ralph E., 272
Gordon, Myron J., 104
Grading system changes, freshman (MIT), 187–188
Graham, Katharine M., 265
Grant, Ulysses S., 196
Gray, Paul E., 126, 157–158, 175–176, 186–187, 200–201, 206–208, 215–216, 218, 227–228, 263–264, 266, 268–271, 274, *275*
Gray, Priscilla K., 264
Great Court (MIT), 138
Great Depression, xi, 6–7
Green, Cecil H., 204
Green, Dwight, 67

Greenewalt, Crawford H., 115, *122,* 136, 207, 236, 238
Greenleaf, Robert K., 111–112
Grissom, Virgil I., 129
Gruenther, Alfred M., 121
Guenette (Heizer), 217
Gund, Graham, 217
Gunness, Robert C., 115
Gvishiani, Dzherman M., 150
Gyftopoulos, Elias P., 186

Hamlet (Shakespeare), 173
Hanify, Edward B., 229–230
Hanley, Edward J., 115, 136
Hansen, Andrew I., 5
Harbison, Frederick H., 60, 65–68, 70, 88
Harrison, George R., 93, 111
Harvard Medical School, 131–132
Harvard University, 81, 92, 109, 140, 165–166, 167, 267
Harvey, Arthur S., 65
Harvey, Evelyn L., 6, 65
Hawthorne, William R., 128
Hazen, Harold L., 93
Heidelberg (Germany), 50, 52–53
Heizer, Michael, 217
Hellmuth, Paul F., 219, 221, 245, 250, 252
Henry V (Shakespeare), 258
Herblock cartoon, 256
Hermann Building bombing (MIT), 201
Hermann, Grover M., 102–104
Herrick & Smith, 176, 229
Hesburgh, Theodore M., 210
Hetherington, Hector, 63
Hetke, Richard, 21
High tech industry, xiii, 232–233
Hill, Albert G., 161, 171, 186, 192, 195, 229–230
Hill, Richard D., 238, 259–260
Hill, Thomas M., 83, 105
Hilles, Susan M., 217, 244, 256
Hiroshima (Japan), 54, 234

Hitchiner Manufacturing Company, 100
Hoffman, Kenneth M., 188, 202
Holland, Jerome H., 183
Holmes, Oliver Wendell, Jr., 56
Homburg Infirmary, 225
Homestead Air Force Base, 109
Horse Race Rapids (Michigan), 12
Howe, C. D., 85
Hudgins, Houlder, 91, 104–105, 108
Hudgins, Vallie, 144, 146
Huguenots, 37
Hulsizer, Robert I., 186
Humphrey, Hubert H., 173
Hunt, Herold C., 97–98, 149
Hunt, Isabel, 97–98
Hunter, Louis, 100
Hurley, Donald, 100
Hutchins, Robert M., 69

IBM, 228–229
Ibrahim, Hassan Hamdi, *224*
Illinois Institute of Technology, 16
Illinois National Guard, 56
Illinois Steel Company, 5
in loco parentis principle, 163
Independent Activities Program (MIT), 187
India business school, 88–89, 97–99, 104–106
Indiana University, 24
Industrial Management Advisory Council, 96
Industrial Management Review, 95
Industrial Relations Center (Princeton University), 68
Industrial Relations Center (University of Chicago), 69–70, 72, 74–75, 79
Instrumentation Laboratory (MIT), 128
Ippen, Arthur T., 209

J. P. Morgan Company, 235–236

Jack C. Tang Center for Management Education, 228
Jacks, Stanley M., 87
Jackson, Shirley A., 157–158
James H. Bowen High School, 8–10, 227
Jamieson, J. Kenneth, 226
Japan, 54, 232–234
Japanese business competition, 232–233
Jefferson, Edward G., 237–238
Jefferson, Thomas, 52
Jenkins, Jack, 9, 19
Jeuck, John E., 68, 77
Johanson, George, 61
John Hancock Mutual Life Insurance Company, 158, 208, 234, 238, 258
Johnson, A. Kenneth, 4, 6, 12–13, 15–16, 65
Johnson, Albert H., 2–3
Johnson, Albin G., 3–4
Johnson, Bruce H., 79, 98, 105, 107, 119, *124,* 137, *147,* 210, 240, *272*
Johnson, Edward L., 4
Johnson, Elizabeth W., 10–11, 52, 70–77, 79, 85–86, 97–98, 100, 104–110, 113, 115–116, 118–119, *124, 130,* 137, 144, *145, 147,* 149, 181, 185–186, 196, 198, 203–204, 209, 215, 219, 221, 240, 243, *262,* 263–264
Johnson, Evelyn. *See* Harvey, Evelyn L.
Johnson, Gullick, 4
Johnson, Howard (ice cream business-man), 240–241
Johnson, Howard Wesley. *See also* MIT; University of Chicago; World War II
Air Force Systems Command and, 109
in Berlin, 209
bird-watching hobby of, 10–11
birth, 1

Johnson, Howard Wesley (cont.)
in Boy Scouts, 10–12, *11*
Campbell Soup Company and, 70–71, *71*, 84
children of, 73–74, 79, 98, 104–105, 107, 119, *124*, 137, *147*, 210, 240, 272
in China, 222
on corporate boards, 84, 112–115, 120–121, 123, 208–209, 234–238 (*see also specific companies*)
in Costa Rica, 265–266
discharge of, army, 59
Du Pont and, 236–238
education of, 7–9, 15–17, 19, 69
in Egypt, 222–224
electrical power outage of 1964, 109–110
environmental issues and, 230–232
Federated Department Stores and, 112–115, 119–121, 123, 144, 234–235
fishing trips of, 12–13, 74
General Mills and, 72–73
at Glasgow University, 59–63
Great Depression and, 6–7
J. P. Morgan Company and, 235–236
John Hancock and, 234, 238
Johnson (ice cream businessman) and, 240–241
leadership and, 277–280
Lexington (Mass.) house of, 98, 116
management and, xiv–xv, 92–93
marriage of, 71 (*see also* Johnson, Elizabeth W.)
Metropolitan Museum of Art in New York and, 260–261
MIT Corporation and, 136, 182–183, 205, 215–241, 263–266
Museum of Fine Arts in Boston and, 146, 244–248, *246*, *254*, 255–261
Northwood (N.H.) house of, 107–108
on not-for-profit boards, 239–240 (*see also specific organizations*)
parents of and parents' families, 2–5, 65, 215
in Prague, 209–210
public posts of, after MIT presidency, 208–209, 234–241
Putnam Funds and, 100
R. N. McMurry and Company and, 69–70
Raymond Tavern house of, 98
retirement of, 273–276
Sadat and, 222–224
siblings of, xxiv, 5, 6, 65, 215
Sloan Foundation and, 271–273
start-up companies and, 238–239
travel of (1975), with family, 240
Washington portraits by Gilbert Stuart and, 255–259
wife of (*see* Johnson, Elizabeth W.)
Johnson, Laura A., 74, 79, 105, 107, 119, *124*, 137, *147*, 210, 240, 272
Johnson, Laura H., 4–5
Johnson, Lyndon B., 108, 111, 150–151, 153–156, 172–173, 208
Johnson (Lyndon B.) Administration, 189
Johnson, Richard A., 5–6, *5*, 65
Johnson, Stephen A., 73, 79, 98, 104–105, 107, 119, *124*, 137, *147*, 210, 240, 272
Joint Harvard-MIT Program in Health Sciences and Technology, 131–133, 225
Jones, Frank S., 142
Jones, John Paul, 120
Jones, Thomas W., 158
Jordan, Vernon E., Jr., 183
Joyce, W. Seavey, 211
Juan Carlos I, 221

Kabat, Jonathan, 172, 174
Kane, Edward R., 238
Kane, Michael A., 132
Karvat, Josef, 209–210

Katsiaficas, George N., 174–175, 196
Kaufman, Gordon M., 87
Keil, Alfred A. H., 128, 216
Kenan Systems Corporation, 238
Kendall Square, 139–140
Kennedy, Donald, 231
Kennedy, Edward M., 150
Kennedy, John F., 108, 111, 129, 153
Kennedy, Robert F., 172
Kent State University, 180
Keohane, Nannerl O., 205
Keyser, Paul V., 207
Killian Court (MIT), 216–217, 264
Killian, Elizabeth P., *103*, *130*, 204, 219
Killian, James R., Jr., 77, 87–88, 103–104, *103*, 113, 115, 117–118, *122*, 125–126, *125*, 130–131, 136, 151, 160, *160*, 172–173, 183, 192–193, 199, 204–206, 208, 211, 219, 229–230, 243–245, 269
Kimball, John, 9
Kindleberger, Charles P., 94, 143–144, 186
King, Martin Luther, Jr., 157, 172
King, Peter S., 105
Kirk, Grayson L., 165
Kispert, Malcolm G., 93
Kissinger, Henry A., 173
Knight, Douglas M., 155
Knight, Frank, 66
Kosygin, Aleksei N., 150
Krebs, William A. W., Jr., 81, *83*
Krensky, Harold, 234–235
Kresge Auditorium (MIT), 144, 165, 176
Krewitz, Elsie, 8
Krugman, Paul R., 232
Kuh, Edwin, 87, 92, 106
Kunst, E. J., 17
Kurtz, Bruno, 9

Lampert, James B., 218, 220–221, 227

Lamson, Roy, 196–197
Land, Edwin H., 96–97, 186, 247, 253
Landau, Ralph, 226, 263
Lane, Saundra, 146
Lane, William H., 146
Laumann, William, 17
Lawrence, Frances (Mrs. James), 252
Lazarus, Cele, 120
Lazarus, Fred, Jr., 112, 115, 120, 149
Lazarus, Gladys, 120
Lazarus, Maurice, 112, 234
Lazarus, Ralph, 112–113, 115, 120, 149, 208, 234–235
Leacock, Richard, 178–179
Leadership, 277–280
Leary, Timothy, 163
Lee, Jenny, 28–29, 31, 60, 62
Lees, Wayne A. R., 17
Leighton, Roger, 210
Leiserson, Avery P., 66
Leland, Simeon, 66
Lettvin, Jerome Y., 163, 202, 246
Letwin, William L., 87
Leventhal, Cyrus, 237
Lever Brothers, 76
Levi, Edward H., 190
Levin, Robert, 10, 12
Levinson, Norman, 127, 128
Lewis Committee (MIT), 188
Lewis, Elma, *246*
Lewis, H. Gregg, 65, 71
Lima (Peru), 210
Lincoln, Abraham, 278
Lincoln Laboratory (MIT), 128, 171, 193–194
Linz (Austria), 209
Little, Arthur D., 186
Little, John D. C., 87
Locke-Ober (Boston restaurant), 169
Lohr, Virgil, 17
London, Irving M., 132
Lorteur, René, 41–42, 50
Louis XIV, 55
Lovell, James A., Jr., *170*

Low, Francis E., 266
Lowell Court (MIT), 217
Lowell, Guy, 247
Lowell Institute, 243
Lowell, Ralph, 244
Luddites, 174
Lumberman's Mutual Fire Insurance Company, 84
Luria, Salvadore E., 165
Lyndon, Donlyn, 128

Ma, Yo Yo, 40
MacArthur, Douglas, 72
MacAvoy, Paul W., 94
McCaffree, Kenneth, 66
McCarthy, Eugene J., 156
McCarthy, Joseph R., 192
McCormack, James J., 93, 128–129, 171
McCormick Hall (MIT), 138, 159–161
McCormick, Katharine Dexter, 159–160
McCormick, Robert, 15
McCormick Tower (MIT), 227
McCoy, Charles B., 236
McCutcheon, John T., 9
McElheny, Victor K., 194
MacElhone, Jack, 31
MacFie, Alec, 61
McGregor, Douglas M., 83, 86–88, 104, 108
MacGregor Hall (MIT), 227
McGregors (owner-editors of Glasgow Herald), 61
McMurry, Robert N., 69
McNamara, Robert S., 155–156, 190
MacVicar, Margaret L. A., 186–187
Magasanik, Boris, 128
Malcolm X, 157
Management
  engineering and, xii
  expansion of concept of, xi–xii
  at Federated Department Stores, 120
  in fifties and sixties, xii
  impact of, in twentieth century, xiv

Johnson (Howard Wesley) and, xiv–xv, 92–93
  leadership and, 277–280
  MIT and teaching, 92
  of Museum of Fine Arts in Boston, 246–248
  in recent decades, xii
  society and, xii
  technology-based companies and, xiii
Mandela, Nelson R., 161
Mann, Robert W., 202, 269
Marquis, Donald G., 87
Marseilles (France), 32–34, 40–42, 50–51
Marshall, Alfred, 61
Marshall, Dale Rogers, 205–206
Marshall, George C., 136
Martin, William Ted, 127, 186
Martin-Marietta, 102
Massachusetts General Hospital, 133
Massachusetts Institute of Technology. See MIT
Materials Science Center (MIT), 164
Mazur, Paul M., 121
MDC special squad, 176
Meade, George G., 196
Medical Department (MIT), 130–131, 225–226
Memorial Day parades (Chicago), 56
Menzel, Donald, 265
Mercer, William C., 80
Merck, 237
Merrill, Esther, 95
Merton, Robert C., 94
Metropolitan District Commission, 166
Metropolitan Museum of Art in New York, 217, 260–261
Meyer, John M., Jr., 235
MFA. See Museum of Fine Arts in Boston
Michelon, L. C., 70
Midwest Regional War Labor Board, 60
MIFA, 250

Miller, Bertie, 9
Miller, Charles L., 142, 170
Millikan, Max F., 89, 104, 180, 189–190
Millis, Harry A., 66
Milne, Walter L., 151, 198–199, 201–203
MIRVs, 168, 195
Mississippi State University, 180
MIT (Massachusetts Institute of Technology)
  aerial views of, *78, 276*
  African Fellows Program, 99, 104, 106
  arts at, 216–217
  Ashdown House, 228
  Building 7 demonstration, *152, 202*
  Building 20, 80
  capital campaign (1975–1980) of, 218–220
  Center for International Studies, 89
  Center for Management Education, 228
  Chemical Engineering Department, 225–226
  civil rights movement and, 157–159
  Commission on MIT Education and, 188
  Committee for the Arts, 216
  Council for the Arts, 216
  curriculum at, during student turmoil, 185–187
  Draper Laboratory, 171, 177–178, 193–195
  drug abuse and, 163
  environmental issues and, 164–168
  Experimental Studies Program, 186
  Faculty Club, 198
  faculty meetings, 144
  financial pressures at, 218, 228
  globalization and, xiii
  Gray as president of, 263–264, 274
  Great Court, 138. *See also* Killian Court
  Hermann Building bombing, 201
  Historical Collections, 217
  Homburg Infirmary, 225
  impacts on, various social, xiv
  Independent Activities Program, 187
  Instrumentation Laboratory, 128
  Johnson (Howard Wesley) and
    Apollo Program, 129
    appointments of, as MIT president, 125–128
    approach to student unrest, 203
    arrival at MIT, 79–80
    athletic and physical education program, 226–227
    AWOL soldier and, 166–167, 182
    at baseball game, student/faculty, *148*
    Calder sculpture and, 138–139, *139*
    Colombia business program, 106–107
    commencement of 1966, 137–138
    commencement of 1970, 204
    corporate consulting, 84
    dormitories and student houses, 227–228
    early years as MIT president, 123–151
    election of, as MIT president, 115–121
    executive development program, 80–83, 85–87, 91
    Fellows in Africa Program, 99, 104, 106
    fund raising, 128
    grading system changes, freshman, 187–188
    Harvard-MIT Joint Center for Urban Studies, 133
    inauguration of, as MIT president, *122, 124*
    India business school, 88–89, 97–99, 104–106
    job offer, first, 75–77
    Joint Harvard-MIT Program in Health Sciences and Technology, 131–133, 225
    laboratory growth, 128–129

MIT (Massachusetts Institute of Technology) (cont.)
Johnson (Howard Wesley) (cont.)
  landscaping campus, 138–140
  Medical Department, 130–131
  in President's House, 144–149
  Program for Senior Executives, 83
  reorganization of departments,
    141–144
  resignation of, as MIT president,
    204–208, 211
  School of Industrial Management,
    76, 91–104, 108, 110–111
  semester system changes, 187
  Sloan School, 112, 115, 271
  Soviet space efforts, 86–87
  teaching award, 84
  thoughts of, after MIT presidency,
    211–213
  Woods Hole Oceanographic Institution, 133–135
Killian Court, 216–217, 264. *See
  also* Great Court
Kresge Auditorium, 144, 165, 176
laboratory debates and, 191–196
Lincoln Laboratory, 128, 171, 193–
  194
Lowell Court, 217
McCormick Hall, 138, 159–161
McCormick Tower, 227
MacGregor Hall, 227
management theory and, 92
Materials Science Center, 164
Medical Department, 130–131,
  225–226
Museum, MIT, 217–218
Museum of Fine Arts at Boston and,
  243
music revolution and, 164
NCR lawsuit and, 228–230
November Actions and, 175–180,
  177, 179, 182, 196
occupation of President's Office and
  (1970), 196–201, *202*
100th anniversary of, 101

picketing of speakers at colleges
  and, 189–191
Pounds Panel and, 174, 191–193
in prewar years, xiv
professor-student relations at, 180–
  182
Radiation Laboratory, 80
Ralph Landau Building for Chemical Engineering, 225
Rostow, Walt W. and, 189–190
ROTC and, 167–168
School of Architecture and Planning,
  101, 124
School of Engineering, 123
School of Humanities and Social Science at, 80, 123–124, 189
School of Industrial Management,
  76, 80, 83, *83,* 85–86, *86,* 91–
  104, 101, 108, 110–111
School of Science, 123
Senior Executives Program, 82–83,
  101
sexual revolution and, 163–164
Sloan Building, 101
Sloan Fellowship Program, 76–77,
  79–82, 85, 101
Sloan School, 94, 112–113, 115,
  118, 123, 139–141, 189, 227,
  247, 271
Sloan teaching award, 84
South Africa situation and, 161
Stratton Student Center, 101, 104,
  166, 198
student movements and, 165–168
Tang Hall, 227–228
Undergraduate Research Opportunities Program, 186–187
Vietnam war and, 153–157, 165,
  172, 201
  protests against, student, *152,*
    165–168
war research at, 168–174, 195
Weathermen and, 174–175, 201
Wellesley program and, 161–162
Whitaker College, 225

Whitaker Health-Sciences Building, 225
Whitehead Institute, 267–270
  Wiesner as president of, 215–217
  Wiesner's inauguration as president, 216
  women's movement and, 159–161
MIT (Massachusetts Institute of Technology) Corporation
  chairmanship of, 204–205
  executive committee of, 136, 182–183
  Johnson (Howard Wesley) and, 136, 182–183, 205, 215–241, 263–266, 270–271
Mitsui Company, 220
Mockler, Coleman M., Jr., 238
Modigliani, Franco, 94
Monet, Claude, 254
Montpellier (France), 37–40, 42–52, 54–55
Moore, David G., 70, 72
Moore, Francis D., 133
Moore, Henry, 217
Moore, Leo B., *83*
Moore, Mrs. David, 72
Morgan Library, 236
Morison, Anne, 135
Morison, Elting E., 76, 81, *86*, 98, 128, 135
Morison, George A., 140
Morris, Frank E., 208
Morse, Richard S., 94–95
Moses, Joel, 266
Moynihan, Daniel P., 133
Mubarak, Muhammed Hosni, 223–224
Mueller, Carl M., 136, 206–208, 218–219, 226, 228, 263, 270–271, 274
Muller-Thym, Bernard J., 94–95
Mulliken, Nathaniel, 98
Multiple warhead missiles (MIRVs), 168, 195
Murchison, Clint W., Jr., 227
Murley, Gladys, 79–80
Murphy, Thomas A., 271
Murphy, William Beverly, 88, 96, 136, 142, 206
Museum of Fine Arts (MFA) in Boston
  art loans to, 146, 217
  attraction to, 253–254
  exhibit schedule of, 250–251
  founding of, 243
  fund raising of, 249–250
  Johnson (Howard Wesley) and, 146, 244–248, 246, 254, 255–261
  Killian (James R.) and, 219
  ladies committee of, 252
  management of, 246–248
  membership of, 252–253
  MIFA and, 250
  MIT and, 243
  Museum School building project and, 250
  president's association and, 259
  Stuart portraits of Washingtons, 255–259
Myers, Charles A., 75, 81, 87–88, 94

NAACP, 157
Nalos, Erwin, 18
NASA, 129, 171
National Academy of Sciences, 230, 232
National Commission on Productivity, 208
National Endowment for the Arts, 247–248, 259
National Gallery of Art (Washington, D.C.), 248–249, 258
National Portrait Gallery of the Smithsonian, 255–257
NATO, 240
Nature Conservancy, the, 231
Navy Air Corps, 19
Navy V–5 Program, 19
NCR lawsuit, 228–230
Nef, John U., 66
Negroponte, Nicholas P., 274

Neurosciences Research Program, 133
New England Mutual Life Insurance Company, 264
New York Times, 118, 190
Newspaper Labor Board, 60
Nichols, Osgood, 192
Nixon, Richard M., 133, 173, 190
Nommensen, Christina, 5
Normandy beaches, 30–31
Northeastern University, 167–168
November Actions, 175–180, *177, 179,* 182, 196
Nuclear Regulatory Commission, 158
Nyhart, J. Daniel, 201

Occupation of MIT President's Office (1970), 196–201, *202*
O'Farrell, Thomas, 72, 81
Ohio State University, 191
Ohira, Masayoshi, 233
Okita, Saburo, 233
Oklahoma A&M, 23
Onassis, Jacqueline Kennedy, 253, *254*
O'Neill, John W., 109
O'Neill, Mary, 109
O'Neill, Thomas P., Jr., 150
Orchestra Hall (Chicago), 190
O'Reilly, Clarence J., 74
Osgood, William B., 244
"Over the hill in October" (OHIO), 18

Page, Walter H., 235–236
Paint River (Michigan), 12–13
Paquette, Leon, 210
Paris (France), 48
Patterson, Ellmore C., 235–236
Patton, George S., 239
Patton, George S., Jr., 239–240
Pearl Harbor (December 7, 1941), 18–19
Pei, I. M., *242,* 248–249, 259, 270–271
Penman, Sheldon, 202

Perkins, James A., 155, 158
Perkins, Richard S., 261
Perot, H. Ross, 256
Personal reconnaissance, 279
Petranic, Muriel A., 273
Pew Memorial Trust, 225
Phi Kappa Psi Fraternity House, 24
Phillips, Thomas L., 238
Physical education program at MIT, 226–227
Pigors, Paul, 75, 87
Pigott, Elizabeth A., 199
Placido, Charlene M., 199
Poggioli, Livio, 41, *44, 51*
Polaroid Corporation, 96–97
Polio menace, 84
Pool, Ithiel de Sola, 128, 202
Porter, William L., 216
Pounds Panel, 174, 191–193
Pounds, William F., 95, 106–107, 125, 127, 142, 174, 216
Powers, Robert E., 10
"Prague Spring," 209
President's Advisory Committee on Labor-Management Policy, 154, 208
Press, Frank, 232
Preston, Lewis T., 235–236
Price, Robert, 10
Princeton University, 68, 161
Proger, Samuel H., 240
Pusey, Anne, 211, 265
Pusey, Nathan M., 133, 151, 155, 165–166, 211, 265
Putnam Funds, 100, 113
Putnam, George, 259

Questrom, Allen I., 235

R. N. McMurry and Company, 69–70
Radcliffe College, 162
Radiation Laboratory (MIT), 80
Ralph Landau Building for Chemical Engineering, 225
Ram, Charat, 89, 105

Ram, Sumitra, 89
Rathbone, Perry T., 252
Raymond Tavern (1795 house), 98
Reagan, Ronald W., 222
Reed, John S., xi–xv
Rees, Albert, 66, 272
Reintjes, J. Francis, 209
Remis, Harry, 250
Renoir exhibit at MFA, 259
Republic Steel Company, 70
Reston, James B., 190
Rike, David L., 121
Ripley, S. Dillon, 257
Rives-Saltes Camp (France), 54
Roberts, Edward B., 95
Robinson, Joseph T., 20
Rogers, Carl, 66
Rogers, Hartley, Jr., 186
Rogers, Malcolm, 260
Rogers, William B., 243
Rolfe, Sidney, 66
Roosevelt, (Anna) Eleanor, 206
Roosevelt, Franklin Delano, 15, 50, 136
Roosevelt University. *See* Central College (Chicago)
Ropes and Gray, 229
Rosen, S. McKee, 17
Rosenblith, Walter A., 45, 126, 131–132, 143–144, 176, 186, *197*, 200–202, 206, 215, 225, 230, 268
Rosenstein-Rodan, Paul N., 94
Ross, John, 128, 186
Rostow, Walt W., 189–190
ROTC, 167–168, 239–240
Rouse, James W., 251
Rubin, Ida, 139
Ruina, Jack P., 171
Rule, John T., 93
Rusk, (David) Dean, 155

Sadat, Muhammed Anwar, 222–223
Sahin, Kenan E., 238–239
Salerno (Italy), 23
Samuelson, Paul A., 94

Sandburg, Carl, 1
Sargent, Francis W., 164–165
Sargent murals at MFA, 249
Saxon, David S., 270
Sayre, Eleanor A., 251
Schein, Edgar H., 87
Schell, Erwin H., 80–81, 108
Schmidt, Helmut, 264–265
Schmitt, Francis O., 133
Scholes, Myron S., 94
School of Architecture and Planning (MIT), 101, 124
School of Engineering (MIT), 123
School of Humanities and Social Science (MIT), 80, 123–124, 189
School of Industrial Management (MIT), 76, 80, 83, *83*, 85–86, *86*, 91–104, 101, 108, 110–111. *See also* Sloan School (MIT)
School of Public Health (Harvard), 131–132
School of Science (MIT), 123
Science Research Associates, 70
Scotland, 59–63
Scott Paper Company, 142
Scripps Institution of Oceanography, 237
Seamans, Warren A., 217
Sears Roebuck and Company, 76
Second Armored Division, U.S. Army, 240
Second Century Fund, 218
Seeler, Albert O., 132, 225
Selective Service Act, 17–18
Sell, Harry B., 17
Semester system changes (MIT), 187
Senior Executives Program (MIT), 82–83, 101
Seton, E. T., 4
Seventh Army, 31
Severance, Donald P., 182
Sexual revolution, 163–164
Seybolt, George C., 244
Shakespeare, William, 258
Shannon, James A., 129–130
Shapiro, Ascher H., 269

Shapiro, Eli, 68, 75–77, 80–81, 83, 86, 87–88
Shapiro, Harold T., 273
Sharp, H. Rodney, III, 238
Sharp, Mrs. Percy, 26–28
Sharp, Muriel, 27
Sharp, Percy, 26–28
Shepard, Alan B., Jr., 129
Shepard, David A., 136
Sherburne, Miriam, 95
Shoemaker, Vaughn, 9
Shrivenham (England), 28
Shultz, George P., 75, 87, 111, 190
Siegel, Abraham J., 87, 94
Sierra Club, 231
Sigler, Andrew C., 235, 251
Silber, John R., 211
Sills, Beverly, 259
Simha, O. Robert, 101
Simonides, Betty L. A., 137, 196, 198
Simonides, Constantine B., 99, 118–119, 140, 157, 161, 176, 180–181, 196, 198–199, 201–203, 206, 215–216
Singer, Arthur L., Jr., 128
Singer, Isadore M., 202
Sizer, Irwin W., 128
Slater, John C., 127
Sloan, Alfred P., Jr., xi, 81, 85, 88, 96, 101–103, *103*, *114*, 119–120, 136, 219, 236, 272–273
Sloan Building (MIT), 101
Sloan Fellowship Program (MIT), 76–77, 79–82, 85, 101
Sloan Foundation, 81, 102, 271–273
Sloan Management Review, 95
Sloan Research Fund, 119–120
Sloan School (MIT), 94, 112–113, 115, 118, 123, 139–141, 189, 227, 247, 271. *See also* School of Industrial Management (MIT)
Sloan teaching award (MIT), 84
Sloan wives group, 85
Smith, Adam, 59–60
Smith, Gregory, 269
Smith, Roger B., 189

Smith, Ross H., 226
Smithsonian Institution, 234, 255–259
Smullin, Louis D., 128
Snow, Welton, 50
Snyder, Benson R., 177, 187
Snyder, Joseph J., 93, 102, 204, 206, 228
Solomon, Ezra, 68
Solomon, Sydney L., 121
Solow, Robert M., 94, 202, 232, 271, 274
Sorolla, Joaquin y Bastida, 146
South Africa, 161
Soviet Union, 86–87, 150
Space research and exploration, 86–87, 129, 169
Sparling, Edward J., 17
Spencer, Lyle M., 70
Sprague, Robert C., 96, 194
Sputnik, 86–87
Stanford University, 109, 165, 267
Start-up companies, 238–239
Stebbins, Theodore E., Jr., 250
Steel industry, Chicago's in 1930s and 1940s, 2–3, 15
Sterling, J. E. Wallace, 165
Stevenson, Adlai E., 68, 72
Sticht, J. Paul, 84, 112–113
Stimson, Henry L., 136
Stoddard, Philip A., 101, 141
Stone & Webster, 147
Stone, Raleigh, 68
Stone of Scone theft, 63
Stratton, Catherine N., *130*, 137, 139
Stratton, Julius A., 87–88, 91–93, 100, 102, 104, 110–111, 113, 117–118, *122*, 125–129, *125*, 137–138, 151, 189, 193, 204–205, 207, 211, 229–230, 243, 269, 273–274
Stratton Student Center (MIT), 101, 104, 166, 198
Strehle, Glenn P., 228
Stuart, Gilbert S., 255, 258

Student Advisory Group (SAG), 172
Student houses at MIT, 227–228
Student movement, 165–168
Students for a Democratic Society (SDS), 174–175, 189
Sullivan, Robert E., 176, 200, 268
Sullivan, Walter J., *170*

Tallman, Gerald B., 77, 79–80
Tang Hall (MIT), 227–228
Tang, Jack C., 228
Tang, Martin Y., 228
Tang, Ping Y., 227–228
Taylor, Robert, 244
Tech Show (1969), 181–182
Technische Universität (Berlin), 209
Technology-based companies, xiii, 232–233
Temin, Christine, 244
Testard family, 42
Tet offensive, 154
3d Division, U.S. Army, 32
33d Division, U.S. Army, 56
Thomas, Charles V., 252–253
Thomas, Lewis, 133
Thompson, Benjamin, 251
Thorn, George W., 133, 136, 206–207
Thornbury, Richard, 70, 81
Thurow, Lester C., 94
TIAA-CREF organization, 158
Time, 179
Tischman, Paul, 139
Tosteson, Daniel C., 132, 237
Townes, Charles H., 100, 102, 109, 111, 115–116, 118, 125
Townes, Frances B., 109, 116
Trenet, Charles, 46
Truman, Harry S., 50, 54
Tsongas, Paul E., 264–265
Tufts University, 167
Ture, Norman B., 66
2678th Regiment (First European Civil Affairs Division), 27

Undergraduate Research Opportunities Program (UROP) (MIT), 186–187
University of Chicago
  Business School at, 70
  changes at, 70–71
  faculty at, 66–68
  Industrial Relations Center at, 69–70, 72, 74–75, 79
  Johnson (Howard Wesley) and, *58*, 64–66, 68–75, 87–88
  Levi (Edward) inauguration as president of, 190
University Hall occupation (Harvard), 165–166
University of Wisconsin, 180
Urbanowicz, Jean, 9
UROP (MIT), 186–187
U.S. Army Report on Civil Affairs Operations in World War II, 51
U.S. Foreign Service examinations, 61–62
U.S. Selective Service, 17–18

V-E Day, 52–53
V-J Day, 54–55
Valley, George E., Jr., 186
Vancouver Island, 17–18
Vandeputte, Amèdée, 38, 41, 44–45
Vandeputte, Francette, 44–45
Vassar College, 161
Vest, Charles M., 274
Vichy French, 35–39, 44, 47
Vietnam war, 153–157, 165, 172, 201, 210
  protests against, student, *152*, 165–168
Villars, Felix M. H., 186
Violet, Jacques, 39
Volcker, Paul A., 208
Volpe, John A., 149
von Hoffman, Nicholas, 70
von Seggern, William E., Jr., 35, 38–41, 43–45, 47–53, *51*, 274

Wade, Emily V., 183
Wade, Jeptha H., 136, 207
Wadleigh, Kenneth R., 141, 187, 198, 201
Wagley, Mary Frances, 183
Waldorf Astoria Hotel, picketing at, 222
Wallis, W. Allen, 88
Walsh, John, Jr., 250
War Labor Board (WLB), 60
Washington portraits by Gilbert Stuart, 255–259
Washington Post, 256
Weatherstone, Dennis, 236
Webb, James E., 129
Weed, Betty. *See* Johnson, Elizabeth W.
Weedon, D. Reid, Jr., 227
Weinbaum, Jay, 17
Weinberg, Arnold N., 132
Weinberg, Robert A., 237
Weisskopf, Victor F., 126–128, 176
Welch, John F., Jr., xiii
Wellesley College, 161–162, 205
Wells, Herman B., 24
Werley, Charles M., 100
Wessell, Nils Y., xxi
West Point (U.S. Military Academy), 161
Whitaker, Helen F., 225, 265
Whitaker, Uncas A., 207, 219, 225
Whitaker College (MIT), 225
Whitaker Foundation, 225
Whitaker Health-Sciences Building (MIT), 225
White, Katharine S. (Mrs. John W.), 252
White, Kevin H., 256
Whitehead, Edwin C., 267–270
Whitehead Institute (MIT), 267–270
Whitehead, James, 41, *41,* 50, *51,* 52
Whitehill, Walter M., 256
Whitin, Thomson M., 87
Whitney Museum in New York, 251
Whittaker, Elizabeth J., 140–141, 199–203, 245, 273

WHOI, 133–135
Whyte, William F., 66
Widnall, Sheila E., 186
Wiesel, Elie, 234
Wiesner, Jerome B., 111, 115–116, 126–128, *127,* 130, 132, 142–144, 150, 157, 176, 181, 186–187, 190, 192, 195–196, 198–199, 201–203, 206–207, 211, 215–219, *216,* 221, 228, 230, 263, 265–271, 273–274, *275*
Wiesner, Laya W., 116, 190, 221, 265
Wilderness Society, 231
Willmore, Kathryn A., 99
Wilson, Carroll L., 94–95, 98–99, 104, 106, 128, 149–150, 209
Wilson, John J., 269
Wilson, Mary B., 104
Wiltsey, Glenn, 17
Windsor Park Lutheran Church, 7
Winquist, Gertrude B., 82
WLB, 60
Women's movement, 159–161
Woodman, Everett M., 89
Woods Hole Oceanographic Institution (WHOI), 133–135
Woodstock (1969), 164
Woolard, Edgar S., Jr., 237–238
World War II
  A-bomb and, 54
  academic changes since, 280
  Battle of Britain and, 15
  Battle of the Bulge and, 50
  Chicago and, 15
  death camps and, 54
  Hiroshima and, 54
  impact of, social, xi
  Pearl Harbor and, 18–19
  start of, 13, 15
  U.S. Army Report on Civil Affairs Operations in World War II and, 51
  V-E Day and, 52–53
  Vichy French in, 35–39, 44, 47

V-J Day, 54–55
veterans, 56–57
Worthen, Jeannette, 9
Wrighton, Mark S., 266
Wulff, John, 180
Wylie, Francis E., 118
Wynne, John M., 85, 88–89, 97,
    103, 105, 115, 118, 141, 157,
    172, 175–176, 180–181, 198–
    199, 201, 206, 215–216

Yale University, 161
Yeats, William Butler, ix
Young, Whitney M., Jr., 183

Zacharias, Jerrold R., 127, 138–139
Zander, Karl, 234
Zeller, Andre, 45
Zona, Anthony J., 199
Zurcher, Arnold J., 85

Picture Credits

Many of the photographs used in this book were provided by the MIT Museum. Some of them originated with the MIT News Office, and others first appeared in *Technology Review.* Wherever possible, photographers are credited and sources indicated.

ii   HWJ portrait by George Augusta. Photograph by Clive Russ. Courtesy of the MIT Museum

xxiv   Photograph by J. Fein, South Chicago, Author's collection

5   Author's collection

11   Author's collection

14   Author's collection

29   Author's collection

33   Photograph by Rosie Rey, Marseilles, France. Author's collection

37   Author's collection

39   Author's collection

41   Author's collection

43   Author's collection

44   Author's collection

51   Photograph appeared in *Midi Libre,* Montpellier. Author's collection

58   Author's collection

71   Author's collection

74   Author's collection

78   Courtesy of the MIT Museum

82   Courtesy of the MIT Museum

83   Photograph by J. Ralph Jackman. Courtesy of the MIT Museum

86   Photograph by J. Ralph Jackman. Courtesy of the MIT Museum

90   Courtesy of the MIT Museum

96   Courtesy of the MIT Museum

103   Courtesy of the MIT Museum

114   Author's collection

122   Courtesy of the MIT Museum

124   Photograph by Arthur Kalotkin '66. Courtesy of the MIT Museum

125   Courtesy of the MIT Museum

127   Photograph by Steven A. Hansen. Courtesy of the MIT Museum

130   Courtesy of the MIT Museum

134   Courtesy of the MIT Museum

139   Courtesy of the MIT Museum

145   Courtesy of the MIT Museum

147   Courtesy of the MIT Museum

148   Photograph by Dov Isaacs '71. Courtesy of the MIT Museum

152   Courtesy of the MIT Museum

160   Courtesy of the MIT Museum

170   Courtesy of the MIT Museum

177   Courtesy of the MIT Museum

178   Courtesy of the MIT Museum

179   Courtesy of the MIT Museum

184   Cartoon by Paul Conrad. © 1969 by the Los Angeles Times. Reprinted by permission. Author's collection

197   Photograph by Steven D. Lipsey, '69. Courtesy of the MIT Museum

202   Photograph Alfred I. Anderson, '71. Courtesy of the MIT Museum

214   Courtesy of the MIT Museum

216   Courtesy of the MIT Museum

220   Photograph reprinted by permission of United Press International. Courtesy of the MIT Museum

223   Prime minister's office, Tokyo. Author's collection

224   Photograph appeared in *Al Ahram*, Cairo, and *Tech Talk*, 1982. Courtesy of the MIT Museum

241   Photograph by Calvin Campbell. Courtesy of the MIT Museum

242   Courtesy of the Museum of Fine Arts, Boston

246   Courtesy of the Museum of Fine Arts, Boston

249   Courtesy of the Museum of Fine Arts, Boston

254   Photograph by Frederick G. S. Clow. Courtesy of the Museum of Fine Arts, Boston

262   Photograph by Susan Weed. Author's collection

265   Photograph by Calvin Campbell. Courtesy of the MIT Museum

267   Chinese Academy of Science, Author's collection

272   Photograph by Barry Swaebe, London. Author's collection

273   Courtesy of Kenan Systems Corporation. Author's collection

275   Photograph by Calvin Campbell. Courtesy of the MIT Museum

276   Photograph by Donna M. Coveney. Courtesy of the MIT Museum